The Business 2.0

B1+ INTERMEDIATE Teacher's Book

Antoinette Meehan, Frances Watkins and Paul Emmerson with Mike Sayer

MACMILLAN

Contents

Additional activities (photocopiable speaking & reading activities) can be found on the Teacher's Resource Disc.

The Business 2.0
B1+ INTERMEDIATE

To the Teacher

The objective of *The* **Business** 2.0 is to help students learn two things: how to do business in English and the language they need to do it. The new language and structures are presented in the Student's Book whilst the eWorkbook provides language practice and extension.

Here is a summary of what you will find in each.

Student's Book
The modules

The Student's Book contains 48 modules in eight units. Each unit deals with a key sector of activity in the business world. There are six different types of module:

1 About business

These modules contain information and language for the topic area of each unit. The focus is on understanding the topic and the general sense of the texts – don't worry too much about details such as new vocabulary.

2 Vocabulary

These modules build on the important words and phrases associated with the topic and provide thorough practice.

3 Grammar

These modules help students practise the grammar in a communicative and meaningful way, in business situations relating to the unit topic. Before they start, students read the *Refresh your memory* box to remind themselves of the key grammar points. Use the *Grammar and practice* section at the back of the book for consolidation.

4 Speaking

These modules develop understanding and speaking skills in typical business situations. In these modules, students build up a checklist of useful expressions to use in the speaking activities. The activities themselves allow students to practise these expressions and their speaking skills in realistic situations with other people.

5 Writing

These modules provide practice for the most important types of document student will need to write at work. They analyse a model text, focus on key language and use both as a basis for doing a writing output activity.

6 Case study

The case studies provide an opportunity to apply all the language, skills and ideas students have worked on in the unit. They present authentic problem-solving situations similar to those students will meet in business.

Internet research

Every module includes an Internet research task to encourage you to explore the topic in more detail. The tasks can be done before or after working on the module. Remember that to search for an exact phrase, you may get more accurate results if you put quotation marks around it.

Other features

In addition to the eight main units, the Student's Book contains the following:

Business fundamentals
This opening section introduces students to basic business principles and vocabulary. It provides a solid foundation for you to build on in the course and will help them get the most out of all components of *The* **Business** 2.0

Reviews
These units can be used in three ways: to consolidate students' work on the units, to catch up quickly if they have missed a lesson, and to revise before tests or exams.

Additional material
This section contains all the extra materials students need to do pair- or group-work activities.

Grammar and practice
This section gives a useful summary of grammar rules with clear examples, and also provides further practice of the essential grammar points in this level of the course.

Recordings
Full scripts of all the audio recordings are provided, allowing students to study the audio dialogues in detail.

Glossary
In each module, there is a short glossary of words students may not know. The definitions for these are in the Glossary at the back of the book. Words in red are high-frequency items, which students should try to learn and use. The others, in black, are words they just need to understand.

eWorkbook

The **Business** 2.0 eWorkbook provides everything you would find in a printed Workbook, as well as extra multimedia resources. It is mainly intended for self-study or home study and contains material to support and enhance the activities in the Student's Book.

Language practice
This section contains activities to consolidate the language presented in the Student's Book. Students can practise grammar, vocabulary, listening, pronunciation, reading and writing.

Watch
This section contains a video clip and worksheet to accompany each unit in the Student's Book. The video clips are episodes of a mini-drama that illustrate the communication and people skills in each unit. The exercises allow students to practise the functional language in the video.

Tests
Students can test themselves at any point in the course using the eWorkbook, by setting either the time or the number of questions. Their test scores are recorded for their reference.

Print and work
This section offers a pen-and-paper version of the activities in the Language practice section. Students can also download the audio tracks required for these activities.

Grammar help
Students can refer to this section for helpful grammar rules and examples.

Word lists
This section contains the key words and definitions from the Vocabulary modules in the Student's Book.

Dictionary
Use the Dictionary Tool to link to the *Macmillan Dictionary* online. http://www.macmillandictionary.com.

Writing tips
This section provides explanations and exercises on aspects of writing, such as spelling, punctuation and paragraphing.

Listen
This section contains all the audio recordings from the Student's Book and eWorkbook, together with the audio scripts. Students can download all the material in this section to a mobile device for listening on the move.

Teacher's Book

This Teacher's Book aims to make using *The* **Business** 2.0 Student's Book easy. It provides ideas for lead-in activities for each unit, for further practice and for extension and personalization activities, as well as answers and recording scripts and additional, photocopiable reading and speaking activities.

Subject background

Each unit begins with a page of background notes about the sector of activity in the business world that is dealt with in the unit. These subject background notes contain lists of useful websites that will provide you and/or your students with more in-depth knowledge and information about the topic of each unit.

Teaching notes

The teaching notes for each module contain the following:
- Classroom procedure and task management notes.
- Ideas for lead-in activities in the *About business* modules.
- Ideas for further practice and extension activities.
- A full answer key for the exercises in the Student's Book.
- Full recording scripts for all the listening activities.
- Suggestions on how and when to use the Internet research tasks.
- Tips for tailoring activities to suit lower- or higher-level classes.

Answer key for *Reviews* and *Grammar and practice*

The full answer key for the *Review* sections can be found after every two units.
The full answer key for *Grammar and practice* is at the end of the teaching notes for the Student's Book units on page 113.

Teacher's Resource Disc

The Teacher's Resource Disc provides a wide range of additional multimedia material to support and enhance your lessons. For each unit you can find:
- a PowerPoint presentation that supplements the language and skills areas for each unit.
- an entertaining video featuring the skills and language taught in the speaking module. The video is supported by worksheets and teaching notes.

The Teacher's Resource Disc also provides a wide range of tests, including unit-by-unit progress tests and two review tests, one after Unit 4 and the second after Unit 8.
You can also find:
- the Student's Book audio, audioscript and glossary.
- the answer key for the exercises in downloadable form.
- additional photocopiable reading and speaking activities which can be used for revision or to fill out a lesson with a higher-level group.

Tips for using this book

Answers

The answers to all the module exercises are on a grey panel at the end of the teaching notes for each exercise. Items that are gapped/missing in the Student's Book are underlined.

Teaching notes

Words, sentences and questions *in italics* are items that can be read out to the class. Expected answers follow in brackets. For example:
'Get students to guess these words.'
This means the same as buying. (purchasing)
When you pay someone money for working, you give them this. (salary), etc.

Words, sentences and questions <u>*in italics and underlined*</u> are items that can be written up on the board. For example:
'If students are unsure of the words, write them in two columns on the board under the headings <u>*Adjectives*</u> and <u>*Nouns*</u>.'

<u>*Adjectives*</u>	<u>*Nouns*</u>
<u>*high*</u>	<u>*height*</u>
<u>*wide*</u>	<u>*width*</u>
<u>*long*</u>	<u>*length*</u>

Terminology

The following terms are used frequently and you may wish to remind students what they mean:
- Scan reading: to read something very quickly to get a general idea of its meaning or to find particular information. It is not necessary to understand every word.

- Skim reading: to read something very quickly to find the main point or particular points. As with scan reading it is not necessary to understand each and every word.
- Listening for gist: to listen to something to get a general idea of what it's about without focusing on specific information or language that's used.
- Brainstorming: to get lots of ideas from a group of students without stopping to evaluate suggestions. The best ideas/suggestions can be discussed after the brainstorming session. It's important to write up all suggestions however unusual they might seem.

We sincerely hope you will enjoy working with *The* **Business** 2.0.
Good luck!

John Allison
Paul Emmerson

Business fundamentals

Subject background

Business fundamentals introduces students to basic business principles and vocabulary. This material is designed to prepare students for the course and to provide a solid foundation on which they can build as they make their way through the material.

The first section, *Company types and structure*, reviews the main sectors of industry, different types of companies and possible business models. This is followed in section two, *Company finance*, by a look at how companies are financed, company accounts and the movement of money in the business cycle. Section three, *Supply chain*, deals with systems which enable products to make their way from suppliers and manufacturers to the customer. Finally, section four, *Recruitment*, looks at how to sell yourself and your skills in the workplace by reviewing possible structures for CVs / résumés and introducing useful phrases for cover letters.

1 Company types and structures

This section focuses on describing different types of industries and businesses and the way they are organized and structured.

LEAD-IN ACTIVITY

Find out how much students know about the terms used in this module. Write the following on the board and ask students to tell you what they think they mean:

PLC   B2C   sole trader   tertiary industry

Alternatively, write some different jobs up on the board and get the students to tell you what kind of company or organization the people doing such jobs would probably work for and what kind of business structure or model the company would be based on, e.g.

- a car mechanic – might work for a garage/car repairers. Garages are often small businesses, such as a partnership or a small-scale limited company. They don't normally manufacture or produce goods but provide a service repairing and maintaining vehicles and often also buying and selling them. Garage's customers may be private individuals, but they may also have contracts with companies, for example to maintain and service a fleet of company vehicles.
- a freelance web designer – would probably work for themselves as a sole trader. If their revenue was big enough, they might consider registering their activities as a limited company in order to pay less tax. He or she would probably work for a number of clients; these might be private individuals but are more likely to be companies of some kind with websites that needed to be designed or maintained.
- a petrochemical engineer – would often work for an oil company, many of which are large multi-national public limited companies, floated on the stock market. The business model would be B2B.

Vocabulary

1 Give students a couple of minutes to read through the chart. Talk the students through the different sections of the chart and make sure they understand that the terms given in the 'business type' section refer to the system in Britain and the United States. Elicit the terms for the equivalent of Ltd or a PLC company in the students' own countries, for example:

France – *SARL (Société à responsabilité limitée): private limited company; SA (Société anonyme): public limited company*

Germany – *GmbH (Gesellschaft mit beschränkter Haftung): private limited company; AG (Aktiengesellschaft): public limited company*

Spain – *S.L. (Sociedad Limitada): private limited company; S.A. (Sociedad Anónima): public limited company*

Students categorize the products and services. Let them compare their answers with a partner.

POSSIBLE ANSWERS:

	Industry type	Business type	Business model
Your internet connection	tertiary (service)	If your internet service is provided by a big telecoms company, this is likely to be a public limited company.	B2C
Your bicycle	secondary (manufacturing)	private limited company	B2B
Spare parts for your car	secondary (manufacturing)	private limited company	B2B2
Your milk and cheese	primary (farming)	private limited company	B2B
Your haircut	tertiary (service)	The hairdresser could be working independently as a sole trader, or be part of a partnership or a private limited company.	B2C
Your dental care	tertiary (service)	Your dentist may be working for a partnership or a private limited company.	B2C

2 Students work in pairs or small groups to match the companies to the business structures. In feedback, ask students with experience of these types of structures to describe how the organization works.

ANSWERS:

Small family business = product structure
Global online retailer = hierarchical structure
Multinational conglomerate = functional structure
Medium-sized manufacturer = matrix structure

Listening

3 1:01–1:05 A good way to approach this is to play the first recording (Mina) with a focus question: *What does Mina's company do?* (mining) Then give students a moment to complete the table for Mina. Let them compare answers with a partner. Then play the other recordings in the same way. Play the recordings a second time if students haven't completed the table on first listening.

ANSWERS:

Speaker 1 – geologist – primary – B2B – PLC – matrix
Speaker 2 – photographer – service – B2C – sole trader – N/A
Speaker 3 – production supervisor – secondary – B2B – Ltd – hierarchical
Speaker 4 – lawyer – service – B2B – partnership – product
Speaker 5 – business development manager – service – B2B2C – PLC – hierarchical

RECORDING SCRIPT

1:01–1:05

Mina: I'm a geologist with a well-known multinational corporation – maybe you even own shares in our company. Our core business is mining – gold, silver, copper, iron and so on. We have a complex structure; each geographical region has a local management structure, but individual product managers also report to different functional managers at HQ – R&D, finance, marketing etc. It's a huge operation, so decision-making can be very slow!

Marty: I'm a freelance photographer, so I run my own business. I do a lot of weddings, parties and so on. Because I'm self-employed, I can do things my way, which is great; on the other hand, it's financially risky. For example, if the business got into trouble, I could lose my home.

Owen: We make furniture for firms like Ikea. I sort of supervise production, and my sister runs the office, but in fact my dad decides everything. He's the General Manager. It's a family business; there are six shareholders altogether, but we can't really do anything without Dad.

Isabelle: I share an office and an assistant with three other lawyers. I specialize in employment law, advising companies on HR issues; my partners each have their own specialization, and Sarah, our assistant, works for all of us. In theory, as managing partner, I'm the boss, but in practice we each look after our own clients. So it's a very flat structure, there's no real hierarchy.

Frank: I work for a hairdressing franchise – my job is to recruit and manage new franchisees; I report directly to the CEO. We help franchisees to set up salons, promote our products, and ultimately, increase our shareholder value. It's good business for them, but although they manage their own Llc, they don't have any real say in how things are done; there's a procedure for everything – and I mean everything!

EXTENSION ACTIVITY

Ask students to prepare a brief presentation of their company structure. Tell them to think in terms of industry type, business model and type, and of company structure. Write the following expressions from Exercise 3 on the board to help students structure their presentation:

We have a simple / complex structure.
The manager reports (directly) to …
I run my own business.
I share an office with …
I specialise in …
I work for …

2 Company finance

This module looks at company finances and introduces or revises the terms for talking about company accounts and the movement of money in the business cycle.

LEAD-IN ACTIVITY

Write the word *Money* on the board. Divide the class into pairs or threes and tell them to think of and write down as many words connected with money as they can in two minutes. In feedback, elicit and write up interesting words (or ask students to come to the board and write their own words), and find out which pair or group thought of most words.

Possible list: (verbs) *pay, buy, sell, lend, borrow, owe, deposit, withdraw, exchange*
(nouns) *profit, loss, costs, revenue, debt, credit, tax, cash, change, loan*
(adjectives) *rich, poor, wealthy, prosperous, profitable*

Reading

1 Ask students to look at the picture and magazine article layout and guess what sort of company Baker's Dozen might be. In feedback, point out that it's a company that makes and sells bread and cakes. Tell students that *dozen* usually means twelve, but that the common English expression *a baker's dozen* means thirteen.

Students read the article and choose the best summary.

ANSWER:

c

Vocabulary

2 Students match the words in bold in the text to the definitions in the diagram. Let them compare their answers in pairs before discussing in whole class feedback.

ANSWERS:

1 revenue 2 cost of goods sold 3 gross profit
4 operating costs 5 operating profit
6 tax and depreciation 7 net profit after tax
8 dividends 9 retained profit

EXTENSION ACTIVITY

Point out the strong stress in some of the longer words and ask students to repeat the words after your model:

revenue *operating* *profit* *depreciation* *dividends*

3 Check the students understand the terms *assets* and *liabilities* and elicit a few examples of each before they start the exercise. They can work on their own to categorize the assets and liabilities and then check their answers in pairs.

ANSWERS:

Current assets: unpaid customer invoices, raw materials, inventory
Long-term assets: office furniture, cars, production machinery, patents, buildings, land
Current liabilities: unpaid supplier invoices, unpaid salaries, unpaid insurance premiums
Long-term liabilities: bank loans, mortgages
Shareholders' equity: money invested in the company by the founders, retained profit

3 Supply chain

This section focuses on describing a supply chain.

LEAD-IN ACTIVITY

Write the following products on the board:

chewing gum *yoghurt* *light bulb*

As a whole class activity, ask students to imagine and describe supply chains for each of these products.

1 Give students a moment to look at the diagram of the supply chain and ask students to describe how it works.

Students read the text and fill in the gaps with the names of the companies in the supply chain.

ANSWERS:

1 High Street PCs Ltd
2 China Keyboards Ltd
3 General Plastics Corp.
4 Electronic Distribution PLC
5 Cherry Computer Inc
6 China Keyboards Ltd
7 Electronic Distribution Ltd

2 Ask students to complete the sentences with the correct preposition. Let them compare their answers in pairs before discussing in whole-class feedback.

ANSWERS:

1 from 2 with 3 to 4 from 5 with 6 to 7 Ø 8 for

3 In pairs, students complete the diagram. In feedback, ask pairs to describe the way the financial supply chain works in their own words.

ANSWERS:

1 goods despatched
2 goods delivered
3 delivery note signed
4 delivery note copy returned
5 delivery confirmed
6 invoice generated

POSSIBLE ANSWER:

The goods are despatched and then delivered to the customer. When the customer receives the goods, the delivery note is signed and the delivery note copy is returned to the supplier. The delivery is confirmed when the supplier receives this. Once the supplier knows the customer has received the goods, an invoice is generated and sent to the customer. Payment is made by the customer after they have received the invoice.

4 Start by eliciting ideas from students verbally. Ask them to say how they think a supply chain might work in each of these sectors, and write up any words students might need on the board.

In pairs, students choose one of the sectors and draw a diagram. Give them time to practise how to describe their diagram then put pairs together to make groups of four. Pairs take turns to describe their diagram.

EXTENSION ACTIVITY

As students describe their diagrams, monitor and listen carefully. Note down any errors or examples of poor language use that you hear. At the end, write up errors on the board and ask students to correct them. If students didn't describe their diagrams all that well the first time, you could get them to describe them again using the corrected language from the board.

4 CVs and cover letters

CVs and cover letters

This module focuses on providing a model text for both a standard CV and cover letter, and on providing practice for students so that they can write their own CV and cover letter.

LEAD-IN ACTIVITY

Bring in copies of your own CV and pass it round the class. Encourage students to ask you questions about your career from the information on the CV, and to make comments about how it could be improved.

Writing

1 Give students two minutes to skim read Lina's CV. Ask a few focus questions: *What is Lina's surname? Which school did she go to? What languages does she (probably) speak?*

Using the model, students create their own CV. It is a good idea (and more realistic) if you get students to write their CV on a PC rather than hand-written. So, if you have access to computers in school, get students to use them. Alternatively, you could set up this task at the end of a lesson and ask students to produce their CV in time for the next lesson.

Speaking

2 In pairs, students ask and answer questions about their CVs. Monitor and check that students have written information for each section. After the discussion, give students time to adapt their CVs based on the question and answer section.

Writing

3 Give students two minutes to skim read the cover letter. Ask a few focus questions: *Who has written the letter? Where is he studying now? Who has he written to?*

In pairs, students re-order the phrases in the cover letter.

ANSWERS:

1 I am keen to gain business experience
2 I have extensive knowledge of
3 considerable experience of assembling computers
4 has given me a strong interest in retailing
5 hard-working and highly motivated intern
6 make a valuable contribution to your organization
7 would be happy to accept any position
8 I will call you next week to answer any questions
9 please feel free to contact me at any time
10 for your time and consideration

4 Students use the model of a cover letter to help them to write their own. You could set this for homework.

EXTENSION ACTIVITY

Bring in some ads for students to look at. You could bring in a job ads page from a newspaper or a website with a variety of jobs on it, (or, if your students have similar professions, you could bring in a page of jobs relevant to them).

Ask students to skim read the jobs and ask some focus questions: *Which job pays best? Which job is most interesting or relevant for you?*

Ask students to choose one of the jobs to apply for. Students must look back at their CVs and cover letters and decide how to rewrite or adapt them so that they are more appropiate when applying for the job they chose.

As a follow-up activity, put students in pairs and ask them to take turns interviewing each other for the jobs they chose to apply for.

1 Corporate culture

Digital resources for Unit 1

eWorkbook

Language practice: interactive & printable grammar, vocabulary, listening & pronunciation practice activities, extra printable reading & writing worksheets
Listen: Student's Book audio, language practice audio
Watch: video & video worksheets
Tests: interactive multiple-choice test
Resources: word list, grammar help & writing tips

Teacher's Resource Disc

Video: video & video worksheets
Audio: Student's Book audio
Tests: progress test Unit 1
Resources: PowerPoint Unit 1, business document Unit 1, photocopiable worksheets, Student's Book answer key, Student's Book glossary

Subject background

What is corporate culture? There are two answers to this question, one non-academic and one academic. In the non-academic approach, the basic definition of corporate culture is 'the personality of an organization', or simply 'how things are done around here'. It includes:

- core values and beliefs.
- corporate ethics.
- rules of behaviour.

Corporate culture can be expressed in the company's mission statement and other communications, in the architectural style or interior decoration of offices, by what people wear to work, by how people address each other, and in the titles given to various employees. Then there is the academic approach to corporate culture (often called 'organizational culture' in this context). There are many gurus in this field, and perhaps the best known is Geert Hofstede. He has developed a Cultural Orientation Model which classifies cultures based on where they fall on five continuums (highly simplified below):

1 Individual vs. collective
(At what level in the organization is behaviour regulated?)
2 Power distance
(Do less powerful parties accept the existing distribution of power?)
3 Uncertainty avoidance
(Do employees feel threatened by ambiguity? How important are rules?)
4 Dominant values
(What are the dominant values? Assertiveness? Money? Job satisfaction?)
5 Short-term vs. long-term
(Do employees expect immediate or deferred gratification?)

Company culture affects employees in many ways. For example:

- the hours you work, including options such as flextime and telecommuting.
- the work environment, including how employees interact, the degree of competition, and whether it's a fun or hostile environment.
- the dress code, including accepted styles of clothing and things such as casual days.
- the office space, including things such as cubicles, window offices, and rules regarding display of personal items.
- training and skills development available to employees.
- onsite perks, such as break rooms, gyms, daycare facilities, etc.
- the amount of time outside the office you're expected to spend with co-workers.
- interaction with other employees, including managers and top management.

Another key issue is whether the company hierarchy is 'tall' (with many layers) or 'flat' (with few layers). This links to the issue of the delegation (or not) of responsibilities. The importance of corporate culture is growing as the result of several recent developments, some of which are listed below.

- Companies are encouraging employees to be more responsible and act and think like owners.
- With the decline of more traditional communities (e.g. neighbourhoods) companies are filling their employees' need to belong to a community.
- Companies are encouraging teamwork.

For all these reasons, organizations need to make their culture explicit, and it is increasingly referred to in mission statements and emphasized in company-sponsored training and company communications.

Useful websites

Websites with background information on company culture include:
http://humanresources.about.com/od/organizationalculture
http://www.answers.com/topic/organizational-culture

For individual companies, look for the 'investor relations' button on the company website. Download the annual report and look at the CEO's opening comments.

Job seekers might be interested in how to research a company before an interview. Try sites like this one: **http://interview.monster.com/articles/compculture**

1.1 About business
Work culture and placements

This module focuses on the culture of the workplace and the unwritten rules of behaviour that can be found in every organization.

Internet research

Students can be asked to do this search before the lesson which will help with the lead-in discussion or after the lesson as a follow-up activity for discussion at the start of the next lesson.

An Internet search of 'work fun' will reveal references to office parties and outings, celebrating employees' birthdays, competitions or contests in which employees win prizes, etc. However, having fun at work can produce benefits for a company. It can contribute to greater job satisfaction, help to improve productivity and morale, reduce absenteeism, and improve employee retention rates. Other factors that would make employees happier at work might be meaningful and challenging work; good people skills in their managers; a pleasant physical environment; good facilities.

LEAD-IN ACTIVITY

Ask students to tell you what their ideal workplace would be like. The purpose here is simply to get students thinking about the topic of corporate culture and what it entails. Encourage students to be as imaginative as they can and to talk about a range of topics: physical environment, working hours, managers, meetings, annual leave, physical environment, business travel, etc.

Discussion

1 Check that students know the meaning of *work placement* (a period of work, usually unpaid, that someone does in order to get experience in the world of work; also known as work experience, and in American English as an internship).

Ask students to discuss the questions in small groups. Useful words and expressions that may arise from this discussion are:
to conform (to follow generally accepted rules).
to fit in (to be in harmony with something or someone).
to step out of line (to behave in a different way from what is expected).
to rock the boat (to do something that causes problems or difficulties).

Take whole-class feedback.

SUGGESTED ANSWER:

It depends on company culture. New employees need to try to work out quickly what is expected in each of the three situations and to adjust to the company culture as soon as they can. To start off though, it's probably safest to dress smartly, not be the first or the last to leave the office, maybe make one or two contributions to a meeting, but more importantly to listen and learn at first.

Scan reading

2 Ask students to read the first two paragraphs of the article quickly, then to close their books.

Get students to explain what happened in the experiment.

Read aloud the three pieces of information that students have to find in the article. Remind students what scan reading is (see page 7).

Students open their books, and read the whole article silently. Help with new vocabulary, if necessary. Remind students to use the *Glossary* on page 152 in the *Student's Book*.

Get students to compare their answers with a partner. Take whole-class feedback.

ANSWERS:

a) The experiment demonstrated how an unwritten rule is created.
b) Below are seven examples of unwritten rules.
   - Nobody should ever climb the ladder.
   - Working long hours is more important than achieving results.
   - The boss is always right, even when he's wrong.
   - If you're not at your desk, you're not working.
   - Nobody complains, because nothing changes.
   - Women, ethnic minorities and the over 50s are not promoted.
   - The customer is king, but don't tell anyone, because management are more interested in profitability.
c) New staff quickly learn when their ideas and opinions are listened to and valued, and when it's better to keep them to themselves; which assignments and aspects of their performance will be checked and evaluated, and whose objectives and instructions they can safely ignore. They learn from the way staff speak to management, to customers and to each other, and from the differences between what is said, decided or promised, and what actually gets done.

Discussion

3 Ask students to keep a list of points made in this discussion as they will be useful for Exercise 6. After each question take whole-class feedback.

Question 1: Ask students to look at the unwritten rules they underlined in the article and to think about how companies can avoid them.

SUGGESTED ANSWER:

Organizations and companies can try to avoid negative unwritten rules by respecting commitments, giving and listening to feedback, defining and applying clear procedures, providing training to develop a positive work culture.

Question 2: Ask the whole class to describe the kind of work that goes on in each type of organization and to suggest some adjectives to describe them, e.g. a government department (*traditional, hierarchical*), a small public relations firm (*relaxed, informal*), a manufacturing company (*highly-structured, organized*).

SUGGESTED ANSWER:

A government department:
- Office etiquette: formal dress code, strict office hours, inflexible, subject to security constraints.
- Relationships with colleagues, management and clients / business partners: hierarchical and formalized.
- Autonomy and initiative: limited, strict procedures for everything.

A small public relations firm:
- Office etiquette: probably very informal, relaxed, flexible, results-orientated rather than time-conscious.
- Relationships with colleagues, management and clients / business partners: friendly and participative, little or no visible hierarchy.
- Autonomy and initiative: wide, but must be justified.

Question 3: Students' answers will vary, but aim to draw out the reasons for their answers.

> **EXTENSION ACTIVITY**
> Ask students to compare the two types of organization in Exercise 3 with their own companies or organizations or ones they know. Encourage them to mention the topics listed in Exercise 3.

Listening for gist

4 1:06, 1:07 Remind students that they are listening for gist (see page 7). Get students to compare their answers with a partner after listening. Check answers with the whole class.

ANSWERS:

1 Sandra was not accepted by her colleagues because they felt that she left work too early. David upset an intern who arrived late.
2 Sandra misunderstood the (unwritten) office rules on working hours. David assumed Monica (the intern) would know to inform him she had a dentist's appointment, but she didn't; Monica misinterpreted David's friendliness as changing the supervisor–intern relationship.

RECORDING SCRIPT

1:06

Sandra:

I got my first placement in a PR firm in Paris. Our teachers had told us to be careful about dress code, being on time, and so on. But I had a problem I really wasn't expecting.

The first day, I arrived at eight thirty and I was a bit surprised because I had to wait an hour and a half for my supervisor to arrive. In fact, most people came in at about eleven o'clock. But everybody was very friendly. They gave me a project to work on and I thought, great, I can really do a good job here and, you know, make a good impression.

Well, for the first two weeks I worked from nine in the morning to about seven in the evening. I didn't really have a social life because I only got home about eight, but, like I said, I wanted to make a good impression. But then gradually, people became less friendly, and stopped talking to me. I couldn't understand why they were giving me these funny looks, especially when I went home in the evening.

Anyway, in the end, I went and asked my supervisor what I'd done wrong. And, in fact, the problem was that most people didn't go home until 9 or 10pm. So because I left at about seven, I was breaking the unwritten rules. They all thought I was lazy! I mean, I knew I was the first to leave, but I arrived at 9am, and I was working really hard, you know?! But as far as they were concerned, you couldn't do any real work before eleven, so arriving at nine in the morning didn't count!

1:07

David:

I'm a department manager in the civil service. The department's actually very informal and friendly – we're all quite young and everyone's on first name terms. We all have lunch together in the canteen and we often go to the pub for a drink after work. We have one or two interns per year. We try to make them feel at home and part of the team, and usually it's fine.

But, a year or two ago, I had a problem with an intern I was supervising. At first, everything was fine. Monica was very bright and friendly, and got on well with everybody. But then one day we had a crisis in the office. My manager needed one of Monica's files for an important meeting at 10am. We couldn't find it, and unfortunately Monica wasn't in the office; she wasn't answering her phone, and she didn't arrive until ten fifteen! In fact, she'd been to the dentist's, but she hadn't told me that she'd be late. Well, as you can imagine, I was stressed out and I made it very clear that this was unacceptable. And Monica just burst into tears, so I had to tell her that, you know, that was unprofessional too.

Anyway, after that, things were never the same. She stopped socializing with the rest of the team; she wouldn't say anything in meetings and she didn't even eat in the canteen with us anymore. I tried to explain that it was my job to tell her when there was a problem, and that it wasn't personal. But she couldn't accept that. For her, a boss was a boss, and a friend was a friend, and you couldn't be a boss *and* a friend.

Listening for detail

5 Play 1:06 and 1:07 again. Pause the recording at appropriate places and ask students to use their own words to describe the mistakes each student and supervisor made.

ANSWERS:

Students' mistakes:
Sandra's story: didn't ask about / was not sensitive to unwritten rules; didn't talk to colleagues
David's story: took friendly culture at face value; didn't accept criticism; didn't learn from the problem
Supervisors' mistakes:
Sandra's story: didn't tell student about unwritten rules; gave student too much autonomy; didn't make sure student met colleagues
David's story: didn't explain local work culture; didn't keep enough distance from intern; didn't understand the intern's confusion

> **EXTENSION ACTIVITY**
> Ask students to work in small groups and describe any experiences they have had themselves as an intern or as a supervisor. They should explain what happened and what mistakes were made. Each group then chooses one story to share with the whole class.

Brainstorming and presentation

6 Remind students what brainstorming is (see page 7). Students could use the ideas they noted down in Exercise 3 to help them write the guidelines.

1.2 Vocabulary
Work organization and responsibility

This module focuses on the vocabulary of organizational structure, role and responsibilities, and employment.

Internet research

Some possible results for this search might be: CIO (Chief Information Officer), CMO (Chief Medical Officer), COPE (Chief Officer for Planning and Environment), CTO (Chief Technology Officer), CSO (Chief Security Officer), CCO (Chief Compliance Officer – responsible for ensuring that a company and its employees are in compliance with government regulations and internal policies), CNO (Chief Nursing Officer), CPO (Chief Police Officer), CFO (Chief Fire Officer).

Students could do a search under 'Chief x-Officer'. CXO is now frequently used as a generic term covering all Chief 'Something' Officers (x = something). Students may come across some humorous examples, such as:
CCO (Chief Chocolate Officer), CIO (Chief Intimidation Officer) and CXO (Chief Xeroxing Officer).

Discussion

1 Ask some students to read the words aloud and check pronunciation. Explain any new vocabulary or allow students to use their dictionaries. Some answers may vary.

Check answers with the whole class.

SUGGESTED ANSWERS:

1 work – *Work* is an uncountable noun referring to a general concept. The other words all refer to specific items.
2 deputy – Your *deputy is* a subordinate who reports to you. The other words refer to people above you in the managerial hierarchy.
3 collaborator – A *collaborator* is someone from a different company who works with you. The other words refer to people who work in the same company as you.

Listening for detail

2 1:08 Ask students why organigrams are useful. In this context, it helps an intern to get a clear picture of the structure of the organization and where responsibilities lie. In other contexts, if the organigram is from a customer's company, it can help you identify contacts; if it is from a competitor, it can help you understand how they run their business.

Give students a few minutes to look at the organigram. Get them to try to predict the words that are needed to complete it.

Remind students that they are only listening for departments and job titles. Play the recording again if necessary. Check answers with the whole class.

ANSWERS:

1 COO
2 Office
3 accountants
4 Business
5 PR
6 R&D (Research and Development)
7 research scientists
8 Engineering
9 technical writer
10 IT Manager
11 web developer
12 support engineers

RECORDING SCRIPT

1:08

Bertram: All right, Sam, welcome to San Antonio. Now, I just want to tell you who's who at Warndar, so you know who to go to when you have questions, OK?
Sam: OK.
B: Now, let's start here in Marketing; I'm the Business Development Manager, and I have a team of four reporting in to me; two salesmen, Jake Smith, our Art Director, and Saidah Hussain, who's our PR Officer. You'll be working mainly with Jake and Saidah in PR, but you're going to report directly to me.
S: All right.
B: As I told you, we're a small company, so the organization is simple for the moment, but we're growing fast, so that's going to change as we hire new staff. For example, right now we don't really have an HR Department – Monica Overstreet, our Office Manager, takes care of HR.
S: Yes, I met Ms Overstreet last time I was here.
B: That's right. She also looks after Finance, and she has two accountants working under her. Now then, as you probably know, Warndar Technologies was founded by Merilyn Warner, our CEO, and David Darren, who's now COO.
S: COO?
B: Yeah. Chief Operating Officer. Basically, David runs the business on a day-to-day basis. Merilyn deals with strategy; she's often away at our parent company in Houston.
S: Uh-huh – so Warndar is a subsidiary of the Irysis group, right?
B: That's right. They took us over a couple of years ago. Anyway, there are three other department heads who all report to David. Roxane Pawle is our IT Manager in charge of IT and Technical Support. She's new – she joined six months ago when our old IT Manager resigned.
S: Really?
B: Yeah. He was appointed Head of IT in a big firm up in Washington. Nice job, but too much stress. They fired him after only three months!
S: Wow!
B: Yeah. Anyway, Roxane has a web developer and two support engineers reporting to her, OK? Now, the biggest department here is R&D. Doug Pearson has seven research scientists in the lab. Doug coordinates our development programs; so he liaises with me in Marketing and with our Program Manager, Herb Monroe. Herb manages the Engineering Department, and he's responsible for building our product package. He has a team of three: two software engineers and a technical writer.
S: OK.
B: All right, I think that's everyone. So, let's go and meet Saidah – unless you have any questions?

3 Ask students to read the questions before they listen to 1:08 again. With lower-level classes, you could pause the recording at appropriate places to allow students to answer the questions one by one.

ANSWERS:

1 Because Warndar is a small company.
2 Because Warndar is growing fast, so it's going to change as they hire new staff.
3 The COO runs the business on a day-to-day basis. The CEO deals with strategy and she's on the board of the parent company.
4 Irysis is Warndar's parent company. It is based in Houston (Texas, USA).
5 Irysis took Warndar over a couple of years ago.
6 Roxane joined six months ago. Her predecessor resigned when he was appointed Head of IT at a big consultancy firm, but was fired after three months.

4 Set a time limit for students to do the exercise, then ask them to check their answers with a partner. Make a list of the key words and phrases on the board: *report to, look after, work under, run (something) on, deal with, take care of, responsible for, in charge of, my role is to …, liaise with*.

ANSWERS:

1 c) 2 e) 3 d) 4 a) 5 b)
6 i) 7 h) 8 j) 9 f) 10 g)

FURTHER PRACTICE 1

Working with a partner, students take turns to make true / false statements about the organigram in Exercise 2, using the words and phrases they have practised, e.g.: *Herb Monroe is responsible for two software engineers.* (True) *Monica Overstreet is in charge of two salesmen.* (False) This could also be done in small groups or as a whole-class activity.

FURTHER PRACTICE 2

Prepare some sentences about the organigram using the words and phrases in Exercise 4. Read them aloud or write them on the board and ask students to correct them, e.g.: *Three accountants report to the Office Manager.* (Two, not three accountants report to the Office Manager.)

The R&D Manager manages seven technical writers. (He manages seven research scientists, not seven technical writers.)

The IT Manager is in charge of one support engineer …, etc.

Students could also prepare their own sentences.

Prepositions

5 This exercise focuses on the use of various prepositions with *to work*. When students have completed the exercise, these phrases can be added to the list compiled in Exercise 4. Students can then refer to this list when they are doing Exercise 6.

ANSWERS:

1 alongside 2 under 3 as 4 at 5 in 6 on

EXTENSION ACTIVITY

To personalize the activity in Exercise 5, ask students to make sentences about their own company or job (or a company or job they know), using words and phrases from Exercises 1–5, e.g.:
I report to the Product Development Manager. My role is to research new products for the over-50s market.
Or: *My sister is a research scientist. She is in charge of a project team with five engineers working under her. She reports to the R&D Manager.*
Students could also bring in organigrams for their own companies or companies they know for comparison and discussion.

Discussion and presentation

6 To introduce the topic, ask if any students have ever had music lessons at a music school. If any have, get the other students to ask questions about the music school. If not, ask students to brainstorm (see page 7) what they think a music school might be like and what might happen there, e.g. they provide lessons in singing and playing instruments; you can get qualifications in music; they put on concerts, etc.

Check that students know the vocabulary in the box. Explain or give examples, if necessary.

7 Circulate while students are speaking. Without interrupting the activity, make a list of any mistakes in the target language for remedial work later. For example, note down the exact words that were used wrongly and write them on the board, but without identifying the student who said them. Get the class to correct the mistakes.

When students have finished their presentations, display the organigrams on a table or wall so that students can see the similarities and differences. Get students to explain why they chose the structure they did.

Defining words

8 This crossword activity focuses on the vocabulary of employment: *demotion, transfer, fire, hire, dismiss, promotion, retire, join, resign, appoint.*

With lower-level classes, you could model one or two simple ways of defining words, perhaps by using some words from Exercise 7, and get them to guess the word:
This means the same as buying. (purchasing)
When you pay someone money for working you give them this. (salary), etc.

EXTENSION ACTIVITY

When students have completed and checked their answers, focus on the meaning and use of these words. For example, ask students the following questions:
Which pairs of words have the same or similar meanings? (hire, appoint; fire, dismiss; resign, join)
Which pairs of words have opposite meanings? (promotion, demotion; hire, fire)
What's the difference between resign *and* transfer? (*resign* – you leave the company completely; *transfer* – you move to another department or branch)
What's the difference between resign *and* fire? (*resign* – it is your choice to leave the company; *fire* – you are forced to leave the company)
What's the difference between resign *and* join? (*resign* – you leave a job; *join* – you start a job)
What's the difference between appoint *and* retire? (*appoint* – you employ someone; *retire* – an employee leaves a job at the end of their working life, usually at 60 or 65 years old)

1.3 Grammar
Past tenses and advice structures

This module focuses on the use of the past simple, past continuous and past perfect. It also introduces a set of advice structures. Students use this language to tell stories and give advice.

Internet research

An Internet search will reveal that present tenses are commonly used to tell jokes. This helps to give the joke immediacy. This search can be done before the lesson and used as a lead in to Exercise 5.

Past tenses

Start by reading the *Refresh your memory* box with students. If students seem unsure of the difference between the three tenses, work through Exercises 1 and 2 in the *Grammar and practice* section (page 122 in the *Student's Book*, answers on page 113 in this book) with them.

1 Ask students to read through the situations carefully and think of things to say. Before they do the activity, check that students know the meaning of:
snoring (making a loud noise when breathing in your sleep).
intern (student or recent graduate who is getting practical experience of the workplace).
kicking (making hard contact with something with your foot).

Students work in pairs to act out the situations. As students do the activity, walk round, listen and note any errors with past tenses. In whole-class feedback, ask a few pairs to act out two or three situations for the class.

End the activity by writing any errors on the board and asking students to correct them.

FURTHER PRACTICE

Ask students to continue with their own ideas or write two or three of the following on the board for further practice:

1 *Why were you listening to music on your MP3 during the meeting?*
2 *Why were you watching a movie on your PC?*
3 *Why were you working in your office on Sunday?*
4 *I saw you on TV yesterday. Why were you watching a football match when you said you were ill?*

Past perfect and past simple

2 Introduce the activity by eliciting possible endings for the first two sentences. Establish that in sentence 1 students have to use the past simple, but in sentence 2 students could use past perfect or past simple. Give students four or five minutes to prepare six endings. Monitor and help with ideas and vocabulary.

Ask students to read through the example dialogue. Then divide them into pairs to act out the situations.

FURTHER PRACTICE

For further practice of past tenses, get students to do Exercises 3–7 in the *Grammar and practice* section (page 122 in the *Student's Book*, answers on page 113 in this book).

Advice structures

3 Ask students to look at the phrases for giving advice in boxes A and B and check that they understand their meaning, form and use. Ask the following questions:

1 *Which five phrases are examples of strong recommendations?* (*You ought to*… and the four phrases in box A)
2 *Which seven phrases are examples of careful or friendly suggestions?* (the rest)
3 *Which phrases are followed by the -ing form of the verb?* (*Have you tried…? How about…? What about…? Have you thought of…?*)
4 *Which phrases are followed by the base infinitive?* (the rest)

Give students a few minutes to prepare things to say in each of the situations 1–6. It is a good idea to ask them to work with a partner when preparing ideas.

Divide the class into groups of four or five. Split the pairs from the previous exercise so that the students will have different things to say. Ask students to take turns to give and respond to advice.

4 Give students a few minutes to prepare things to say in each of the problems 1–6. Working in the same groups, ask students to take turns to give and respond to advice.

EXTENSION ACTIVITY

Ask students to discuss other situations when they might use strong recommendations (e.g. with a subordinate) and when they might use careful or friendly suggestions (e.g. with a colleague or a boss). Ask them to think of examples, e.g.:
You ought to get to work on time. (to a subordinate)
You might want to ask the other managers what they are doing about this problem. (to a boss)

Listening for detail

5 1:09 Check that students know the meaning of *CFO* (Chief Financial Officer). Ask the students to listen to the whole story once and answer the question: *Why did the CFO jump in?* (He didn't jump in, he was pushed in.)

Then ask individual students to read the sentences aloud. Check pronunciation and explain any new vocabulary, e.g. *to do very well for yourself* (to be successful). The meaning of *crocodiles* will be clear from the photograph!

Play the recording and get students to identify the event that happened first in each pair of sentences. For lower-level classes, you could pause the recording at appropriate moments to allow them to answer the questions one by one. Check answers with the whole class.

ANSWERS:

2 The CEO showed the executives the pool.
3 The CEO challenged his team.
4 There was a loud splash.
5 Everyone ran back to the pool.
6 The CFO climbed out of the pool.
7 The largest crocodile's mouth shut -snap- behind the CFO.
8 The CFO asked the CEO who was responsible.

RECORDING SCRIPT

1:09

Do you know the one about the CFO and the crocodiles? Well, there was this CEO, who was giving a party for his executive team. Over the years, the boss had done very well for himself, so he was proudly showing the executives around his luxurious country house. Anyway, at the back of the house, he had built the largest swimming pool any of them had ever seen. Absolutely huge, you know? But the pool was full of very hungry crocodiles. So, the CEO said to his executives, 'The most important quality for an executive is courage. Without it, you will never become a CEO like me. So, this is my challenge to each of you: if anyone can dive into the pool, swim through those crocodiles and reach the other side, I will give them anything they want. My job, my money, my house, anything!' Well, of course, everyone laughed at the challenge and nobody took it very seriously. Anyway, they had just started to follow the CEO towards the barbecue when suddenly there was a loud splash. Everyone turned around and ran back to the pool where the Chief Financial Officer was swimming for his life. The crocodiles had almost caught him when he reached the edge of the pool. He had just managed to climb out of the pool when he heard the mouth of the biggest crocodile close shut – snap – behind him. Well, the CEO shook the CFO's hand and said, 'I'm really impressed. Until you dived into that pool, I never imagined you had such courage. You accepted my challenge and now anything I own is yours. Tell me what I can do for you.' The CFO was still recovering from the swim. He looked up at the CEO and said, 'You can start by telling me who the hell pushed me into the pool!'

6 Ask students to try to complete the sentences with a partner. Remind them that they should choose one of the past tenses practised in this module – the past simple, the past continuous, or the past perfect.

Play 1:09 again, pausing after each sentence to allow students time to check or write in their answers. Check answers by getting students to read the completed sentences aloud.

ANSWERS:

1 had done; was proudly showing
2 had built
3 had just started; was
4 turned around; ran back; was swimming
5 had almost caught; reached
6 had/'d just managed; heard

Telling a story

7 Give students time to think of an interesting plot for their story. Encourage them to take brief notes and then in pairs tell each other their story. Remind them to use appropriate past tenses. As students do the activity, walk round, listen and note any errors with past tenses. In whole-class feedback, ask a few students to tell their story for the class.

End the activity by writing any errors on the board and asking students to correct them.

For further practice on how to tell or write a good story, get students to do Exercises 8–12 in the *Grammar and practice* section (pages 122–123 in the *Student's Book*, answers on page 113 in this book).

Giving advice

8 Ask students to match the sentence halves individually. Then get them to read aloud the correct, complete sentences.

ANSWERS:

1 b) 2 d) 3 e) 4 c) 5 a)
6 g) 7 i) or h) 8 j) 9 f) 10 h) or i)

FURTHER PRACTICE

Working with a partner, get students to add one or two extra pieces of advice for new employees, perhaps referring back to earlier parts of the module, e.g.:
You should be punctual.
It's important to adapt to the culture of the company.
You ought to ask permission if you need to go to the doctor or dentist in working hours.
It's a good idea to be professional at all times.

9 Give students a few minutes to read their roleplay notes. Help with any new vocabulary, e.g. Student A, *black looks* (expressions of anger or disapproval); Student B, *sombre* (serious). Tell students not to read the sentences aloud, but to put the situation into their own words. Ask students to add ideas of their own to make it more interesting.

Circulate while students are speaking and assist if necessary. Make a note of any mistakes you hear for remedial work at a later stage.

For further practice of advice structures, get students to do Exercises 13–16 in the *Grammar and practice* section (page 123 in the *Student's Book*, answers on page 113 in this book).

1.4 Speaking
Meetings one-to-one

This module focuses on the ways of using diplomatic language to deal with difficult meetings.

Internet research

A search for the key words 'learn English' will generate a wide range of possible resources for learning English. You could ask students to investigate one or two of them, and report back to the class on their usefulness. This search task can be done at any point: during, before or after this module.

Discussion

1 The questionnaire focuses on personal relationships and behaviour at work. Read through the statements with students before they answer them.

SUGGESTED ANSWERS:

Answers depend on local and work cultures.

1 In most English-speaking cultures, this is the norm, with the notable exception of Africa, where superiors, and frequently peers, are addressed by their surname. Use of the first name is also unusual in much of Asia, and in Germany.
2 Some cultures, like France, make a clear distinction between business and personal life. Others, like the Swedish furniture company Ikea, organize regular social events where all levels of staff are expected to mix freely.
3 In most Latin cultures, managers will expect subordinates to perform tasks like making coffee. Some staff in Nordic cultures may be shocked and even insulted by such a request.
4 This usually depends more on the type of work involved than on local or work culture. Personal calls for staff in production may be very unwelcome, whereas in departments like sales or marketing there is usually no particular problem.
5 This is the case in many English-speaking and Nordic cultures, especially in the USA. In Latin and Asian countries, the opposite is often true, with a certain kudos or even machismo associated with working late.
6 This probably depends on the organization as much as on the culture: in large scientific meetings, for example, the majority of attendees will not be expected to speak.
7 Some organizations welcome and even encourage junior staff to suggest improvements; this is usually less well accepted in smaller companies, where the management feel more personally involved and responsible for the way things are done.
8 Some companies have a policy of not hiring couples and will more or less actively dissuade staff from entering romantic relationships. Other companies accept that relationships will occur, but when they do, will move the partners to separate parts of the organization. In extreme cases, one member of the couple may be asked to resign.

Listening for detail

2 1:10, 1:11 Check that students understand the adjectives. Explain any unfamiliar vocabulary, e.g.: *diplomatic* (being skilful or tactful) *frank* (honest, direct).

You could also get students to pick out the adjectives with negative connotations, e.g.: *impatient, dogmatic, threatening, insincere, weak.*

Remind students that they should listen not only to what Simon says, but also how he says it. Play both versions of the conversation. Get students to compare their initial impressions about Simon's behaviour with a partner and then play the recording again.

ANSWERS:

Version 1: impatient, firm, authoritarian, threatening, frank and possibly objective and dogmatic
Version 2: objective, a good listener, diplomatic, friendly, understanding, insincere and possibly weak

RECORDING SCRIPT

1:10

Version 1
Simon: Morning, Tiffany. Good weekend?
Tiffany: Oh, yes, it was cool. And you?
S: No, not really. Listen, Tiffany, come into my office, I need to talk to you.
T: Oh, no, what now?
S: Look, I hear you had a problem with Maureen on Friday.
T: Oh, that. Yeah. That idiot refused to help me! Who does she think she is?!
S: You mustn't talk about your colleagues like that. Maureen is a very experienced assistant and a valuable member of the team.
T: Maybe, but she still refused to help me.
S: Yes, but she had a good reason to refuse. Maureen was very busy on Friday and you didn't ask for help: you demanded her immediate attention. As a future manager, you should show respect to all the staff.
T: But I was just trying to finish the job.
S: Well, you won't get results from people like Maureen if you're rude.
T: Look, I was tired. I had a difficult week, OK?
S: Tiffany, everyone gets tired, and I'm getting tired of your attitude. You apologize, or there'll be trouble. Do you understand?
T: Me? Apologize to some stupid little secretary? No way!

1:11

Version 2
Simon: Morning, Tiffany. Good weekend?
Tiffany: Oh, yes, it was cool and you?
S: Yeah, I had a good weekend too – apart from having to finish off this report. How about you? What did you do?
T: I went to the swimming pool yesterday. Gorgeous weather.
S: Mm, sounds good. Er, Tiffany, have you got a minute?
T: Sure.
S: Come in. I just wanted to have a quick word. I hear you had a problem with Maureen on Friday.
T: Oh, that. Yeah. That idiot refused to help me! Who does she think she is?!
S: Well, Tiffany, I think perhaps you should be more careful about how you talk about your colleagues. Maureen is a very experienced assistant and a valuable member of the team.
T: OK, but she still refused to help me.
S: Well, you might want to think about why she couldn't help you. Maureen was very busy on Friday, and I understand you didn't really ask for help so much as demand her immediate attention. We try hard to respect all our staff here. As a future manager, I think you ought to do the same.
T: But I was just trying to finish the job.
S: Well, I understand that, and I appreciate that you work hard and that you expect other people to show the same commitment. But, don't you think you might get better results from people like Maureen by being a little more diplomatic?
T: Yeah, OK. I'm sorry, you're right. I was tired. I didn't mean to be rude.
S: OK. It can happen to anyone. Why don't you ask Maureen to have a coffee with you, and just clear the air? OK?
T: OK. Thanks, Simon.

3 Ask students to discuss the questions with a partner. Then, in whole-class feedback, elicit from students the main differences between Simon's language in the two versions of the conversation. Point out that the tone of voice he uses is also different. In Version 1 it sounds abrupt and slightly aggressive; in Version 2 it is firm but not aggressive.

SUGGESTED ANSWERS:

1 Simon's approach in the second version is more successful because it is more diplomatic. He isn't aggressive in the way he criticizes Tiffany's behaviour *'I think perhaps you should think about how you talk to you colleagues'*, so he avoids putting her on the defensive. He gets her to consider Maureen's point of view *'You might want to think about why she couldn't help you'*, but also demonstrates an understanding of Tiffany's position *'I appreciate that you work hard and expect other people to show the same commitment.'* He also uses persuasive tactics appealing to reason, rather than simply giving an order *'Don't you think you might get better results from people like Maureen by being a little more diplomatic'*. All this makes it much easier for Tiffany to respond calmly.
2 Whether or not there are situations when the style in Version 1 is more acceptable might depend both on the culture of the students' country and the culture of the company in question. There are work cultures in which a more 'direct' and authoritative / authoritarian approach might not only be acceptable but would be expected. The senior colleague might even lose the respect of his junior if he didn't respond forcefully. This is particularly but not exclusively true of work environments where there is a strong hierarchy, such as the armed forces, or where work is physically demanding and can be dangerous such as an oil rig or construction site.
3 Students' own answers

EXTENSION ACTIVITY

To draw attention to the effects of these two different approaches, ask students how Tiffany's response to Simon at the end of Version 2 differed from her response at the end of Version 1. (At the end of Version 1 she was angry and confrontational; at the end of Version 2 she apologized for her behaviour.)

4 1:11 This exercise focuses on specific examples of Simon's language in Version 2 of the conversation. Ask students to try to complete the expressions before they listen. Then play 1:11 again.

ANSWERS:

You <u>might</u> want to …
I think <u>perhaps</u> …
It <u>seems</u> to me that …
<u>Don't</u> you think …?
Why <u>don't</u> you …?

EXTENSION ACTIVITY

Ask students to look at the audioscript on page 139 of the *Student's Book* and find examples in Version 2 of the following: modals for giving advice (*might, should, ought to*) and introductory phrases (*Have you got a minute?; I just wanted to have a quick word …, I think perhaps …; I understand that, but …*)

Diplomatic advice

5 Students could work with a partner to make these comments more diplomatic. Point out that more than one answer is possible and encourage them to try two or three options in each case.

When they have finished, ask students to read their revised comments aloud, paying attention to intonation.

SUGGESTED ANSWERS:

1 Wouldn't it be better not to disturb your co-workers?
2 It seems to me that you need to prioritize if you want to meet deadlines.
3 You might want to delegate more if you want to finish the job.
4 I think perhaps you shouldn't eat at your desk.
5 You'd do better not to make personal calls at work.
6 Actually, I think if you ignore your colleagues, you can't expect them to help.
7 Wouldn't you agree that you should take care of your life-work balance if you don't want to get ill?

FURTHER PRACTICE

Give students a few more prompts and get them to create diplomatic statements, e.g.:
Don't take three-hour lunch breaks.
You shouldn't arrive late every morning.
You won't make a good impression if you fall asleep at meetings.
If you work too hard, you'll get stressed.

6 Ask students to practise reading the dialogue in pairs. Then get them to rewrite the dialogue using more diplomatic language.

Circulate while students are speaking and assist if necessary. When students have finished, ask three or four pairs to perform their dialogues for the class. Decide, as a class, who was most diplomatic.

SUGGESTED ANSWERS:

A: I think perhaps that it wasn't a good idea to disagree with your boss this morning.
B: Well, it seems to me that I was right.
A: Wouldn't it be better not to be so aggressive?
B: I don't think it's any of your business.
A: Wouldn't you agree that you won't progress in the company if you can't accept criticism?
B: OK. I see your point.
A: Wouldn't it be better to change your attitude a little?
B: Sure. You're right. I'll try to change.

EXTENSION ACTIVITY

Write the following sentences on the board (without the underlines) and ask students to underline the two key words, which carry the stress, in each sentence. Check the answers then ask students to practise saying the sentences paying attention to the strong stresses and the rhythm.
(key words underlined)
1 I <u>hear</u> you had a <u>problem</u>.
2 <u>Perhaps</u> you should be more <u>careful</u>.
3 You <u>ought</u> to do the <u>same</u>.
4 I <u>appreciate</u> that you <u>work</u> hard.
5 I didn't <u>mean</u> to be <u>rude</u>.
6 It can <u>happen</u> to <u>anyone</u>.

Roleplay

7 These roleplays review the language practised in this module and allow students the opportunity to develop their own skills in problem-solving.

Remind students to use the diplomatic language they practised in Exercises 4–6.

Discuss the best kind of directive language to use, if they feel it is necessary. This is more likely to be the advice structures practised in module 1.3, Exercises 3 and 8, than the language used by Simon in Exercises 2–4. Remind students of the phrases they learnt to express strong recommendations, i.e. *you should …, it's wise to …, you ought to …, it's important to ….*

Give students time to read roleplay 1 and think about what they want to say. Tell them to put the situation into their own words, adding ideas of their own to make it more interesting.

While students are speaking, circulate and assist where necessary. Make a note of any common mistakes in the target language for remedial teaching at a later stage.

When students have finished, choose or ask one or two pairs to present their roleplay to the class. Write these two headings on the board:
Things I liked:
Things that could be improved:
While the rest of the class is listening to the roleplay, they should make notes under these headings for a feedback discussion at the end.

Ask students to work with a new partner to do roleplay 2. Repeat the procedure.

1.5 Writing
A placement report

This module focuses on writing reports and the language and style used in them.

Internet research

An Internet search for 'find internships' will generate a wide range of websites which will undertake to match applicants to meaningful work placements. Internships are available in a number of industries, including retail, finance, banking, etc. The websites also offer guidance on how to make a successful application.

Discussion

1 Elicit ideas from students about what Henry's placement report might contain and the style it might be written in. Don't worry at this stage if the ideas are incomplete – the exercises that follow will draw out the important points that need to be made.

SUGGESTED ANSWER:

It will contain information about his work experience, colleagues and managers, the company, the department(s) he worked in and what he learned while he was at the company. It will be written in a formal style.

Model

2 Ask students to cover the report extracts and just read the section headings. Ask them what kind of things they would expect to find in each section. Suggested answers in brackets.

Observations about the company (details about the company and the department he worked in); *Appendix* (extra information which may be of interest, but is not required in the main body of the report); *Introduction* (some background information answering some or all of the questions *who, what, when, why, how*); *Professional achievements* (the skills and experience he gained); *Experience during work placement* (the tasks Henry performed).

Get students to skim the report and do the matching task with a partner. Check answers with the whole class.

ANSWERS:

1 c) 2 e) 3 a) 4 d) 5 b)

Analysis

3 Students work with a partner. Check answers with the whole class. Get students to explain the reasons for their choices.

ANSWERS:

1 d) Professional achievements and conclusions
2 c) Introduction
3 e) Experience during work placement
4 d) Professional achievements and conclusions
5 a) Observations about the company
6 d) Professional achievements and conclusions
7 a) Observations about the company or c) Introduction
8 a) Observations about the company

Language focus

4 You could do this as a whole-class activity, getting students to call out the formal phrases in the report as they find them.

ANSWERS:

1 under the supervision of Mr Geoffrey Thomson
2 customers were contacted by telephone
3 it became clear that
4 The order of the items was therefore modified ...
5 To obtain a similar result through media campaigns would cost millions.
6 most impressive
7 was a major challenge
8 Fortunately, I was able to apply the knowledge I had acquired in marketing in year two of my degree ...
9 the results of my study were extremely well received

EXTENSION ACTIVITY

Get students to work in small groups to summarize some key differences between the informal language of the phrases in Exercise 4 and the formal language of the corresponding phrases in the report in Exercise 2.
In formal language:

- colloquial words and phrases are not used, e.g. *guy, cool, worth a fortune*
- passive tenses are used more often, e.g. *were contacted, was modified, were well received*
- sentences are longer and more complex
- things are expressed in a positive way, e.g. *a major challenge* not *difficult and exhausting*
- exclamation marks are not used.

Output

5 1:12 Ask students what things they think Jason might tell Alex about his placement. Use the headings in Exercise 2 as prompts. Students listen and take notes individually, then compare their notes with a partner. Play the recording two or three times, if necessary.

Make sure students keep these notes for use in Exercise 6. Check answers with the whole class.

SUGGESTED ANSWERS:

- three months near Birmingham at a place called Diftco
- they export construction equipment
- it was all right
- a bit crazy there – people worked really hard, sometimes from eight in the morning to nine or ten in the evening
- in charge of preparing shipping documents
- did international trade last semester – it helped a lot to understand what was going on
- boss very strict but, OK – she didn't scream at me when I did something wrong.
- once sent a container to Austria instead of Australia
- really strong accent – I didn't understand half of what he said
- sophisticated automatic system
- can't ever completely eliminate human error
- good placement for first-years, but second-years should have more management responsibility
- was hoping to get some management experience, but I mostly worked alone
- learned quite a lot in three months
- wouldn't like to work there

RECORDING SCRIPT

1:12

Alex: Hi, Jason!
Jason: Oh, hi, Alex.
A: Do you feel like going out tonight? There's a new Will Smith movie on at nine fifteen!
J: Oh, yeah. Look, I'd love to, but I've got this essay to finish, and then I've got to write my placement report.
A: Placement? Oh, that's interesting, I didn't know you did a placement. What did you do?
J: I spent three months near Birmingham at a place called Diftco. They export construction equipment.
A: Oh, yeah, good job was it?
J: It was all right. They're a bit crazy there. People worked really hard, sometimes from eight in the morning to nine or ten in the evening.
A: Hmm ... Sounds like school!
J: Yeah! Anyway, I was in charge of preparing shipping documents. It was lucky we did international trade last semester. It really helped me understand what was going on.
A: Preparing shipping documents, eh? Sounds boring. Didn't like international trade much myself. Did you get on well with your boss?
J: Oh, she was very strict. But, OK, I suppose. She didn't scream at me or anything when I did something wrong.
A: Why, did you get things wrong a lot?
J: Nah. Only once when I sent a container to Austria instead of Australia.
A: You're joking!
J: Well, it wasn't my fault. This guy on the phone had a really strong accent. I didn't understand half of what he said.
A: So you sent a container to Austria? What an idiot!
J: Well, I bet you wouldn't do any better. Anyway, it was interesting 'cos they had this really sophisticated automatic system, but you can't ever eliminate human error completely.
A: Yeah, right, the guys at IBM only tested their systems with monkeys, they didn't expect you to be using them!
J: OK, OK ... Now, if you've finished taking the mickey, I've got an essay to write.
A: No, come on. I'm just joking. I'm really interested in Diftco. I need to find a placement for next summer.
J: Well, it's a good placement for first-years, but I think second-years should have more responsibility. I was hoping to get some management experience but I mostly worked alone, so it wasn't that great.
A: You wouldn't recommend it, then?
J: No. I learned quite a lot in three months, but I certainly wouldn't like to work there.
A: Mm, I see what you mean.
J: Listen, now I've told you all about it, you couldn't help me with the report, could you? If we finish by nine, we can still make it in time for the movie. Look, I've already made these notes. You just have to write them up for me ...

6 With lower-level classes, you could again do this as a whole-class activity. Write down the headings from Exercise 2 on the board:

Introduction, *Experience during work placement*, *Observations about the company*, *Professional achievements* and *Appendix*.

Write up these notes and the notes from Exercise 5 under the headings.

If you don't have time in class to write the whole placement report, you could write the introduction or the first sentence of each paragraph as a whole-class activity to get students started. Students then finish the report for homework.

MODEL ANSWER:

I was employed for three months at Diftco, near Birmingham, under the supervision of Ms Witten. The objective of the internship was to gain management experience in an industrial environment. Diftco exports construction equipment and is one of the most profitable firms in the region.
I worked in the Export Office most of time, where I was in charge of preparing shipping documents. I was also responsible for checking containers in the warehouse, where the equipment is assembled and packed. I successfully learnt to use the automatic bar code system used in the warehouse. This is a sophisticated automatic system, which assigns a code and a position to every component in the warehouse. However, it was interesting to discover that even such a sophisticated tool can never completely eliminate human error. Perhaps the most valuable lesson I learnt was to double-check information. The importance of careful checking was emphasized when I unfortunately sent a container to Austria instead of Australia, because I had misunderstood my correspondent on the telephone.
The company is successful and well organized, with a very motivated, hard-working and dedicated staff. However, I feel I would be more effective in an environment with more variety and less routine paperwork. One area of the company's activity leaves room for improvement, and that is the problem of waste in the warehouse. A more systematic policy of recycling would help to solve this problem.
The course module in international trade studied last semester was extremely valuable in understanding how a company like Diftco works. Thanks to this preparation, I was able to establish a good rapport with the export staff. On the other hand, communication with the warehousemen was much more difficult, mainly because many of them do not speak English.
Overall, the internship was a positive experience, which allowed me to gain significant experience in three months. However, I mostly worked alone and therefore did not achieve the goal of acquiring management experience. A placement at Diftco would be most valuable for first-year students; second-year students would benefit from a position with greater management responsibility.

Appendix: A Daily journal, B Copies of letters to and from Ms Witten, supervisor

EXTENSION ACTIVITY 1

Ask students to bring in some examples of reports they have received or written themselves. Compare them with the examples in this module – can they find the same elements? How would they change or improve their reports?

EXTENSION ACTIVITY 2

As a whole-class activity, get students to brainstorm a list of guidelines entitled 'Tips on writing effective reports'. This might include the points below.

- Use a clear structure.
- Use informative headings.
- Write in a formal style.
- Use a clear layout, e.g. bullet points, numbers, etc.
- Send it to the right people.
- Don't write too much – if it's too long, people may not read it.
- If the report is long, write a summary.
- Check it carefully for typing and factual mistakes.
- Get a colleague to read it for you before you send it.

1.6 Case study
Counselling

This module focuses on living and working abroad and the use of counselling skills and counselling language to discuss problems. On the Teacher's Resource Disc, you will find more related practice material, including a video (with worksheets) featuring an example situation for students to analyse and discuss.

Internet research

An Internet search about living and working in Japan, the UK or the USA will reveal numerous websites dealing with culture shock in general terms and the difficulties of adjusting to a new cultural environment. Many of them offer advice on how to tackle this problem. They also offer background information into the history of the country and practical information about everyday concerns such as work, study, accommodation, shopping, healthcare, banking, taxes, etc.

Students' investigations could be focused in various ways, e.g. they could research culture shock – what it is and what to do about it – or they could look into one or two topics in some detail.

Students could do this search before the lesson as preparation for the activity in Exercise 7.

Discussion

1 Give students a few minutes to brainstorm with a partner. Then, collect ideas and make a list on the board. Keep this list of ideas – it will be useful for Exercise 7.

SUGGESTED ANSWERS:

culture shock in general, language problems, homesickness, food, climate, housing, schools, family members don't make the adjustment, cultural differences at work and outside work

EXTENSION ACTIVITY

If any students have already worked abroad, ask them to share their experiences with the class.

Listening for detail

2 1:13 Read through the handout with the students before they listen. Working with a partner, get them to predict which words might fill the blanks and which skills are needed. Then play the recording. Check answers with the whole class.

ANSWERS:

Counselling = helping someone manage a personal problem using their own resources
Counselling skills = listening, talking, helping, assisting, exploring problems
The three phases of counselling = Phase one = Talk;
Phase two = Think; Phase three = Act

RECORDING SCRIPT

1:13

Now, before we go on, I'll just summarize the three points we've already discussed. Firstly, the goal of counselling is to help another person manage a personal problem using their own resources. Secondly, counselling is about listening, not about telling. It's about talking to someone and helping, not about persuading or manipulating. And, counselling is about assisting and exploring problems. It's not about reassuring someone or solving their problems for them. Thirdly, the three phases of counselling.
Phase one, talk. This is where you encourage the problem holder to talk about the problem, and to start to understand how they feel about the problem and why they feel that way.

Phase two, think. This is where you encourage them to think about the problem and reassess it. You help them to see their situation from a new perspective, so that they can consider the different options for dealing with the situation. And phase three, act. This is where you help them to choose their own solution and to establish an action plan to manage the problem. OK, are there any questions?

3 Be aware that some students may not wish to discuss personal problems so point out that they could talk about less personal issues. Circulate while students are talking and assist where necessary.

Take whole-class feedback, drawing out the similarities and differences between students' own experiences and what was said in the lecture. Some possible differences might be:
you helped someone with a problem: you didn't know what to say or do; they asked you to come up with solutions; they talked for ages and you got bored; etc.
someone helped you with a problem: they didn't really listen to you; they didn't ask how you felt; they tried to tell you what to do; etc.

Counselling language

4 This handout gives a comprehensive list of important counselling skills. Read it through with students so that they get the overall idea of what is involved. You could then do the matching task as a whole-class activity.

ANSWERS:

1 How did you feel?
2 So you're saying that …?
4 Right.
5 You were surprised?
6 So, to sum up, …
7 What are the options?
8 What would happen if (+ *past tense*)?
9 What's your first priority?
10 Why not start by *-ing* …?

5 Ask students to work with a partner to add more phrases to the counselling skills. Then take whole-class feedback, making a list of all the phrases students suggest. Keep this as it will be useful for Exercise 6.

SUGGESTED ANSWERS:

1 What did you do?
2 So what you mean is …
4 That's interesting.
5 Really? You actually (said) …?
6 So, basically, …
7 What alternatives can you see?
8 Would that get the result you want?
9 Where do you think you need to start?
10 Before you do anything else, why don't you …?

EXTENSION ACTIVITY

To put the counselling language in Exercises 4 and 5 into context in a whole-class activity, give students a few simple scenarios and get them to 'counsel' you, e.g.:

I have trouble getting on with my office mate. He's very untidy and noisy and is always making lengthy personal phone calls. He interrupts me a lot and I can't concentrate on my work.

I have too much work to do and I can't manage it all. I'm getting very tired and stressed. Last week I took two days sick leave because I couldn't face going into the office. My boss doesn't want to know – she just tells me to get on with it.

You will need to be able to respond spontaneously to what students say as the conversation unfolds. Encourage students to use as many of the counselling skills they practised in Exercise 4 as possible.

Roleplay

6 These roleplays review the language practised in this module and allow students the opportunity to develop their own counselling skills.

Give students who are going to play *Problem holder A* time to read the notes and think about what they want to say. Remind them to put the situation into their own words, adding ideas of their own where possible. While they are doing this, the *Counsellor* can review the counselling skills language practised in Exercises 4 and 5. The *Observer* should also review the handout in Exercise 4.

While students are speaking, circulate and assist where necessary. Make a note of any common mistakes in the target language for remedial teaching at a later stage.

When students have finished, take some whole-class feedback on how the roleplay went – what was easy, what was difficult, what they might do differently next time, etc.

Then, repeat the procedure with problems B and C.

Writing

7 Remind students about the discussion they had in Exercise 1. If it's appropriate, get them to refer to the results of their Internet research. Read through the phrases in the box and check that students understand them.

Give students a few minutes to write their emails. With lower-level classes, or if time is limited, the emails could be quite short, mentioning just one problem. Then get students to exchange emails and write their responses. Remind them to use as many of the phrases in the box as possible.

With higher-level classes, students could give their problem email to two or more students. The responses should be written on separate pieces of paper. The writer of the problem could then choose which response helps them the most.

If there is time, or for homework, get students to write a second email to the person who responded to the problem. In this email, they could thank them for the advice and say what they plan to do next.

2 Customer support

Digital resources for Unit 2

eWorkbook

Language practice: interactive & printable grammar, vocabulary, listening & pronunciation practice activities, extra printable reading & writing worksheets
Listen: Student's Book audio, language practice audio
Watch: video & video worksheets
Tests: interactive multiple-choice test
Resources: word list, grammar help & writing tips

Teacher's Resource Disc

Video: video & video worksheets
Audio: Student's Book audio
Tests: progress test Unit 2
Resources: PowerPoint Unit 2, business document Unit 2, photocopiable worksheets, Student's Book answer key Student's Book glossary

Subject background

The phrase 'customer service' refers to pre-sales (enquiries), sales itself (including order processing) and post-sales (returns, complaints, etc.). The phrase 'customer support' is usually limited to post-sales only.

Customer support is important because:

- in an age when many competing goods and services don't differ greatly from each other, the quality of customer support can make all the difference.
- good customer support leads to repeat business.
- a 'silent complainer' tells all their friends.
- customers have expectations of good service set by other companies.

Customer support staff are usually given pre-defined 'performance standards' which serve as guidelines in their day-to-day work. Here are some typical examples of such standards.

- Get it right first time.
- Only make promises that are realistic.
- When you 'inherit' an error from elsewhere in the organization, do not pass it on again (instead refer it to your supervisor if you cannot deal with it).
- Make all written work clear and simple (use standard formats where available).
- Treat customers with the maximum courtesy and helpfulness at all times.
- Leave all records and files in a state that they can be easily dealt with by someone who does not normally handle them.
- Answer all telephone calls within three rings, then give a name and a friendly greeting.
- Direct the conversation so that you identify the needs of the customer as soon as possible, then provide that information at the time it is needed.

Most customers are satisfied if their complaint is dealt with quickly and helpfully. They only get irritated or angry when their attempts to complain lead them nowhere.

Many modern companies see complaints as an opportunity. They are an excellent way of discovering problems, and once the cause of the complaint has been eliminated it should never happen again. So an efficient complaints procedure leads directly to constantly improving quality.

In addition, customers whose complaints have been resolved satisfactorily tend to become strong, long-term customers. The reason is simple: they are impressed with the care and attention given to their complaint – and how that contrasts with the indifference they have met in other companies.

A key skill for customer support staff is active listening. This means:

- letting the customer fully explain the problem with no interruptions (except for clarification questions). Only move to the problem-solving part of the conversation when they have 'let off steam'.
- paying full attention while the customer is speaking. From time to time give a brief summary of what they have been saying. This shows that you are listening and are on common ground.
- resisting the urge to argue, defend or excuse. Apologize sincerely and acknowledge any inconvenience caused.
- using the other person's name.
- making written notes of key points.
- if the conversation is face-to-face, then maintaining frequent eye contact and an open body posture leaning slightly towards the other person.
- as the conversation progresses, focusing on positive action for the future.

Useful websites

The UK's professional body for customer service has a website:
http://www.instituteofcustomerservice.com
Follow the links for 'Information Centre' and then 'Glossary of terms' for useful teaching material.
These two sites have useful background information:
http://en.wikipedia.org/wiki/Customer_service
http://money.howstuffworks.com/customer-service.htm

2.1 About business

Call centres

This module examines the growth of call centres in the Philippines. It describes how the industry has developed and the challenges it faces in the future. The module also looks at the technology involved in cloud computing.

Culture notes: The Philippines is a nation composed of over 7,000 islands in the Pacific. It has an ethnically and culturally diverse population of almost 100 million people. The capital is Manila. The Filipino language, Tagalog, is related to Malay and spoken as a first language by about a third of the population. There are about 41 pesos to one US dollar.

Internet research

An Internet search for 'call centre racist abuse' will yield articles on the abuse experienced by Indian and Filipino call-centre employees from their customers in the UK and USA. They often experience shouting, swearing, and racist comments from angry customers. Some customers resort to this kind of abuse when they are not happy with the service, but some are also angry because the call centre jobs have been outsourced and employment has been lost in their own countries. Call-centre employees are taught to remain calm and polite and not to respond to the abuse, but some have left their jobs because they find the abuse difficult to take.

Possible solutions for combating this type of abuse: allow staff to warn customers that this behaviour is not acceptable; allow them to hang up on abusive customers.

You could ask students to do this search as preparation for the first exercise in this module or as a follow-up to the lesson.

LEAD-IN ACTIVITY

Establish that students know what a call centre is (a call centre provides customer service by telephone, e.g. for water, gas and electricity companies; mail order shopping; airlines; insurance companies, etc.).

Get students to talk about their own experiences of call centres, if they have any, and what impressions they got of them. Prompt with questions like:
How long did you have to wait for a response?
Was the operator pleasant and helpful?
Was your problem solved?
How long did it take?
Did your experience influence your opinion of the company?, etc.

Discussion

1 Get students to discuss whether the location of a call centre matters. Take whole-class feedback and make two lists on the board of reasons why it does or does not matter where a call centre is located. Refer back to the lists once students have done Exercises 1–6 to see how their views match those presented in the article and the interview.

SUGGESTED ANSWERS:

Reasons why it matters:
when people have a problem, it's reassuring to have someone who is culturally and linguistically the same on the end of the line; there may be language problems with non-native speakers – their use of language may be unclear or impolite; native speakers with strong accents sometimes make it impossible for non-natives in call centres to understand; it's hard for non-natives to deal with rude or sarcastic customers because they don't understand their tone or mood; some customers worry about the working conditions of foreign workers abroad – they don't want to be using a service which is underpaying or exploiting people

Reasons why it doesn't matter:
Modern technology means that location is irrelevant in terms of cost and quality of the line; English is a world language and speakers in many developing countries often speak it exceptionally well; as call centre jobs are highly-prized in countries like India but considered dead-end jobs in Europe, you are more likely to get a brighter, more polite, more motivated call centre employee in developing countries; most people want good service or advice so the culture and accent of the call centre employee is irrelevant.

Scan reading

2 Ask students to read through the six statements first. Get them to deduce from the statements and the headline what they expect the article to be about, and which statements they expect to be true and which they expect to be false. Elicit ideas and guesses.

Check the meaning of the expression *don't put all your eggs in one basket.* (Don't focus all your resources on one hope, possibility or avenue of success.)

Then give students a few minutes to read the article briefly and silently. Ask them to write *T* (true) or *F* (false). Remind them to use the *Glossary* on page 152 in the *Student's Book*. Check answers with the whole class.

ANSWERS:

a) F b) T c) T d) T e) F f) F

Summarizing

3 Students match the headings to the correct paragraphs. You could support them by doing the first as an example. Ask students to find reasons in paragraph A why the heading 'Culture change' is an appropriate heading.

Get students to compare their answers with a partner. Take whole-class feedback.

ANSWERS:

1 E 2 A 3 C 4 D 5 B

Reading for detail

4 Students could do this exercise with a partner, and then compare their answers with another pair. Tell them to refer back to the text to research and check answers.

ANSWERS:

Strengths: cultural links; bars, restaurants and shopping malls; national language; tax breaks
Weaknesses: experienced managers
Opportunities: unreliable infrastructure to bus employees to and from work; replace up to half their staff
Threats: consultancy projects; night shifts; four million college graduates

EXTENSION ACTIVITY

Divide the class into groups of four. Tell two students in each group to look at the text and find reasons why it is a good idea to open a call centre in the Philippines. Tell the other two students to find reasons why it is still a good idea to open a call centre in India. Students compare their findings and decide which country they would choose.

Listening

5 1:14 Read through the introduction and questions with the class. Check that they understand what *cloud computing* is (the practice of using a network of remote servers hosted on the Internet to store, manage and process data) and ask them to predict what the head of customer relations at Groupon® is going to talk about.

Play the recording. Students listen and note answers to the questions. Let students compare their answers in pairs. Play the recording a second time so that they can add to their notes.

After whole-class feedback, ask students what they think is the best aspect of the way that Natterbox® operates.

ANSWERS:

1 It transfers them to the right salesperson, and if that person is not at his or her desk, it is pushed through to their mobile. If they don't pick up, it records a voicemail.
2 It recognizes the location of the call and sends it to someone local.
3 The agents come from all the regions covered by the company and have cultural familiarity and local knowledge.
4 It avoids frustration by making sure customers get through to the right person and not a machine.
5 Theoretically they coud be working anywhere in the world, even at home.

RECORDING SCRIPT

1:14

Interviewer: Groupon is currently the world's fastest growing company, with 35 million registered users all around the world. How do you keep so many customers happy?
Manager: Well, one of the key factors has been cloud computing. We're now in 45 countries around the world, and we got there in about a year and a half. If it wasn't for the cloud architecture we have in place, we could never have done that.
I: Can you give us an example?
M: Well, we've recently adopted Natterbox. Basically, it's software that decides how valuable or how urgent a call is, and then transfers that call to the best person to answer it. If an important client calls and the salesperson is not at their desk, the call is pushed through to their mobile. If they don't pick up, the system records a voicemail that can be accessed online.
I: So, if the salesperson is on the road, or in a restaurant ...
M: They still get the call. Yes.
I: And where do your call centre staff work?
M: Well, we provide customer service for England, Wales, Scotland, Ireland and Denmark from our call centre in London. But we employ agents who come from all those regions, each with their own cultural familiarity and local knowledge. Natterbox recognizes the location of the incoming phone numbers and directs the call to a customer service agent from the right region.
I: So if I'm calling from Scotland, the person who answers the phone will be Scottish, and if I'm calling from Denmark ...
M: The agent will be Danish.
I: Excellent!
M: Yes. It also means we answer every call. Before we had Natterbox, our customer service department wasn't handling around 50% of the calls – they were just coming in and getting lost. And people hate it when a machine answers their call, it's very frustrating. With Natterbox, they get through to the right person straight away.
I: So, in theory, the sales person or the customer service agent could be anywhere in the world; in London, in India or in the Philippines, in a call centre or working from home?
M: Exactly.

Roleplay

6 Divide the class into groups of three and tell each group to decide which student will play which role. Give students a few minutes to read their roleplay notes and prepare their arguments. Circulate and assist where necessary. Remind students to look back at the article and the notes they made in Exercise 4.

When students are ready, ask them to carry out their meetings. In the end, they must agree on one call centre solution.

You could use the following procedure to provide structure for the students' meetings.

1 Tell Student A in each group that they will chair the meeting. Elicit a few phrases to the board that the chair might use to structure the meeting, e.g.:
We're here today to talk about …
I'd like to begin by …
What's your view on this?
Do we all agree that …
2 Brainstorm ways of expressing opinions in meetings (revising the meetings language from Module 1), e.g.:
I think perhaps …
In my opinion, …
Would it be a good idea to …
3 Tell the chair to encourage the two other speakers to express their views first before saying what they think.

As students do the activity, walk round, listen and note any errors. End the activity by writing any errors on the board and asking students to correct them.

2.2 Vocabulary

Customer service and telephoning

This module explores a range of vocabulary and expressions for describing problems and dealing with customer service.

Internet research

An Internet search for 'golden rules of customer service' will reveal a number of listings. After students have done Exercise 9, they can carry out their Internet search and look for ideas to add to their own.

Adjectives

1 Give students a few minutes to read the adjectives in the box and check that they know the meanings. Allow them to use their dictionaries to look up any new words. Students' answers to this exercise may vary from those given below – in that case, accept any answers that students can justify.

SUGGESTED ANSWERS:

annoyed (B), cheerful (H), difficult (C), frustrated (B), grateful (C), helpful (H), knowledgeable (H), patient (H), persuasive (H), pleasant (H), reassuring (H), satisfied (C), sympathetic (H), upset (C)

EXTENSION ACTIVITY

Ask students to tell you where the strong stress lies in each adjective in the box. Tell them to underline the strong stress.

To explore the meanings of the adjectives further, get students to divide them into two groups:
positive emotions: *cheerful, grateful, helpful, knowledgeable, patient, persuasive, pleasant, reassuring, satisfied, sympathetic*
negative emotions: *annoyed, difficult, frustrated, upset.*
This will also help students to prepare for Exercise 3.

ANSWERS:

Stress on second syllable: *annoyed, appreciative, frustrated, persuasive, upset*
Stress on third syllable: *reassuring, sympathetic, understanding*
In the other words, the stress is on the first syllable

Listening for attitude

2 1:15–1:22 Play the extracts one by one and have students identify the appropriate adjectives or play all the extracts and check answers at the end. Point out that there is usually more than one possible answer in each case. When you check the answers, ensure that students are putting the stress in the correct place in each word.

SUGGESTED ANSWERS:

1 reassuring, pleasant, sympathetic
2 frustrated, annoyed, upset
3 knowledgeable, helpful
4 grateful, satisfied
5 sympathetic, patient
6 persuasive, pleasant
7 grateful, satisfied
8 cheerful, helpful, pleasant

RECORDING SCRIPT

1:15–1:22

1 Operator: Now, don't worry, Madam. This is just a minor problem that a few customers experience at first. It will only take a few minutes to resolve.
2 ... or if you would like more information about our products, please press four.
Customer: All I want is to speak to a human being, not a stupid, condescending, brainless piece of ... silicon!
3 O: All right, sir. Yes, it is an unusual problem, and it's a little complicated, but you'll be pleased to know there is a solution.
4 C: Oh, that's wonderful. You're so clever! Thank you so much!
5 O: I fully understand your position, sir, and I would feel exactly the same way myself.
6 O: Alternatively, the simplest solution is to upgrade to the professional version of the software. The extra cost is only around one euro per month. I think you'd agree that that's excellent value, wouldn't you?
7 C: Oh, thank you so much. You're so patient. I bet nobody else has these problems. I just feel so stupid!
8 O: A very good morning to you, and thank you for calling the helpline. How I can help you today?

Describing problems

3 Students work with a partner to match these ten sentences to the appropriate devices. Check answers.

SUGGESTED ANSWERS:

1 When I switch it on, nothing happens. (photocopier, PC, mobile phone)
2 It broke down on the way to work. (car)
3 It keeps crashing. (PC)
4 There's something stuck inside. (photocopier)
5 I can't switch it off. (photocopier, PC, mobile phone)
6 It's not working properly. (car, photocopier, PC, mobile phone)
7 It won't start. (car, PC)
8 It's out of order. (photocopier, PC)
9 I think it's a complete write-off. (car, photocopier, PC, mobile phone)
10 The battery's dead. (car, PC, mobile phone)

FURTHER PRACTICE

Give students a few minutes to look at the sentences again. Then get them to close their books and reconstruct the sentences from one-word prompts that you give them:
stuck (There's something stuck inside.)
order (It's out of order.), etc.

Collocations and antonyms

4, **5** and **6** Exercises 4–6 bring together a number of useful words and phrases for talking about customer service problems. Students could complete these exercises individually or with a partner. Circulate while they are working and assist where necessary. Check answers with the whole class.

When students have finished, get them to pick out any words or phrases which are new to them or that they are unsure of, and review their meaning and use.

ANSWERS:

Exercise 4

1 identify the symptoms
2 diagnose the fault
3 sort out a problem
4 talk the customer through the process
5 escalate the problem to the supervisor
6 arrange a visit from our technician
7 exchange the product
8 give a full refund

Exercise 5

1 a) 2 d/e) 3 c) 4 b) 5 d/e) 6 g) 7 f)

Exercise 6

1 switch off 2 disconnect 3 unscrew 4 remove
5 release 6 Lift out 7 insert 8 push into
9 Fasten 10 Replace 11 screw in 12 turn on

Phrasal verbs

7 Students match verbs with the definitions. Ask them to compare answers with a partner before checking them with the whole class.

ANSWERS:

1 d) 2 c) 3 a) 4 b) 5 f) 6 g) 7 h) 8 e)

EXTENSION TASK

Mime is a fun way of checking words. For example, mime someone talking on the phone, then act out hanging up, speaking up, holding on, etc. Ask students to say which phrasal verbs you are miming.

8 Students work in pairs to complete the crossword with phrasal verbs. Check answers with the whole class.

ANSWERS:

1 S												
2 P	U	3 T	Y	O	U	T	H	R	O	U	4 G	H
E		A									E	
A		K									T	
K		E		5 G	E	T	B	A	6 C	K	T	O
U		D							A		H	
P		O							L		R	
		W					7 H	O	L	D	O	N
8 H	A	N	G	U	P				B		U	
									A		G	
									C		H	
									K			

Discussion

9 Lead in to this activity by writing the following words on the board at random:

polite *listening* *time* *responding* *valued* *training* *friendly* *efficient*

Ask students if they think any of these words are important when talking about good customer service. Tell students to use some of these words when thinking of their golden rules.

Set students a time limit to write down as many rules as they can. Then get students to call out their ideas and write them on the board until you have a comprehensive list of ideas. Get students to expand on what they mean by each statement, if necessary. Keep this list for reference in the modules that follow.

SUGGESTED ANSWERS:

The customer is always right.
Make the customer feel valued and important.
Be courteous and friendly at all times.
Give customers what they want.
Always deliver what you promise.
Pay attention to detail.
Deal with problems quickly and efficiently.
Choose the right people to do the job.
Train your customer service staff to the highest standards.
Don't stand still – keep reviewing what you do and how you do it.

EXTENSION ACTIVITY

Students work in groups. They are a team of consultants with the task of improving customer relations in the following businesses:

- a beauty salon
- a dry-cleaning service
- a coffee shop
- a car repair shop.

They should think of ideas for each business that will attract and keep new customers.

Give students a time limit and circulate and assist where necessary. When students have finished, get each group to present their ideas, explaining why they think they will work.

2.3 Grammar

Questions and instructions

This module focuses on different ways of asking questions, making requests and giving instructions.

Internet research

An Internet search for 'FAQ learning English' reveals that the most frequently asked questions are usually about how to improve the four skills (reading, writing, listening, speaking), grammar and vocabulary. Other questions refer to studying abroad, examinations, learning English for work purposes, and how to study online.

Students could be asked to choose one question that particularly interests them and search for the answer to it on several different websites.

Asking questions

Read the *Refresh your memory* box with students. Write a few examples on the board and get students to match them to the rules given in the box:
Are you listening? (auxiliary verb + subject + main verb)
When will he arrive? (question word + auxiliary word + subject + main verb)
Who telephoned? (*who* is the subject so no auxiliary verb is needed)

Listening

1 1:23 Focus students on the photo in the *Student's Book*. Ask *What type of TV programme is it?* (a quiz show) *What are the people doing?* (answering questions, winning prizes, etc.). Tell students that the quiz show is called *Guess the Product*. Ask them to guess what format the show might take.

Play the recording, pause before the contestant gives the answer, and ask students to summarize the features of the product (it's found in every office; it's small enough to put in your pocket; it uses electricity; it is connected with computers, but you don't use it to speak to people. It isn't expensive; it has replaced the floppy disk). Accept all guesses about what the mystery product might be, but don't confirm the correct answer yet.

Play to the end of the game so that students can check the answer.

ANSWER:

a USB memory stick

RECORDING SCRIPT

1:23

Presenter: Welcome back to *Guess the Product*. Our next mystery product is a fairly simple but extremely useful piece of technology. Panel, you've just ten questions to help you 'guess the product'!
Contestant 1: OK. Is it advertised on TV?
P: No, it isn't.
Contestant 2: Do you use it for work?
P: Yes, you do.
Contestant 3: Would you find one in every office?
P: Yes, you would.
C2: Can you put it in your pocket?
P: Yes, you can.
C3: Did it exist twenty years ago?
P: No, it didn't.
C2: Does it use electricity?
P: Yes, it does.
C1: Do you use it to speak to people?
P: No, you don't.
C2: Is there a connection with computers?
P: Yes, there is.
C1: Does it cost more than $30?
P: No, it doesn't.
C3: Can you use it to store data?
P: Yes, you can. All right, that's ten questions. Now, have you 'guessed the product'?
C3: We think it's a USB memory stick.
P: Yes! Well done! You have correctly 'guessed the product'!

2 Give students time to look at the questions and remember, guess or predict them, but tell them not to write anything yet. Then play **1:23** again. Tell students to listen carefully and to write the questions once the recording has finished.

Let students compare their questions with a partner. Draw attention to the formation of questions using auxiliary verbs.

ANSWERS:

1. Is it advertised on TV?
2. Do you use it for work?
3. Would you find one in every office?
4. Can you put it in your pocket?
5. Did it exist twenty years ago?
6. Does it use electricity?
7. Do you use it to speak to people?
8. Is there a connection with computers?
9. Does it cost more than $30?
10. Can you use it to store data?

FURTHER PRACTICE

Ask students to think of other questions the quiz team might have asked to find out about the product.

3 Divide the class into groups of four or five. One person in each group must think of a product and the others must ask questions to find out what it is. When the group have guessed the product, another person must choose another product.

Add a competitive element by telling the groups that they can only ask ten questions before they have to guess the product. To help students with this activity, you could bring in some pictures of products or simply write the name of some products on cards. You could match the products to students' areas of interest or the work they are involved with.

Monitor the groups as they do the quiz. Make a note of any incorrect questions you hear for remedial work at a later stage.

Asking questions

4 Divide the class into small A groups and B groups with three or four students in each group. Make sure there is an equal number of A and B groups as this will affect Exercise 5.

Ask students to look at their list of answers and elicit one or two possible questions to get them stated. Monitor the groups and prompt with ideas and vocabulary as they do the task.

SUGGESTED QUESTIONS:

How many days are there in a year? 365
Who was the founder of Microsoft®? Bill Gates
What is the largest sporting event in the world?
the Olympic Games™

5 Divide the class into pairs. Make sure there is an A student and a B student in each pair. Students take turns to ask and answer questions.

If you think students need more practice of questions before they continue, work through the exercises in the *Grammar and practice* section (page 124 in the *Student's Book*, answers on page 113 in this book).

Making requests

6 Give students a few minutes to complete the sentences and put them in order. Then elicit which words need to be followed by the *-ing* form of the verb (in sentence 2 *mind* is followed by the *–ing* form; in sentence 6 to is used as a preposition so needs to be followed by the *-ing* form).

Ask students what features the most direct sentences have (they're shorter and less complex) and what features the most polite sentences have (they're longer, with introductory phrases leading up to the request).

ANSWERS:

Ordered from most direct to most polite:
5 Do you think you could possibly fax me the details, please?
4 Would you mind faxing me the details?
2 Can you fax me the details?
6 I was wondering if you would have any objection to faxing me the details?
1 Fax me the details, will you?
3 Could you fax me the details, please?

7 With a partner, students say each request aloud and reply with the responses given here. They should be able to hear what works and what doesn't work and identify the inappropriate ones.

ANSWERS:

e) No, no problem.
The negative is appropriate for 2 and 6, but not for the others.

Roleplay

8 Read the list of requests with students and get them to comment on how 'big' each one is, i.e. how much trouble will it cause the person you are asking? Is the request fairly simple / undemanding or is it more substantial? Point out that this will influence how direct or indirect the request will be. Remind students about appropriate tone of voice – the more demanding the request, the more tentative their tone might need to be.

Circulate while students are speaking and assist where necessary. When they have finished, ask some pairs to present their requests and responses.

If students need more practice with making requests, work through the exercises in *Grammar and practice* section (page 125 in the *Student's Book*, answers on page 113 in this book).

Giving instructions

9 If students are uncertain about the six modal verbs here, work through Exercises 13 and 14 which provide simple definitions of each one in *Grammar and practice* section (page 125 in the *Student's Book*, answers on page 113 in this book).

Students could work alone to complete Steve's side of the conversation, then compare their answers with a partner. Check answers with the whole class, referring to the definitions given on page 125 in the *Student's Book*.

ANSWERS:

1	don't	6	'll need to / 'll have to
2	'll have to / 'll need to	7	don't
3	needn't / don't have to	8	needn't / don't have to
4	Don't	9	don't
5	might have to	10	needn't / don't have to

10 1:24 With a partner, get students to try to complete and put them in order. You might want to point out that not all of his lines are questions. Ask students to note down what he says. Then play the recording. Get students to dictate their lines to you and write them on the board. Take whole-class feedback on the versions they wrote themselves – some of them may be perfectly acceptable.

RECORDING SCRIPT

1:24

Steve: OK, Pete. First of all, you open the printer. No, wait a minute, don't just open it, select 'change cartridge' from the menu.
Pete: From the menu? Do I have to switch the printer on?
S: Er, yes, of course you have to switch it on, otherwise you can't use the menu!
P: Oh, right. What about the computer?
S: No, that's all right, you needn't switch the PC on, just the printer.
P: All right. So, the printer's on, select 'change cartridge', OK, and open the printer. What now?
S: So now you gently remove the old cartridge. Don't force it. If it's difficult, you might have to pull it back first, then upwards.
P: Backwards, then upwards. All right, I've got it.
S: OK, so now you can install the new cartridge. You'll need to remove the adhesive tape first, but be careful you don't touch the printed circuits – they're very fragile.
P: You needn't worry. I'm being very careful. OK, that's it.
S: Right. It'll ask you if you want to align the new cartridge, but you needn't bother. Usually it's fine as it is.
P: OK; what about the old one? Can I just throw it in the trash?
S: Oh, no, don't throw the old cartridge away. You can recycle them.
P: Oh, yes, right. Listen, that's great. I really appreciate your help. Is there anything I can do for you?
S: No, that's all right, Pete. You needn't worry. Just buy me a coffee some time!

11 Read through the list of topics with students. Give them a few minutes to come up with at least two ideas of their own, if necessary. Remind students to start by making a request – refer them back to the language in Exercise 5. They should also try to use the modal verbs and reformulate their answers to show understanding, if they can.

Conversations should begin something like this:
A: Would you mind explaining how to change the oil in a car?
B: No, no problem.

2.4 Speaking

Dealing with problems by telephone

This module deals with appropriate language and intonation for a telephone helpline conversation, and focuses on explaining problems, diagnosing causes, giving instructions, and promising help. On the Teacher's Resource Disc, you will find more related practice material, including a video (with worksheets) featuring an example situation for students to analyse and discuss.

Internet research

The BBC World Service radio programmes typically include news, business, science and nature, health, technology, entertainment, sports, etc. so students should be able to find something to interest them. Lower-level students might prefer to choose a short programme.

Remind students that they are listening to get the general meaning of the programme and to pick out three interesting points. They may need to listen to the programme two or three times to do this. Students could make a note of any new vocabulary they learn connected with the topic.

Giving instructions

1 To prepare students for this task, ask them to draw a 3x3-square grid like this and to number it as shown.

1	2	3
4	5	6
7	8	9

Ask them to do the following without letting anyone else see:
Draw a small circle in the middle of square 1, and a slightly bigger circle in the middle of square 9.
Join the circles with a straight line that goes diagonally through square 5.
Draw small crosses in the middle of squares 3 and 7.
Join the crosses with a curved line that goes through squares 4 and 2 and which touches the top left-hand corner of square 5.
Ask students to compare their drawings with each other.
Tell them they are now going to give similar instructions to their partner so that their partner can draw the sign they are describing. The signs are typical signs that you might see on public transport or on road signs.
Before they begin, you could check that students know the following words that may be useful: *square, triangle, semi-circle, corners, curved, straight, along (the line), the middle of, diagonal, vertical, horizontal.*

ANSWERS:

Student A will describe a 'no mobile phones allowed' / 'switch off mobile phones' sign.
Student B will describe a 'disabled access' / 'disabled toilets' sign.

Listening

2 1:25 Read the questions and get students to predict the kind of things that might be said, given that this is a telephone conversation on a software helpline.

Play the recording and check answers with the whole class.
Ask students:
Did the helpline operator handle the call well? Was the customer satisfied?

ANSWERS:

1 The customer can't import spreadsheets into a Superword document.
2 The operator promises to ask the spreadsheet specialist to call back in a few minutes.

RECORDING SCRIPT

1:25

Helpline: Thank you for calling the Superword hotline. Please hold the line.
Dean: Good morning. Dean speaking. How can I help you?
Customer: Oh, good morning. Yes, I'm afraid your programme isn't working properly.
D: Oh, I'm sorry to hear that. What exactly seems to be the problem?
C: Well, the thing is, I can't put those automatic table thingies in my documents.
D: I'm sorry, it's not a very good line. Could you speak up a little?
C: Yes, sorry. I'm on my mobile. Is that better?
D: Yes, that's much better, thank you.
C: All right. Anyway, I was just saying, I can't insert those tables.
D: Oh, I see. You're having trouble importing spreadsheets into a Superword document?
C: Yes, that's right.
D: All right, I'll put you through to our spreadsheet specialist.
C: Thank you.
D: Hello?
C: Yes?
D: I'm sorry, the number's busy. Could I ask her to get back to you in a few minutes?
C: Yes, that's fine.
D: OK, then. So, you're on 0680 425 232?
C: That's right.
D: And could I have your name please?
C: Wyndham. Delia Wyndham.
D: Is that Wyndham with a 'y'?
C: That's right. W-Y-N-D-H-A-M.
D: Thank you, Ms Wyndham. I'm sure we'll be able to sort it out.
C: Thank you very much.
D: Not at all. Goodbye.

3 Divide the class into pairs to read through the checklist and decide which expressions were in the conversation.
Play **1:25** again. Pause from time to time to allow students to write down the expressions they hear. Check answers with the whole class.

ANSWERS:

1 b) 2 a) 3 b) 4 a) 5 b) 6 a) 7 b) 8 b)
9 b) 10 a) 11 a) 12 b)

Improving a conversation

4 You could get a student to read the part of the customer, while you read the part of the helpline operator so that you can exaggerate the negative tone of the operator. Ask the rest of the class:
How does the helpline operator sound? (e.g. rude and aggressive) *How would you feel if a helpline operator spoke to you in this way?* (e.g. annoyed).
With lower-level classes, get students to first tell you how they could improve the conversation (make the sentences less direct / longer; use a more polite tone of voice).

During the activity, circulate and assist where necessary. Choose one or two pairs to present their conversations to the class.

Get students to turn to the second conversation on page 115 in the *Student's Book*. This time get two students to read the conversation aloud. Ask students: *How does the hotline operator sound?* (e.g. bored / uninterested). Repeat the rest of the procedure as above.

SUGGESTED ANSWERS:

Conversation 1

Helpline: Superword helpline. Hold the line, please ... Thank you for holding. May I help you?

Customer: Yes, I'm afraid I'm having a problem with your program.

H: I'm sorry to hear that. Let me sort that out for you.

C: Yes, I'd appreciate that.

H: All right. What sort of problems are you having?

C: Well, I can't print PDF files.

H: Sorry? I'm afraid it's not a very good line. Could you speak up a bit?

C: Oh, sorry, yes. Is this better? I was just saying that I can't print PDF files.

H: I see. In that case, I think it would be best to speak to our PDF expert.

C: All right, can you put me through?

H: Well, I'm afraid he's not available at the moment, but I can ask him to call you back. When would be convenient for you?

C: Tomorrow morning?

H: That would be fine. On this number, Ms, er, ...?

C: Gearhirt. Jamila Gearhirt.

H: Could you spell that please?

C: Yes, of course. That's G-E-A-R-H-I-R-T.

H: All right, Ms Gearhirt. Tomorrow morning at about 9 o'clock, then?

C: Yes, that's perfect. Thank you very much.

H: You're welcome. Goodbye.

Conversation 2

Helpline: Good afternoon. May I help you?

Customer: Oh, hello. Is that Autosales?

H: Yes, sir. Pamela speaking. How can I help you?

C: Oh, good. Well, I'm calling about the new car I bought last week. It won't start.

H: Oh, I'm very sorry to hear that. It must be very annoying for you.

C: Well, can you do something about it?

H: I'm afraid the mechanics are all out to lunch right now, sir.

C: Well, can I leave a message?

H: Yes of course. Could I have your name, please?

C: It's McCready. Alistair McCready.

H: Ah, yes, Mr McCready. All right, I'll make sure someone calls you back first thing after lunch.

C: All right. Well, I'll be expecting your call. Goodbye.

H: Goodbye, Mr McCready.

Handling problems

5 1:26 Read the questions with the students and then play the recording. You could pause the recording after the customer's question, *What do I tell them?* and see if students can predict what the operator says, before playing through to the end.

ANSWERS:

1 The customer can't use Word because there is a power cut.
2 The operator tells the customer to take his computer back to the store because he is too stupid to own a computer.

RECORDING SCRIPT

1:26

Operator: Customer support. May I help you?

Customer: Yeah, well, I'm having trouble with Word.

O: Well, let me sort that out for you. What exactly seems to be the problem?

C: It doesn't work. It won't accept anything when I type.

O: I see. How long have you been having this problem?

C: Well, about ten minutes.

O: And was it working properly before that?

C: Sure. I was just typing away, and all of a sudden the words went away.

O: You mean they just disappeared?

C: Yes. Just like that.

O: So what does your screen look like now?

C: Nothing.

O: Nothing?

C: It's blank. Like I said, it won't accept anything when I type.

O: Uh-huh. Have you tried hitting 'Escape'?

C: Yes. Nothing happens.

O: OK. Did you quit Word?

C: I don't know. How do I tell if I quit?

O: Can you see the toolbar on the screen?

C: What's a toolbar?

O: OK, never mind. Can you move the cursor around on the screen?

C: There isn't any cursor. I told you, I can't type anything.

O: I see. Does your monitor have a power indicator?

C: What's a monitor?

O: It's the thing with the screen on it that looks like a TV. Does it have a little light that tells you when it's on?

C: I don't know.

O: Well, could you look on the back of the monitor and find where the power cord goes into it? Can you see that?

C: Yes, I think so.

O: Great. Now you just have to follow the cord to the plug, and tell me if it's plugged into the wall.

C: Er, yes, it is.

O: All right. Now, when you were behind the monitor, did you notice that there were two cables plugged into the back of it, not just one?

C: No.

O: Well, there are. I need you to look back there again and find the other cable.

C: ... OK, here it is.

O: Good. Could you tell me if it's plugged securely into the back of your computer?

C: I can't reach.

O: Uh-huh. Well, you don't have to touch it. Can you just see if it's plugged in?

C: No. It's too dark.

O: So, you mean the lights are off?

C: Yes.

O: Well, couldn't you just turn on the light?

C: I can't.

O: No? Why not?

C: Because there's a power cut.

O: A power ... A power cut? Ah, OK. I can handle this now. Listen, for the power cut, I'll have someone call the electricity company. For your Word problem, do you still have the boxes and manuals and packing stuff your computer came in?

C: Well, yes. I keep them in the closet.

O: Good. I'd like you to go and get them, to unplug your system and to pack it up just like it was when you got it. Then I want you to take it back to the store you bought it from.

C: Really? Is it that bad?

O: Yes, I'm afraid it is.

C: Well, all right then, I suppose. What do I tell them?

O: Tell them you're too stupid to own a computer.

6 Divide the class into pairs to read through the checklist and complete the expressions. Play **1:26** again, pausing at appropriate places to allow students time to check the expressions. Get students to read the expressions aloud and check for pronunciation.

ANSWERS:

Explaining the problem
I'm having <u>trouble</u> with Word.
It doesn't <u>work</u>.
It <u>won't</u> accept anything when I type.
Nothing <u>happens</u>.
I <u>can't</u> type anything.

Diagnosing the causes
Was it <u>working</u> properly before that?
What does your screen <u>look</u> like now?
Have you <u>tried</u> hitting 'Escape'?
Did you <u>quit</u> Word?
Can you <u>move</u> the cursor around?
Does your <u>monitor</u> have a power indicator?

Giving instructions
Could you <u>look</u> on the back of the monitor?
Now you just <u>have</u> to follow the cord to the plug.
I <u>need</u> you to look back there again.
I'd like <u>you</u> to go and get them.
Then I <u>want</u> you to take it back to the store.

Promising help
I'll <u>have</u> someone call the electricity company.

EXTENSION ACTIVITY

Write the following questions from the recording in Exercise 5 on the board:
<u>*What does your screen look like now?*</u>
<u>*What's a toolbar? Did you quit Word?*</u>
<u>*Does your monitor have a power indicator?*</u>

Read the questions out and explain that intonation falls at the end of the *wh-* questions and rises at the end of the *yes / no* questions.

Ask students to listen again and repeat. Give them further practise by asking students to read out the questions in Exercise 6 under the heading *Diagnosing the causes.*

Roleplay

7 Make sure students understand the technical problems listed. For their own ideas, students could use a real problem that they have experienced themselves. Remind students to use the language from Exercise 6 and the appropriate intonation.

With lower-level classes construct a conversation using one of the problems as a whole-class activity.

To consolidate the language work, get students to write down one or two of the conversations for homework.

EXTENSION ACTIVITY

Brainstorm ways of finishing a phone call, e.g:

- Signal that you would like to end the call
  Well, it's been good talking to you.
  Is there anything else we need to discuss?
  I'm afraid I have to go – I have a meeting in five minutes.
- Confirming action
  Can we just go over what we've agreed to do?
  Could you put that in an email for me?
  I'll put that in writing and send it to you later today.
- Promising action
  I'll take care of that. *I'll get back to you about that.*
- Closing statements
  It's been very nice talking to you.
  See you at the meeting next week.
  Well, I really must go now.

Students should practise saying these expressions with the appropriate intonation in some telephone conversations.

2.5 Writing

Formal and informal correspondence

This module explores aspects of formal and informal style in different kinds of business correspondence.

Internet research

'Email risk policy' refers to the range of issues that companies need to be concerned about in their use of email. It covers, for example, privacy issues, sexual harassment, bullying, online libel, theft of confidential information, etc. This can lead to losses in productivity, financial loss, and damage to a company's reputation. Companies may find themselves involved in costly legal proceedings as a result of email misuse or abuse. Companies should have a clear policy in place to cover these eventualities.

Students could also be asked to search news or business websites for items about the misuse or abuse of email, and report back to the class on any interesting stories they find which illustrate the risks involved.

Discussion

1 Remind students to think about grammar, vocabulary, style, opening, closing, etc. when they are discussing the differences between formal and informal correspondence.

Give pairs a few minutes to discuss and note down their answers, then take feedback from the whole class. Make a list on the board of all the points they raise. Keep this list, and add to it throughout the lesson as other points come up.

SUGGESTED ANSWER:

Depending on the language, typical features which distinguish formal from informal or neutral styles are: use of titles or specific form of address; use of polite / familiar 2nd person pronoun; absence / use of 1st person pronoun; absence / use of conventional polite expressions; use of indirect / direct style; use of formal / informal vocabulary; absence / use of contractions; use of references; reference to previous correspondence; length of sentences; layout constraints.

Model

2 Question 1: Ask students to skim read the emails quickly to identify who the emails are from.

ANSWERS:

4 a customer service department
3 a senior colleague
1 a junior colleague
2 a customer

Question 2: Students can work with a partner to decide which two emails are formal and which two are neutral / informal. Ask them to give reasons for their answers.

ANSWERS:

Formal messages: 1, 2
Neutral / Informal messages: 3, 4

Language focus

3 Students should re-read the emails in Exercise 2 more closely to complete the grid.

With lower-level classes, you could do the first email as a whole-class activity. When the grid has been completed, elicit from students the differences between the two columns, i.e. in the formal column, the expressions are usually longer and more complex; in the informal column, they are shorter; unimportant words are omitted; vocabulary is less formal / more colloquial, etc.

ANSWERS:

Formal	Neutral/Informal
Greeting Dear Ms Reckett, Dear Sir or Madam,	 Hi James, Dear Miss Roebotham,
Opening I am writing with regard to ... I am writing to enquire about ...	 Re your email Thanks for your mail.
Requests I was wondering if you could ...? I would be very grateful if you could ...	 Give me a ring ... Can you just ...?
Closing I would very much appreciate any help. Thank you for your help.	 Hope this helps. Don't hesitate to get back to me if ...
Salutation Yours sincerely, Yours faithfully,	 Cheers, Regards,

4 Get students to read each pair of emails and refer back to the emails in Exercise 2 to decide which two writers have changed style and why.

Point out that it is usually good practice to write a first email to someone in a fairly formal style, and then to adjust (or retain) this style according to the response that you receive.

ANSWERS / SUGGESTED ANSWERS:

Question 1
James has adapted to Margaret's informal style after confirming that she remembers him from the party.
Max has switched to Miss Roebotham's formal style after discovering that she is not in fact an old friend.

Question 2
Email 5
Thanks ➔ Thank you ...
Cheers ➔ Yours sincerely
Email 6
I would be very grateful if you could ...➔ Can you ...?
I would like to express my gratitude for ...➔ Thanks for ...
Email 7
I've attached ... ➔ Please find attached ...
Hope this helps. ➔ Do not hesitate to contact us again if you need any further information.
Email 8
I was wondering if you would mind coming ... ➔ Could you come / Why don't you come ...?
Yours sincerely ➔ Best wishes

Output

5 Before students start this activity, explain the context to the whole class, i.e. Students A and B work for Relopharma, a pharmaceuticals company. Student A works in the Accounts Department and Student B in the Information Systems Department. Student C works for Nakisoft, a software company specialising in accountancy software, and one of Relopharma's suppliers. The task is for students to write and reply to a number of emails.

Get students to predict the kinds of things they might be asked to write about. It doesn't matter if they don't get the right answers – the idea is simply to get them thinking about the topic.

To help students focus on the task, ask them to tell you the style they will use (this will depend to some extent on the contents of the emails, but as they are all colleagues a fairly neutral style would be most appropriate). Remind them that to clarify or explain anything in the email – if something is unclear, they should 'email' back for clarification. The emails should be fairly short and to the point, but still polite.

Give students time to read the instructions and circulate to assist with understanding them, where necessary. Remind students that they have already practised much of the language needed to do the task in earlier parts of the unit, i.e. explaining the problem, giving instructions, making requests, etc. Once students are sure what to do, get them to start writing. Higher-level students could be asked to write within a time limit.

While students are writing, circulate and assist where necessary. When they have finished the task, ask groups of students to read a string of emails aloud. Get the rest of the class to comment on the following questions:
Is the correspondence effective?
Is the style appropriate? If not, can you (either the person who wrote it or a classmate) *suggest ways of improving it?*

EXTENSION ACTIVITY

Use this matching exercise to extend students' formal vocabulary. For lower-level classes, give both the informal and formal words. You could dictate the words or write them on the board. With higher-level classes, you could give just the informal words, and get them to work out the formal words for themselves, possibly with the help of a dictionary. (The informal / formal words are presented in the correct order. You will need to mix up one list of words so that students have to match them to the correct equivalent.)

Informal	Formal
to say sorry	*to apologize*
enough	*sufficient*
secret	*confidential*
quickly	*promptly*
to tell	*to inform*
late	*overdue*
to get in touch	*to contact*
to move	*to relocate*
to ask	*to enquire*
help	*co-operation*

2.6 Case study

Cybertartan Software

This case study examines the problems faced by a contact centre – customer dissatisfaction, staff recruitment and retention, rising costs – and how they might be tackled.

Internet research

FLSA stands for *Fair Labor Standards Act*. This is a law in the USA which deals with employment issues, including minimum wage, overtime pay, record-keeping, and working conditions for children. It covers full-time and part-time workers in the public and private sector. Employers who violate the Act may be fined or prosecuted.

The FLSA does not require employers to give employees meal or rest breaks, but if they do, they should usually be paid for short breaks (up to about 20 minutes), but not for longer breaks (usually lasting at least 30 minutes).

According to the FLSA, employees should be given bathroom breaks, but there are no federal laws that refer to the number and duration of bathroom breaks. This is covered by regulations issued by the Occupational Safety and Health Administration (OSHA) in the USA.

Students can research these issues in the employment laws of their own countries and report back to the class. Possible discussion questions are:
Did they find out anything that surprises them?
What effect do they think these laws might have on productivity and morale among workers?
Do you disagree with any of the regulations?
What would you change?

Discussion

1 Read the list of customer problems with the whole class and ask them to give you some real-world examples of each one. This could be things they've experienced themselves or things they've heard about.

With lower-level classes you could give one or two examples of your own to get them started, e.g. you got poorly translated instructions with an electronic product you bought; you were put on hold for a long time by a bank or insurance company and the call cost you a lot of money; the waiter / waitress in a coffee shop was very unfriendly and the service was slow, etc.

With a partner, get students to pick the three things that annoy them most. Take whole-class feedback, asking students to raise their hands for each problem listed in the box. Ask individual students to say why the problem annoys them.

Give students a few minutes to discuss what a customer could do about these problems. The solutions could be realistic or imaginary, i.e. what would you really like to do, even though it might be very difficult or impossible to achieve, but would be very satisfying!

SUGGESTED ANSWERS:

Customers can make a complaint; send a product back to the manufacturer; refuse to buy specific products or use specific shops, etc.

Scan reading

2 Remind students what scan reading is (see page 7).
Question 1: Get students to read the email silently and look for the four problems. Ask individual students to tell you what the problems are.

Question 2: Answer this as a whole-class activity. Ask individual students to explain the links in their own words.

ANSWER:

Question 1
customer satisfaction, recruitment problems, high staff turnover, need to reduce costs
Question 2
Customers are dissatisfied because there aren't enough advisers and because they are kept on hold to increase call charges; more money rather than less is required to recruit and keep good staff.

Reading for detail

3 Ask students to read the statements silently. Then read the email aloud. Get students to raise their hands when they hear the answer to the statements. Tell them that they will need to look at the email and the pie charts to find the answers.

Ask them to give the words from the email which match the true statements, correct the false statements, and explain the 'it depends' statements.

ANSWERS:

1 T
2 F (employees and customers are dissatisfied)
3 F (average call 12 minutes @ £0.50 / minute = £6: cost of call = £4.50)
4 D (it depends – perhaps not if hold time is reduced)
5 T
6 F (only 'very dissatisfied' tripled)
7 T

Listening for detail

4 1:27 Play the first two lines of the interview – the interviewer's question and Laurie McAllister's response – and elicit the answer to the question. Ask:
What other problem does she mention? (salaries)
How does the problem with salaries affect the contact centre? (The salaries haven't kept pace with the cost of living and the company can't attract workers to the area.)

Get students to discuss briefly why they think working conditions and job satisfaction are more important to the workers than salary. Do they feel the same way about their own jobs?

ANSWER:

the shift system

RECORDING SCRIPT

1:27

Interviewer: So, Laurie, these recruitment and turnover problems we're having – is it just a question of money?

Laurie: Well of course salaries are not terribly attractive these days. They were quite good a few years ago when the centre opened, but they haven't really increased with the cost of living, especially now house prices are so expensive here, so we're finding it more difficult to attract people from outside the area. But, actually, salaries are not the biggest problem. Basically there are two reasons why our turnover is high: working conditions and job satisfaction.

I: I see. What's the matter with working conditions? We give them free coffee, don't we?

L: Well, things are very different now from when we started. In the past, the volume of calls was much lower, so things were more relaxed. Advisers had time to chat or have a cigarette between two calls. Now, the workload is much heavier, and the supervisors have to be very strict about breaks. Two bathroom breaks per day, and twenty minutes for lunch. There's a lot of unhappiness about that. And punctuality, well, the bus service here is totally inadequate. A lot of advisers can't afford a car, so transport is a real problem, especially at night.

I: Yes, I can see why that's a problem.
L: And there are little things, you know, like having your own personal space. When you share your desk with your colleagues on the other shifts, you can't really personalize anything.
I: Hmm ... Maybe there are things that can be improved there. What's the problem with job satisfaction?
L: Time, mostly. Our software products have become so complex that customers need more and more help. There are more calls than we can answer, so advisers have to keep them as short as possible. That's frustrating because there isn't time to build a relationship with the customer; sometimes there isn't even time to explain the solution properly. And then of course they say if they can't spend longer on the phone, they would like to send out instructions by email.
I: Yes, well, the customers would like that too, but we can't charge them for it like we can phone calls!
L: Exactly. And we really need to give the advisers more training, especially the new people, but there just isn't time. They often have to read out instructions from the manual; it's not much fun answering questions when you don't really understand the answers yourself!
I: No. I can see that.
L: Of course the thing they really don't like is the shift system. They work one week in the morning, from 6am to 2pm, one week in the afternoon from 2pm to 10pm, and one week nights, 10pm to 6am. I mean, it's OK for young, single people, but it's impossible for women with children, so that's a whole category of the population we have virtually no chance of employing. And some people actually like working nights, so they would happily swap their day shifts with other colleagues who don't want to work nights – but the company won't let them. It's company policy, but it's too rigid, it's just not realistic. Anyway, perhaps you should talk to the advisers themselves – get it straight from the horse's mouth, as they say.

5 Read the statements aloud or get students to read them aloud and predict what effects they might have on the workers at the contact centre. Then play **1:27** again. Pause the recording after the answer to each statement and allow students a few minutes to make notes. Check answers with the whole class.

ANSWERS:

1. This leads to high staff turnover.
2. Supervisers have to be strict about punctuality and breaks.
3. Punctuality is a problem.
4. Advisers can't personalize their work space.
5. Customers need more help; there are more calls than the centre can answer, so advisers have to make calls as short as possible.
6. Advisers have to read out instructions from the manual; explaining things they don't understand themselves is not satisfying.
7. There is no chance of employing women with children.

Solving problems

6 Read through the instructions and the agenda with the whole class. As a reminder, you could get students to list the problems experienced at the Kirkcaldy contact centre. Students then use this list to prepare their presentations. Then in groups, students should brainstorm solutions and make recommendations.

Writing presentation slides

7 Before students prepare their slides, brainstorm what makes an effective slide (use only short phrases or sentences; use headings and bullet points to make the text easier to read and remember, etc.). Don't go into too much detail at this stage as Unit 7 deals with this in more depth.

Remind students that the slides are just about their recommendations, and each recommendation should have three parts – what it is, why it's a good idea, and what the expected results will be.

Circulate while students are working on their slides and assist where necessary.

Presentations

8 To help students with their presentations, you could give them a list of useful phrases, e.g.:
First of all, I'd like to ...
Let's look at the problem of ...
That's all I have to say on ...
Now let's move on to ...
That brings me to the end of my presentation.
Are there any questions?

The presentation should be fairly short and concise. One student in each group could be nominated to give the presentation, or each student could present one recommendation.

FURTHER PRACTICE

Get students to write a short report from the consultants to Hamish Hamilton, consisting of a summary of the situation and the recommendations they have made in their presentations.

EXTENSION ACTIVITY

Students rank these factors related to job satisfaction from most important to least important. They could do this individually first, and then discuss their answers in small groups.

- *good interpersonal relationships with colleagues*
- *job security*
- *promotion prospects*
- *interesting, challenging work*
- *a good salary and bonuses*
- *independence / autonomy to act*
- *good communications and information flow within the organization*
- *opportunities for personal growth and development*
- *a good manager*
- *benefits package (healthcare, gym membership, etc.)*
- *company pension scheme*

Review 1 and 2 Answer key

Review 1

(page 34 in the *Student's Book*)

Corporate culture

1

1 b)
2 e)
3 a)
4 c)
5 d)
6 f)

2

1 deadline
2 insight
3 appraisal
4 workload
5 commitment
6 etiquette
7 overview
8 predecessor
9 outcome
10 threaten

3

1 of
2 in
3 for
4 with
5 under
6 with
7 after
8 to
9 on
10 of

4

1 in charge of
2 responsible for
3 deals with
4 looks after
5 takes care of

5

1 F
2 T (mostly, but can depend on hierarchy in a company)
3 F
4 F (Chief Operations Officer)
5 T
6 T
7 F (Research and Development)
8 F (subsidiaries)
9 T
10 F (organigram)

6

1 was working, started, had never thought
2 had already been, spoke, was parking

7

1 Actually
2 seems
3 might
4 could
5 Don't
6 Wouldn't

8

1 analysis
2 description
3 evaluation
4 observation
5 suggestion

Review 2

(page 35 of the *Student's Book*)

Customer support

1

1 clean environment
2 satisfied customer
3 high staff turnover
4 subsidized meals

5 heavy workload
6 hourly rate
7 competent staff
8 dead-end job

2

1 annoyed (also: annoying)
2 competent
3 frustrated (also: frustrating)
4 grateful
5 helpful
6 knowledgeable
7 persuasive
8 reassuring (also: reassured)
9 satisfied (also: satisfying)
10 rude

3

1 push in
2 replace
3 offer
4 escalate
5 call
6 replace

4

Helpline operator: Before I can <u>sort out</u> the problem, I first need to <u>locate</u> exactly where the fault is.

Customer: OK, no problem, we can do that. But if it's still not working properly, can you <u>replace</u> the product, or at least <u>give</u> me a refund?

Helpline operator: Yes, that's possible, but I'm not authorized to do it. I would first have to <u>escalate</u> the problem to my supervisor.

5

I'll <u>look</u> into it, <u>sort</u> it out, and <u>get</u> back to you tomorrow.

6

1 through
2 down
3 in
4 on
5 through
6 down
7 into
8 on
9 up
10 up

7

1 monitor
2 toolbar
3 crash
4 upgrade
5 cartridge
6 plug in
7 attach
8 customer
9 supplier
10 guarantee

8

1 regard
2 would
3 grateful
4 could
5 attached
6 hesitate
7 get back to
8 further
9 appreciate
10 urgently

9

1 need
2 Q4
3 threat
4 linked
5 suggest
6 counting (could also be *depending*)

3 Products and packaging

Digital resources for Unit 3

eWorkbook

Language practice: interactive & printable grammar, vocabulary, listening & pronunciation practice activities, extra printable reading & writing worksheets
Listen: Student's Book audio, language practice audio
Watch: video & video worksheets
Tests: interactive multiple-choice test
Resources: word list, grammar help & writing tips

Teacher's Resource Disc

Video: video & video worksheets
Audio: Student's Book audio
Tests: progress test Unit 3
Resources: PowerPoint Unit 3, business document Unit 3, photocopiable worksheets, Student's Book answer key, Student's Book glossary

Subject background

Product is one of the famous '4 Ps' of marketing (the others being *Price*, *Place* (i.e. distribution) and *Promotion*. In the past, when business people talked about 'products and services' the term *product* referred only to manufactured goods. Nowadays the distinction between a product and a service is increasingly blurred, so that a bank can offer 'financial products' and a manufacturing company can offer a service (e.g. customizing their products).

When developing a new product, a company needs to take into account a wide range of factors:

- the origin of any new product ideas: customers? sales staff?
- the fit with the existing product line.
- manufacturing questions like: 'How easy will it be to make this new product with our existing equipment?'
- pricing, distribution and promotion of the new product.

The feasibility of new products depends very much on production and operations as well as marketing. If a product cannot be manufactured for a reasonable price then it cannot be sold for one.

Designing and developing a new product involves a number of different stages.

1 Research: Market research to find out customers' needs; technical and scientific research and development of a more fundamental nature (R&D); prioritizing research into different projects; lead time between starting a project and the product coming to market.
2 Design: Deciding the specifications to include in the design brief (features, size, weight, materials, etc.); screening out poor designs and choosing the final design; limitations in the production technology available; designing for manufacture (an easy process will lower production costs and mean fewer defects); designing for ease of disposal at the end of the product's life.
3 Prototype: Deciding how many working models to build; coordination between marketing and production when evaluating the prototype; which to prioritize: speed to market or more time for a better product?
4 Consumer tests: Choosing the target group for the test; deciding what to measure and how to measure it; modifying the prototype on the basis of the test results.
5 Full production: Set-up of machines and machine tools; supply of materials and parts; run time (time taken for a batch of products to go through the process); estimating consumer demand.

When the finished product is finally on the market, sales staff will need to know:

- its functions (what it does).
- its features (selling points).
- its customer benefits (how the features and functions make the customer's life easier).
- improvements that have been made (in what ways it's better than previous models).
- possibilities for customization.
- how it compares with competitors' products.

Packaging is of course a key issue in the product mix, and its importance is often underestimated. Amongst other things, it a) attracts the buyer's attention, b) advertises the benefits of the product inside, c) lists the contents of the product inside, d) protects the product during handling and e) contributes to convenience and ease-of-use.

Useful websites

In terms of Internet resources for further study, this is a good online magazine with free access to some articles and a sign-up newsletter:
http://www.designnews.com

The following site has a 'body of knowledge' (BOK) for new product development, including a link to a glossary:
http://www.npd-solutions.com/bok.html

3.1 About business

Packaging

This module examines the packaging of products from the point of view of manufacturer and consumer.

Internet research

'Universal design' refers to the design and delivery of products and services that can be used by everyone, regardless of age, ability, or situation, with the aim of promoting equal access for all. In packaging, this would mean that the packaging used must be accessible to a wide range of people, including the elderly, infirm, disabled, etc.

Students could research some examples of universal design in packaging and present the products to the class. For example, a liquid soap dispenser for children which is designed with a broad base and easy-action pump so that it is accessible to small hands; easy-open packaging of hearing aids, consumers of which are likely to be elderly people with little strength in their hands; easy-open ring-pulls on drinks so anyone can open them, etc.

It would be useful for students to do this search before the module as it will provide them with a good base of background knowledge about the subject of packaging. Or, students can use it as a follow-up activity to the lesson.

LEAD-IN ACTIVITY

Get students to write down every product they have bought or used in the last 24 hours which has been packaged in some way. Give them a few examples of your own to get them started, e.g. a doughnut in a paper bag; sandwiches in a plastic container; a notebook which a sales assistant put in a plastic carrier bag; a CD, etc.

Ask students to put a tick next to each item of packaging that was essential and a cross next to the packaging which was not essential. Get students to estimate what percentage of the packaging used was non-essential.

Discussion

1 Bring in examples of pre-packaged goods, e.g. items of food and drink, stationery, batteries, a bottle, a carton, etc. Teach any new vocabulary, e.g. *cellophane*, *blister pack*, *child-proof top*, *cardboard*, *container*, etc.
Students can also look at photographs and identify the types of packaging they see in them.

Hold the items up so that everyone can see them or pass them around so that students can handle them.

Discuss the topics listed in the *Student's Book* and make a list on the board of the points made.

SUGGESTED ANSWERS:

Packaging should protect the product whilst it's being transported, display the product to its advantage on the shelf, resist pilfering (e.g. be large enough to prevent the small product being hidden in a pocket), be a practical shape for transportation and storage, carry text for instructions, etc.

Listening for gist

2 1:28 Read the questions with the students and play the whole interview through. Get them to compare their answers with a partner. Then take whole-class feedback.

ANSWERS:

1 He thinks packaging is the best way to communicate the difference that makes your product the best choice.
2 New China Packaging uses cross-functional 'task forces' to develop packaging concepts.

As a follow-up, discuss these questions:
Do you agree with Charlie Wang's view that packaging is the best way to communicate the differences between products? Does packaging influence your choice of purchase, or are there other factors?

Check that students understand the meaning of *cross-functional task force* (a group of people with different backgrounds or expertise working towards a common goal. It could include people from finance, production, marketing, human resources and might involve employees from all levels. Some members of the group might also come from outside the organization, e.g. suppliers, customers). Do not develop this theme yet, as it comes up in more detail in Exercise 4.

RECORDING SCRIPT

1:28

Interviewer: Mr. Wang, you often say that packaging is 'the manufacturer's last chance to seduce the customer.' Why is that?

Wang: Yes. In today's highly competitive marketplace, many products are almost identical. So branding is not enough. That's especially true here in Asia, where there may be literally hundreds of competitors making the same product in the same city. You have to differentiate; you have to communicate the difference which makes your product a better choice. I agree with Jack Trout when he says, 'Every aspect of your communications should reflect your difference. The bottom line is: You can't overcommunicate your difference.'

I: So, packaging is the best way to communicate your difference?

W: Exactly. You know, 75% of purchasing decisions are made at the point of sale. And because most stores are self-service, your product is alone on the shelf, surrounded by its competitors. According to Wal-Mart – and they're the world's largest retailer, so they should know! – your product has to pitch its promise to the customer in three seconds or less, from up to fifteen feet away. If your packaging is not attractive, effective and distinctive, how are you going to communicate its difference?

I: OK, so packaging is critical, and manufacturers spend millions of dollars on it. So why are there so many failures?

W: The big problem is a lack of communication. Typically, there are several different groups of experts, all working in their own specialized field: market research people who know nothing about design, designers who know nothing about manufacturing, and production people who know nothing about consumer needs. Traditionally, you keep your design team well away from business and manufacturing constraints because you don't want to limit their creativity. Unfortunately, the result is inevitably a compromise. You start out with an original, creative idea, but then you find out it's impractical, for reasons of cost or technical limitations. So, it gets watered down, simplified, adapted. In the end, you are left with a package which is easy to make, easy to transport and within budget, but it's no longer what the consumer wanted! So, you get focus groups where consumers don't really like any of the concepts that are presented. That means, either you start all over again, or you have to choose the least unpopular option!

I: How do you avoid this problem at New China Packaging?

W: Well, basically, what we do is to build what we call a 'task force'. This a cross-functional team with people from all the different departments involved in the project. We put them all together in a hotel, with all the tools they need to produce mockups and prototypes. Then we literally lock the door and we don't let them out until they produce something that everybody is enthusiastic about!
I: And do you include consumers in the task force?
W: Yes, indeed. We need the end user's input right from the beginning. Everything is consumer-led. And, because we know that what consumers say they need and what they really need are frequently two different things, we also observe them using the product. Frequently, we can detect behaviours and needs that the consumer is not even conscious of.
I: Really? Uh-huh. So, who else is involved?
W: Marketing, manufacturing, designers, consultants – everyone who has a stake in the product.
I: And how long does the process take?
W: Traditionally, months or sometimes years. But today, our task forces can usually deliver an optimal solution in one week, sometimes less. And remember, when they deliver, every aspect of the package is consumer-validated, realistic and feasible. So, this extremely short turn-around means that the manufacturer can react very, very quickly to changes in the market, almost in real time.

Listening for detail

3 Read the statements aloud or get students to read them aloud and see if they can respond to any before they listen again. Then play **1:28** again. Check answers with the whole class. Get students to correct the false statements.

ANSWERS

1 T 2 F 3 F 4 T 5 F 6 T 7 T 8 F

Discussion

4 Get students to do this with a partner. Ask students to think of and discuss advantages and disadvantages in each situation then take whole-class feedback.

SUGGESTED ANSWERS:

1 The advantages could be getting a range of different perspectives on the suitability of the candidate and that he or she is approved by all the different departments they will have contact with in the company. The disadvantage is that it would be possible to end up with the most popular candidate rather than the one best suited to the job in question.
2 The advantage is that the developers will have the broadest possible perspective of the company's needs. They are likely to produce a better product that takes into consideration the requirements of all the stakeholders. The disadvantage could be that the developers would need more time to process the information and sort out what is most relevant.
3 The advantage could be that the whole company could contribute in personalizing the deal to the customer's particular needs. The disadvantage is that if the special deals are primarily financial, this is essentially a matter for the sales department who need to spend time cultivating customer relationships without interference from elsewhere. From the customer's perspective, they probably prefer to deal with the same point of contact.
4 The advantage of a cross-functional task force for creating training programmes is that it would be very useful in determining the exact needs of personnel at all levels and in different job functions as well as financial and technical constraints. The disadvantage could be that the technical knowledge and understanding required might be very different from one department to another.

EXTENSION ACTIVITY

Get students to comment on how they think cross-functional task forces would work in their jobs / company, or if they have any personal experience of them.

Scan reading

5 Get students to look at the photo. Ask: *What is the man doing? Is he trying to eat this product? Look at his face – how do you think he feels?* Read the caption '... consumers use all kinds of tools and knives ...' and ask: *Have you ever used a knife or another tool to open the packaging of a product?*

Read the questions with your students. Ask if they can predict the answers to the questions before they read. If necessary, explain *triggers* (causes).

Give students a few minutes to read the text silently, underlining the words that help them with the answers to the questions as they read. Remind them what scan reading is (see page 7). Remind students to use the *Glossary* in their *Student's Book* on page 153. Check answers with the whole class.

ANSWERS:

1 'Wrap rage' is a new term used to describe the irritation and loss of self-control experienced when struggling to open wrapping / product packaging.
2 It's especially prevalent amongst seniors: 70% of over 50s experience wrap rage-related injuries.
3 It's triggered by sterile food packs, child-proof packaging, packaging that protects products during transport, packaging that stops thieves from stealing products, ring-pull cans, price tags and overpackaging.
4 There is pressure on manufacturers to meet stringent protection standards at low cost.

Paraphrasing

6 Students could do this exercise with a partner. Allow them to use dictionaries. Remind them to re-read the sentence in which the phrase occurs so that they can see it in its full context. Check answers with the whole class.

SUGGESTED ANSWERS:

1 to decrease the amount of stock that disappears from shops because it is stolen by customers or staff
2 the factors which most often cause people to become frustrated and irritated with packaging
3 people can even lose their temper trying to remove labels with prices from some products
4 something which enrages people who feel strongly about ecology
5 after a long period of discouragement there are signs of hope
6 Basically, unless they respond, they'll lose customers.

EXTENSION ACTIVITY

Ask students to share any similar experiences of their own with packaging. Ask them if they can they identify one item of packaging which they find particularly difficult or annoying?

Discussion

7 Read the instructions with the whole class.

With lower-level classes, brainstorm answers to the questions to help them get started, and write any useful vocabulary on the board. Students could also refer to the results of their Internet research on universal design and packaging.

Get each group to present their packaging solution using the questions in the *Student's Book* to provide a structure for their presentation. Groups should also be prepared to take questions from the rest of the class.

SUGGESTED ANSWERS:

1 Most commonly used materials are plastic and cardboard or paperboard. Paperboard is cheap, recyclable, easy to print on, plastic is more versatile and more secure. Other materials such as metal, glass and wood are unlikely to be used for this type of product.

2 and 3 Anything is possible, but preferably not a standard, rectangular box with pale or dark colours and small photos and print.

EXTENSION ACTIVITY

As a follow-up, get students to evaluate the packaging solution using the criteria in the discussion activity on page 36, i.e. protection, identification, transport, storage, display, security.

Alternatively, they could discuss the pros and cons of each packaging solution using the points mentioned by Charlie Wang in the listening activity on page 36, i.e: *Is the design attractive, effective and distinctive? Does the packaging help to communicate the difference between this product and other products? Will this packaging help to persuade consumers to buy the product?*

3.2 Vocabulary

Specifications and features

This module practises describing products and outlining their main features in a product presentation.

Internet research

Two common ways of recording vocabulary are to use vocabulary notebooks or word cards. In a vocabulary notebook students might record, for example, individual words, pronunciation, useful phrases or chunks of language, word families, collocations, or lexical sets. They could also use mind maps or make their own dictionaries.

Encourage students to find and try out as many different techniques as possible so that they can find the ones that suit them best.

Discussion

1 Give students a few minutes to put the stages of product development in the right order. Check answers with the whole class by calling on students to read the sentences aloud.

ANSWERS:

The most likely chronological order:

[6] Beta test the product by users in typical situations.
[5] Conduct market studies to test the concept.
[8] Launch the product.
[4] Draw sketches and build mockups.
[7] Go into production.
[3] Draw up specifications for the product.
[1] Generate new ideas in focus groups and brainstorming meetings.
[2] Screen out unfeasible or unprofitable ideas.

FURTHER PRACTICE

To provide further practice of the collocations, get students to close their books and give you the correct verb in each case, e.g. *to ____ ideas, to ____ ____ unprofitable ideas, or the noun, e.g. to test the ____, to launch the____.*

Reading for detail

2 When students have completed the sentences, get them to read them aloud. This is an opportunity to check that students can say numbers with decimal points, e.g. *thirty-one point four,* and the abbreviations *g* (grams), *cm* (centimetres), *kg* (kilograms).

If students are unsure of the words, write them in two columns on the board under adjectives and nouns.

high *height*
wide *width*
long *length*

You could also check that students know how to say the three dimensions shown in the picture, e.g. '31.4 by 45.4 by 7.6'.

ANSWERS:

1 The large FedEx Box is 31.4 cm wide and 45.4 cm long. It is 7.6 cm high. When empty, the box weighs 400 g; it can be used to ship small parts or computer printouts up to 9 kg in weight.

2 The FedEx Tube is 96.5 cm in length and 15.2 cm in height and width. With a weight of 450 g when empty, it can be used to ship plans, posters, blueprints, etc. weighing up to 9 kg.

Describing products

3 Students could put a range of items from their pockets and bags on the desk in front of them to do this activity. Without naming it or pointing to it, each student in turn describes an object while the other students guess which one it is. Circulate and check that students are using the target language correctly.

Collocations

4 Read through the words in the box and the compound adjectives with the class. Draw students' attention to the meanings of some of the adjectives, e.g. *eye-catching* and *attention-grabbing* have similar meanings; *waterproof* (does not let water through) is different from *water-resistant* (offers only some protection from water damage).

ANSWERS:

1 energy-saving / labour-saving devices
2 fire-retardant / water-resistant materials
3 waterproof / shockproof personal stereos
4 child-resistant / tamper-resistant packaging
5 future-proof / fool-proof technology
6 eye-catching / attention-grabbing design

Elicit from students any other compound adjectives they might know, and some possible collocations, e.g. *heat-resistant (materials), stain-resistant (materials, clothing), time-saving (device), rainproof (jacket), soundproof (room), bullet-proof (car, vest).*

Listening for gist

5 1:29–1:34 Play the six conversations and allow students to choose the correct collocations individually before checking answers with the whole class. Get students to pick out the words or phrases they heard which helped them arrive at the answer.

ANSWERS:

1 shockproof personal stereos
2 a labour-saving device
3 eye-catching / attention-grabbing design
4 child-resistant packaging
5 water-resistant materials
6 fool-proof technology

RECORDING SCRIPT

1:29–1:34

1
A: I want to listen to English while I go jogging. Is that possible?
B: Oh, yeah. Jogging, cycling, skiing ... whatever you like. Nothing can stop it. I even dropped mine down two flights of stairs, and when I picked it up, it was still working.
2
C: I hear you bought one of those new robots. What do you think of it?
D: It's fantastic! I used to spend hours cleaning the flat. Now I can just program the robot and sit back and watch it work.
C: That's incredible! I must get one ...
3
E: I really like the colour. It's a beautiful car!
F: Yes, and it's an interesting shape too. Quite unusual. Very different from other cars in this category, isn't it?
4
G: Mum, what's in this bottle? I can't open it!
H: Give that to me, dear. You mustn't touch that. It's for cleaning the kitchen, and it's dangerous. Fortunately, they put it in a special bottle that children can't open ...
5
I: Quick, it's starting to rain and there's a pallet of those electronic toys outside!
J: OK, I'll move it straight away. But don't worry – the boxes are made of special paperboard. A little rain won't do any damage.
6
K: Are you sure I'll be able to record TV programmes? I mean, I'm not very good at anything technical.
L: Oh, yes. No worries. My five-year-old can operate this model. It's dead easy.

For further practice, students could work with a partner to produce similar short conversations using more of the collocations in Exercise 4 and/or the additional ones listed above.

6 1:35 Ask students to listen to the start of the presentation and tell you what the ChartTech i3 is (an integrated nautical information system). Play the first two paragraphs of the recording and then pause so that students can give you the answer. Ask them to brainstorm what kinds of features it might have.

Then play the rest of the presentation, pausing, if necessary, to allow students to make notes about the three main features of the ChartTech i3. Ask students to note down the name of each feature and a brief description of it in their own words. Check answers with the whole class.

ANSWERS:

one-finger navigation, underwater radar and fishfinder, communications functions

RECORDING SCRIPT

1:35

Good afternoon, everybody. Imagine you're on a fishing trip. It's the middle of the night. It's dark, it's foggy, and you're sailing your boat between dangerous rocks. Are you afraid? Not at all. You are supremely confident, checking and adjusting your route with just a touch of a finger on a screen. How do you do it?
Well, I'm here today to tell you about the ChartTech i3, an extraordinary, nautical information system, where a touch-controlled screen enables you to operate several different navigation functions with a touch of the finger.
Let's start with the Touch Screen Command. Just by touching the screen, you can view and change charts, calculate distances, create a route and a lot more. The large colour display screen automatically shows you a bird's-eye view of where you are and where you're going.
Moving on to what's below the water, thanks to the radar overlay, you see exactly what the fish are seeing and the Touch Screen 3D Fishfinder, will help make your fishing trips are considerably more successful!
Now, can I just turn to communications? The ChartTech i3 can send fax, email and voice messages. You can request and receive weather reports based on your actual GPS position. And you can even automatically monitor vital onboard systems when you're away from your boat.
So, I'll just sum up the ChartTech i3's main features. Let's just go back to our midnight fishing trip. First, Touch Screen Command lets you navigate between the rocks with just one finger and a bird's-eye view. Secondly, the underwater radar and fishfinder shows you where the rocks are, and where the fish are hiding. Finally, the communications function mean you can receive and send important data on the weather, your location and your boat at any moment.
I'd like to finish by inviting you to try the ChartTech i3 for yourself. Our website has an incredibly realistic simulation that you can try out without ever getting your feet wet. Thank you very much.

Listening for detail

7 Get students to try to complete the expressions before they listen again. Then play **1:35** again so that they can check their answers.

ANSWERS:

1 about 2 with 3 on 4 to 5 up 6 back 7 by

8 Do this matching exercise with the whole class. Play the recording again. This time, get students to focus on the structure of the presentation and the five stages identified here. They can also practise repeating the expressions aloud.

ANSWERS:

a) Beginning the presentation (1, 2)
b) Moving to a new point (3, 4)
c) Returning to a point made earlier (6)
d) Ending the presentation (5, 7)

Presentation

9 Give students a few minutes to choose an electronic product that they want to present. They can use the products in the photos or their own ideas. Remind them of the work they have done on product specifications and features, the nouns and compound adjectives they have practised, and the structure of the presentation they listened to.

Students could make some notes about their product and the points they want to make so that the structure is clear. Each student in the group could then be asked to prepare one or more parts of the presentation, depending on the size of the group. Circulate and assist where necessary.

You could ask groups to do their presentation for the whole class. The rest of the class could listen and check that it follows an appropriate structure and provides clear information. While students are making their presentations, make a note of any common mistakes in the target language for remedial teaching.

3.3 Grammar

Relative clauses, articles and noun combinations

This module practises articles, relative clauses and noun combinations in the context of writing a business and technology trivia quiz, expanding notes and defining words.

Internet research

Searching an online dictionary for the noun 'information' will reveal that it is an uncountable noun. Its informal form is *info*. It is used with *about* and *on*. Some typical collocations are: *information technology*, *information retrieval*, *information overload*; some typical constructions are: *a piece of information* and *a mine of information*.

In addition to providing definitions, phonetic transcriptions, and example sentences, online dictionaries allow students to hear audio pronunciations and find links to other useful websites. When they are browsing different online dictionaries, get students to conduct searches for the same word(s) in two or more dictionaries. This will allow them to do a more accurate comparison between them.

Defining relative clauses

1 Start by reading the *Refresh your memory box* on relative clauses with the students. If students seem unsure of how to use them, work through some or all of exercises 5–10 in the *Grammar and practice* section (page 126 and 127 in the *Student's Book*, answers on page 114 in this book) before they do the exercise.

Divide the class into small groups of three or four to do the quiz. Then, in whole-class feedback, check the answers and ask students to say which relative pronoun is used in each question and why.

ANSWERS:

1 the first television (the televisor)
2 Marie Curie
3 mass production (the assembly line)
4 Marconi
5 franchising
6 the computer mouse

2 Students prepare their own quiz of five to six questions. It is a good idea to ensure that they have internet access while preparing so that they can verify the information they want to test in the quiz. Monitor and help with vocabulary and make sure students are using defining relative clauses.

When students are ready, match groups and ask them to challenge each other by asking and answering their questions. When they have finished, find out which team got most answers right.

EXTENSION ACTIVITY

Alternatively, you could make this a class quiz. Team 1 ask their questions and the other groups must write their answers. Then Team 2 ask their questions, and so on until all the teams have asked their questions. At the end, ask teams to provide the answers and find out which team got most right.

Non-defining relative clauses

3 Ask students to look at the photos on the page, (which show, from left to right, Oprah Winfrey, Mark Zuckerberg, Victoria Beckham and Steve Jobs). Ask students to tell you what they know about the four people.

Read the sentences about Steve Jobs as a class so that students get an idea of what is required. Then divide them into pairs to do the task. Tell students to concentrate on people they know about.

At the end, elicit some of the best long sentences from the class and comment on any good uses or inappropriate uses of non-defining relative clauses that you heard.

SAMPLE ANSWERS:

2 Oprah Winfrey, who is one of the richest women in the world, started *The Oprah Winfrey Show* in 1985, which is still broadcasted in the US today.
3 Walt Disney, who started Walt Disney Co., invented Mickey Mouse, who is the world's most famous cartoon character.
4 Mark Zuckerberg, whose life has been made into a movie, is the renowned founder of Facebook, which is an easy-to-use social networking service.
5 Ben Cohen and Jerry Greenfield, who were lifelong friends, set up Ben & Jerry's, which re-named one of its ice-creams 'Yes Pecan' in honour of Barack Obama's election as U.S. President.
6 Jeff Bezos, who studied computer science, set up Amazon, which launched the Kindle e-book reader, in his garage.
7 Sergey Brin and Larry Page, whose company's slogan is 'Don't be evil', set up Google, which is famous for free applications like Google Earth.
8 Richard Branson, whose first business was a student magazine, owns the Virgin group, which has more than 400 companies including Virgin Galactic, which plans to take tourists into space.
9 Muhammed Yunus, who is from Bangladesh, and who received a Nobel Prize, founded the Grameen Bank, which provides micro-credit – small loans.
10 Victoria Beckham, whose husband is a famous footballer, and who is also known as Posh Spice, is a Director of Beckham Brand Ltd., which owns a range of 'Intimately Beckham' perfumes.

EXTENSION ACTIVITY

You could make this an online research task. Ask pairs to choose one of the people, products or organizations and to find information about them on the Internet. Once they have the information, they must produce a description using non-defining relative clauses.

Discussion

4 In groups, students decide on their top three and present their list to the class.

Articles

5 Start by reading the *Refresh your memory* box on articles with students. If students seem unsure of how to use them, work through Exercises 1–4 in the *Grammar and practice* section (page 126 in the *Student's Book*, answers on page 114 in this book) before they do the exercise.

Students could work with a partner to insert the missing articles. Check answers with the whole class, getting students to explain the reason for their choice.

ANSWERS:

- In 1485, Leonardo da Vinci made detailed drawings of – parachutes. He also made sketches of a/the helicopter and a/the tank. The first helicopter that could carry a person was flown by Paul Cornu at the beginning of the twentieth century. During the First World War, – tanks were first used in – France in 1917.
- Bar codes were invented by Silver and Woodland in 1948. They used – light to read a set of concentric circles, but it was two decades before the arrival of – computers and – lasers made the system practical.
- The first computer was built in 1943, more than 100 years after Charles Babbage had designed the first programmable device. In 1998, the Science Museum in London built a working copy of Babbage machine using his original plans and (the) materials that would have been available at the time. It worked just as Babbage had intended.

Expanding notes

6 1:36 This exercise and Exercise 7 allow students to do further practice on articles within a real-world context of expanding notes. Write the notes on the board before playing the recording. Once they have listened, get students to come to the board to insert the missing words. Or, elicit the missing words from students and write them on the board yourself. Make a list of the words which have been omitted: *the, this, it's, I, it, there are, be, have,* etc.

RECORDING SCRIPT

1:36

Message: Please record your product review and your rating out of five after the beep. Thank you for your feedback.
Customer 1: This is easily the best phone I've had so far. It's the perfect phone for the basic user. I have already bumped it and dropped it a few times but it's still going strong. The battery life is incredible. Overall, it's a real workhorse – there are no frills, but it does what a cellphone needs to do. I rate it five out of five.

7 1:37,1:38 Circulate while students are discussing how to expand the notes. Refer them to the list of omitted words on the board. Get students to read their sentences aloud and compare versions before listening to the recording.

RECORDING SCRIPT

1:37

1

Message: Please record your product review and your rating out of five after the beep. Thank you for your feedback.
Customer 2: I hate this phone. It's too small – I can't open the flip cover with one hand. There's no screen on the outside to see the caller identity. The reception is horrible. It drops calls probably 30% of the time. There is a very long key delay, which is incredibly annoying. I am anxiously awaiting the day I can upgrade and get rid of this monstrosity. I rate it zero out of five.

1:38

2

Message: Please record your product review and your rating out of five after the beep. Thank you for your feedback.
Customer 3: I've had the phone for about three weeks. I like the size and the design. The features are good too. It's easy enough to use, and it has survived a couple of drops. However, the alarm clock won't work anymore. I'm not too sure about the internal antenna. I hate having a full signal when making a call, only to have a dramatic drop when I put the phone to my head. Everybody says it's the telecom company's fault, not the phone, or maybe I just got a bad one. We'll see. I'm going to try the 9200 next. I would give it a rating of three out of five.

EXTENSION ACTIVITY

Reverse the procedure and get students to reduce some complete sentences to note form. To do this, you or they could bring some suitable texts to class, such as reports, email messages, etc. Or, you could provide appropriate sentences on individual slips of paper and pass them around for students to rewrite.

Defining words

8 Get students to work with a partner to do the exercise. Check answers with the whole class.

ANSWERS

1 c) 2 a) 3 d) 4 b)

Definitions game

9 Give students a few minutes to read the instructions and look up any new words in their dictionaries. Remind them to use what they practised in Exercise 8 to help them prepare their definitions. However, they should start their definitions: *This is* … or *These are* … to avoid giving the answer, e.g. from Student B: *This is a container that is economical with material.*

FURTHER PRACTICE

Get students to look for similar examples of noun combinations in written material they are familiar with, e.g. company brochures or websites, real documents from the workplace, such as reports or market surveys, advertisements, or newspapers. You could focus this work by giving groups of students a specific area to look at, e.g. websites of packaging companies, car advertisements, annual reports, etc.

3.4 Speaking

Presentations – structure

This module focuses on how to organize and deliver an effective product presentation. On the Teacher's Resource Disc, you will find more related practice material, including a video (with worksheets) featuring an example situation for students to analyse and discuss.

Internet research

This research will be particularly helpful for Exercise 9, so ask students to do the search before they do that task. Students will find a range of websites offering a wealth of tips on how to make effective presentations. After individual research, get students to compare and exchange their answers to the questions.

You could also use this information as the basis for a poster or handout providing a detailed list of presentation tips for future reference.

Brainstorming

1 If students need help getting started on this brainstorming activity, give them a list of topics to think about, e.g. structure of the lesson, lecture or presentation, content, delivery, teacher / speaker, visuals, pace, timing / length. At this point, students should simply note down key words and phrases. Take whole-class feedback and make a list on the board. Get students to expand on their basic points by giving examples to clarify what they mean or anecdotes about real situations they have experienced.

SUGGESTED ANSWERS:

well-structured, well-researched, well-prepared, well-targeted, well-paced, entertaining, sense of humour, varied, interactive, interesting voice, good eye-contact, smart appearance, clear and attractive visuals, not too long

Listening for gist

2 1:39 Play the first part of the recording, up to 'enormous potential for this product'* and ask students:
What is wrong with the opening of this presentation?
How does it compare with the points in the checklist in Exercise 1?

Then play the rest of the presentation and get students to check what they hear against the list of qualities of a good presentation. Check answers with the whole class, getting students to make complete sentences, e.g.:
The speaker is very hesitant. It makes him/her sound uncertain.
The information isn't well-structured, which makes it a bit confusing.

RECORDING SCRIPT

1:39
Version 1
Man:
Um, shall I start then? OK, I know, erm, I know you're going to be very excited by the Pingman, like me! So, I'm sure you'll have lots of questions. And, perhaps we'll take questions after the demonstration.
OK, er, we've done lots of tests, which have all been very positive, and, er, there are lots of different markets for the Pingman, children, adults, dogs, businesses, and so on. We think there's an enormous potential for this product.* Until now, GPS tracking systems have been too bulky, too heavy and too unreliable indoors to be used as personal tracking devices. Our Pingman weighs only 75 grams, and, well, we'll show you how it

works in a few minutes... on the, er, Internet. So, you know, you can connect to the Internet from anywhere in the world, and just ping your user to know exactly where they are. Within one metre ... er. Nobody else has a product like this on the market, so we want you to approve the investment, because there's a huge market.
Woman: What do you mean by 'ping'?
Man: Oh, yes, on the Internet, you tell a satellite to send a signal to the device, and the device answers the signal, and then the satellite can calculate the device's exact location.
Anyway, it only weighs 75 grams, did I say that already? Yes, er, 75 grams, it's five centimetres in length and about three point five centimetres wide, so, about half the size of a cellphone, and there are different models for children or adults. Tests were really positive, and our sales forecasts are excellent. There's also a model for animals; it's built in to a collar so, if you lose your dog, for example, you just ping it from the Internet to know where it is. So, er, unless you want to ask questions, I think we'd better have the demonstration. Oh, I forgot to mention profitability. We think it will, er, will be profitable. Very profitable. OK, are there any questions? No? No questions? Um, OK then, let's have the demonstration. It's, er, at the back of the room. Yes. Er, ...

3 With lower-level classes you could give some sentence stems to help students formulate their suggestions for improvement: *The speaker should / could ...; Instead of ...* (*-ing* verb), *the speaker should / could ...*, etc. Take whole-class feedback.

SUGGESTED ANSWERS:

Aspects to improve: structure, voice, pace, stress and intonation, hesitations.

Listening for detail

4 1:40 Play Version 2 of the presentation and get students to listen and note answers to the questions. Let students compare their answers with a partner before discussing as a class in open feedback. Play the recording again if students aren't sure about their answers.

ANSWERS:

1 by asking questions
2 To present the Pingman, a new GPS tracking device; to demonstrate the prototype and to ask Board members for investment.
3 15 minutes; the next step is a hands-on demonstration.
4 Some time has been allowed for questions at the end, but the speaker tells board members to feel free to interrupt with any urgent questions.
5 Section 1: background to the project and current offer on the market; section 2: prototype and specifications and data taken from tests, focus groups, market studies; section 3: business plan.
6 the second and third sections
7 The speaker says he wants to wrap up the presentation and summarizes what has been said.
8 Go to the back of the room to see R&D staff.
9 The speakers says thank you.
10 Suggested answers for what has improved in Version 2:
- The presentation is better prepared with fewer hesitations.
- The speaker addresses the audience's interests and gets them involved.
- The speaker's voice is firmer, clearer, more audible, more confident and persuasive.
- The pace is more appropriate.
- Stress and intonation give variety and interest and convey the speaker's enthusiasm.

RECORDING SCRIPT

1:40

Version 2
Good morning, everybody. Would you like to know at all times exactly where your young child or teenager is? How comforting would it be to know that your elderly mother is safely back home from the shops? How much would it be worth to know precisely where your sales reps or technicians were? And how much time would you save if you knew where your dog was hiding?
Well, here's the answer. I'm here this morning to present the Pingman, a revolutionary new personal GPS tracking device and to ask you, members of the Board, to approve the investment needed to start production.
Now, I know you're going to be very excited by the Pingman, so I'm going to give you a quick overview of the product in about fifteen minutes. After that, there'll be a hands-on demonstration, and I've allowed some time for questions and discussion after that. But if you have any questions that can't wait, feel free to interrupt me. OK?
I've divided my presentation into three sections. First of all, I'm going to talk to you about the background to this project and the current offers on the market. After that, I'll be talking about the prototype, the specifications and the data we've collected from tests and focus groups. Finally, I'd like to present a business plan which will show you why we expect the return on investment on this product to be considerable.
Is everybody happy with that agenda? OK, so, let's start with the background. Now, GPS tracking systems are not new, but until now they've been too heavy, and too unreliable indoors to be used as a personal tracking device. What's new about the Pingman is that we can build it into a wrist strap or collar small and light enough to be worn comfortably by a small child or a dog. For the first time, it will be possible to locate the wearer via the Internet, anywhere in the world, indoors or out, 24 hours a day ...
... does that answer your question? OK, so, I'd like to wrap up the presentation and move on to the demonstration. Let me just summarize what I've already told you. Firstly, I explained why there is a huge market just waiting for this product. Secondly, I presented the different specifications for the child, adult and animal versions we intend to launch, and the positive reactions we've had during trials. Last, but not least, I have given you the strongest possible reasons why you should approve this investment: extraordinary sales forecasts, strong cash flow and unprecedented profitability.
Now, if you'd like to move to the back of the room, our R&D staff are ready to start the demonstration and to answer your questions. Thank you very much for your attention.

5 1:40 Read through the language in the table with the students. Then ask students to work in pairs to complete the expressions. Play Version 2 again, pausing at appropriate places, while students complete the expressions.

ANSWERS:

Hook
How would you like to know …?
How much would it be worth to …?

Objective
I'm here this morning to present the Pingman …

Agenda
Feel free to interrupt me.
I've divided my presentation into three sections.
First of all, I'm going to …
After that, I'll be talking about …
Finally, I'd like to present …

Summary
I'd like to wrap up the presentation.
Firstly, I explained why …
Secondly, I presented the different specifications …
Last, but not least, I have given you …

Call for action
These are the reasons why I am asking you to …

Close
Thank you very much for your attention.

EXTENSION ACTIVITY

Put students into groups to discuss solutions for the following 'presentations problems'. What would they suggest that the speaker does in each case to change or improve their approach?

a) *Norman is very nervous about giving presentations. He is an expert in his field so the content of his presentations is good, but gets very nervous and forgets what he wants to say.*
b) *Olivia always overruns when she gives a presentation. She finds it difficult to be concise and never finishes on time.*
c) *Dieter doesn't speak clearly and never looks at his audience when he gives a presentation. He plays with the keys or loose coins in his pocket. His audience often becomes bored and restless.*
d) *Marie's presentations are usually very boring. She prepares detailed handouts and usually reads aloud what is written on them, adding comments as she goes.*

Students can refer to the work they have done in this module to help them or they can use their own ideas. Take whole-class feedback.

As a follow-up, ask students if they have experienced any of these problems. If they have experienced any other problems, they could share them and the rest of the class could suggest ways of dealing with them.

Pronunciation

6 **1:41** Students could do this exercise on pausing and intonation with a partner. Encourage them to say the words aloud so that they can hear what they sound like. When they have finished, ask a couple of students to read their paragraphs aloud and get the rest of the class to comment. Then play the recording and have students check their answers. See answers for Exercise 8 on the next page.

RECORDING SCRIPT

1:41
I've divided my presentation into three sections. First of all, I'm going to remind you of the background to this project and the current offer on the market. After that, I'll be talking about the prototype, the specifications and the data we've collected from tests, focus groups and market studies. Finally, I'd like to present a business plan; this will show you why we expect a return on investment that is without precedent for our company. Is everybody happy with that agenda?

FURTHER PRACTICE

Play **1:41** again. Stop at each pause so that students can repeat it quietly to themselves, either with their eyes closed or by reading the words from the book.

7 Ask students to look at the text in Exercise 6 and underline the key syllables and key words according to the stress. They should also link words by drawing a line. Circulate while students are doing the task but don't correct any mistakes.

8 **1:41** Play the recording so that students can check what they have underlined and linked. Finally, get individual students to read the paragraph aloud, bringing intonation, stress, and linking together in a naturalistic way.

ANSWERS:

I've divided my presentation into three sections. ↘ |First of all, ↗ I'm going to remind you of the background to this project ↗ | and the current offer on the market. ↘ |After that, ↗ |I'll be talking about the prototype, ↘ |the specifications ↘ |and the data we've collected from tests, focus groups and market studies. ↘ |Finally, ↘ |I'd like to present a business plan; ↘ |this will show you why we expect a return on investment that is without precedent for our company. ↘ |Is everybody happy with that agenda?

EXTENSION ACTIVITY

For homework, students could record themselves reading the paragraph. They could then play it back and assess their own delivery.

Presentation

9 This activity may require two lessons, with part of it done for homework. Read the instructions with the students. First, get students to decide which product they are going to present and what they want to say about it. The decisions they make here will also feed into the content of the presentation.

Then get students to review the work they did in earlier exercises in this module. This will help when it comes to preparing what they are going to say.

Students can divide the presentation among two or more people, but should ensure that there is a smooth transition from one speaker to the next.

You could spend some time discussing the last question (*How can you avoid an embarrassing silence at the end of your presentation?*) as this hasn't been covered in the material so far.

Possible answers to this question:

- Don't be afraid to let a minute or two go by before someone asks a question – people can be hesitant at first, but once one person has asked a question, others are likely to follow.
- Say: 'One question that people often ask is ….' This approach will often relax your audience and encourages them to start asking questions.
- If there are no questions, invite audience members to speak to you afterwards or contact you by email with any questions.

10 Once students have prepared their presentations and have had time to practise delivering them, get groups to present to the whole class. If you have time, students can assess each other in a supportive way by referring to the list of qualities for a good presentation in Exercise 1 and the presentation tips they gathered as a result of their Internet search. They could also listen out for appropriate use of expressions, intonation, etc.

A quicker, alternative method of assessment would be simply to ask students to identify two things they liked about the presentation and two ways in which they think it could be improved.

3.5 Writing
A product description

This module focuses on the features and benefits of consumer products and requires students to write their own production description.

Internet research

Students will find a range of different games and other products in response to a search for open source software. Remind students that they should write a short description and try to 'sell' the software to classmates.

Discussion

1 Check that students understand the difference between *a feature* (a factual statement about a product) and *a benefit* (the value or advantage customers get from the product; a positive outcome or result that will make them want to buy it).

Read the vocabulary in the box and get students to pick out the four features and their corresponding benefits. Students can then discuss questions 1 and 2 with a partner or in small groups. Get them to make lists of one or two features and benefits for each product, to show that they have understood the difference.

Other products they might discuss are a digital camera, a bike, or a watch.

ANSWERS:

(feature, followed by benefit)
ABS – safe braking and cornering; alloy wheels – head-turning good looks; 3.0l V6 engine – power on demand; automatic climate control – air-conditioned comfort

Model

2 Ask students to look at the name of the product and the headline. Ask them to predict what sort of product it is and what they expect to read about in the article.

Students read the description quickly and note the main benefits. Let students compare their answers in pairs.

ANSWERS:

Main benefits:
- available in many languages.
- works on all computers.
- stores data in international open standard format.
- can read and write files from other softwars packages.
- free to download and use.
- create documents; analyse data; design presentations.

Analysis

3 Get students to read the sections again and number the sections. Let them compare their answers in pairs.

Get students to try to differentiate the features and the benefits in the text. At this stage, accept all answers as this is dealt with in more detail in the next exercise.

ANSWERS:

1 background
2 overview of benefits
3 compatibility
4 details of features and benefits
5 invitation

Language focus

4 When students have completed the task, focus on the language used to describe benefits and features as this will be useful for the writing task in Exercise 5. This text, for example, uses:

- the present simple tense to give the effect of immediacy.
- *will* to promise things, e.g. *you'll start to appreciate the extras.*
- *can*, e.g. *you can create, you can integrate.*
- the first conditional, e.g. *If you're used to using other office suites, you'll feel completely at home …*
- imperatives, e.g. *use, produce.*
- a number of adjectives and adverbs to get the message across, e.g. *easily, impressive, dynamic, powerful, effective.*
- comparatives to get the message across, e.g. *more compatible, more international, more accessible, more open.*

ANSWERS:

2 OpenOffice.org 3 gives you everything you'd expect in office software.
3 You can publish your work in Portable Document Format (PDF) and release your graphics in Flash (SWF) format – without needing any additional software.
4 If you're used to using other office suites – such as Microsoft Office® – you'll be completely at home.
5 You can of course continue to use your old Microsoft Office files without any problems …
6 You can easily integrate images and charts in documents.
7 Use built-in charting tools to generate impressive 2D and 3D charts.
8 produce everything from simple diagrams to dynamic 3D illustrations and special effects.

5 Students could do this reformulation exercise in small groups. When they have finished, get groups to read their sentences aloud.

SUGGESTED ANSWERS:

2 You can download this amazing audio manager software – free!
3 Run Creole Audio Manager without problems on any Mac or PC computer.
4 You can search for music on the Internet, download it and organize your music files on your computer.
5 Listen to radio and watch TV online.
6 Creole lets you burn your favourite music onto CDs.
7 If you're used to using other audio players, you'll be completely at home; Creole Audio Manager is really easy to use.
8 You can even display song lyrics and sing along in Karaoke mode!

FURTHER PRACTICE

Write the following features on the board or dictate them to students:
50-number speed dial
One-click business reports
Open 24 hours
Batteries included
With a partner or in small groups, get students to note down what products each of these features could refer to and some benefits that users might get from them.
Give students a few minutes to exchange ideas and encourage them to be imaginative. Take whole-class feedback.

POSSIBLE ANSWERS:

50-number speed dial: phone – fewer keystrokes; quick and easy to use; I won't waste time by misdialling
One-click business reports: website – you can see the latest news very quickly and easily; you can use the time you save to do other things.
Open 24 hours: supermarket you can shop whenever you want; if you feel like ice-cream late at night, you can get some.
Batteries included: child's toy – the product is ready to use; you don't have to spend more money on batteries; you don't have to make another shopping trip to buy batteries.

> **EXTENSION ACTIVITY**
>
> Get students to think of the features and benefits of some everyday objects, e.g. a toothbrush, a cushion, a bar of chocolate.

Writing

6 Read the notes with the whole class. They are structured in the same way as the text in Exercise 2, which can act as a model for students' own writing.

Circulate while students are writing and help where necessary. Students should write a first draft, making sure they have several benefits. They could then exchange their texts with another student for feedback. When they are reading each other's texts, students should be able to easily identify the benefits and should also look for the appropriate use of language.

Students then revise their texts. Display the finished texts on a table or on the wall so that students can read them all. If you wish, get them to choose the best two or three texts, i.e. the ones which make them want to buy the product.

MODEL ANSWER:

The iPad killer is here!
The new Torrent tablet PC does everything an iPad® can do, and more. It's smaller, lighter and stronger than other leading tablets, and as for good looks, you'll love the Torrent's attention-grabbing design. Best of all, the Torrent costs less than half the price of an iPad®!

More content, more easily
The Torrent gives you everything you ever wanted from a tablet. It's so compact (only 1cm thick) that you can slide it into a pocket or handbag. Unlimited free cloud storage means that you can enjoy your complete media library everywhere you go. As for apps, you'll have access to more than 50,000 fantastic ways of making everyday life easier!

Child's play
If you're used to having to navigate complex multiple menus, you won't believe how simple and completely intuitive the Torrent is – it really is child's play, and your kids will love it. Accessing all your favourite movies, TV shows, albums, books, magazines and newspapers is as simple as taking a book off the shelf.

What else is cool about the Torrent?
With its shock-proof aluminium case and Gorilla Glass screen, anywhere you can go, the Torrent will go too. It's even water-resistant for those inevitable coffee spills! The Torrent is so light you won't even notice it's in your pocket. With the latest battery technology, you can enjoy up to 15 hours non stop entertainment.
Whether you're downloading new content, watching favourite soaps from your collection in the cloud, enjoying multi-player video games or just surfing the Web, the Torrent's WiFi and 3G connections are lightning fast; with built-in Satnav, you'll never be lost, and if inspiration hits you while you're on the road, Office software lets you work just as efficiently as at work. Need to contact colleagues or family, or show friends where you are and what you're doing? With front and rear cameras, you can video-conference and send photos and video any time, any place. And the Torrent comes with a two year guarantee, giving you real peace of mind.

Try it today
We're so sure you'll love the Torrent that we're offering a two week, no quibble, money back guarantee. Try the Torrent for two weeks; if you're not 100% satisfied, we promise to give you a full refund with no questions asked. What do you have to lose? Try the Torrent today!

3.6 Case study
Big Jack's pizza

This module draws together the work on product packaging and making an effective presentation by asking students to consider ways that a pizza company could strengthen its brand and improve its packaging.

Internet research

An Internet search for 'pizza box advertising' will reveal the ways in which companies use pizza boxes and other fast food containers to advertise their products and services.

It would be most useful if students could do this search before the final task in Exercise 6.

Discussion

1 Before students start this exercise, get them to brainstorm the names of some fast food chains in their town or city, and write them on the board. At this point just write down the names and the kind of food they sell. Then give students a few more minutes to discuss with a partner or small groups how each of them tries to differentiate itself from its competitors. They might mention factors such as price, taste, service, quality, range of meals, special offers, etc.

Scan reading

2 You could do this as a whole-class activity by reading the first question aloud and giving students a few minutes to find the answer in the texts. They should then raise their hands when they have found the answer. Wait until most of the class have raised their hands and then call on a student to give you the answer. Continue in this way until students have answered all the questions.

ANSWERS:

1 A pizza franchise with 23 restaurants in Hong Kong with takeout and home-delivery activities.
2 The President & CEO (and presumably the son of the founder, Big Jack).
3 value: large pizzas at low prices
4 less than one third
5 attracting new franchisees
6 loss of market share to international majors
7 convenience – proximity of stores and 24/7 delivery service; the banal product
8 a new range of pizzas, new promotional ideas, a new logo and colour scheme, a new box

Listening for gist

3 1:42 Before students listen, go back to the texts in Exercise 2 and re-read the four points on the agenda. Get students to predict what kinds of things might be discussed under these headings at the marketing meeting. Then play the recording. Remind students that they are listening only for definite decisions. For lower-level classes you might like to point out that they will hear the word 'agree' around the discussion of things that have definitely been decided.

ANSWERS:

1 To introduce a new range of fusion cuisine pizzas.
2 To bring in brand-building and packaging consultants.

RECORDING SCRIPT

1:42

Jack Jr: OK, so, we all agree on that then? A completely new range of pizzas for the 21st century, featuring fusion cuisine with the best of contemporary Chinese and Western influences? Great. We'll need at least five really new recipes, so see what you can come up with.

Mick: We'll need new names for each new pizza, then, Jack ...

J: Of course, but we can come back to that later. OK, so, can we move on to point two – new promotional ideas? What suggestions do we have? Billie?

Billie: Well, obviously with the new pizza range we should do a relaunch. And what about doing specials at different times in the year? You know, New Year, National Day, Dragon Boat Festival ...

J: Well, Billie, it's been done before, but I guess we could do that. Why not? Mick?

M: What about BOGOF?

J: I'm sorry?

M: You know, B.O.G.O.F. – buy one, get one free. Two pizzas for the price of one. And another idea would be to have a two-pizza box. The pizzas stay hotter when you have two in a box.

J: Hmm ... I'm not sure that's a direction we really want to go in. The franchisees won't like it, and we want to get away from the idea that Big Jack's is just good for filling your stomach.

M: Well, what about a gourmet club? Customers get special privileges if they become members. Or feature different national cuisines each month – Indian in the first month, Thai in the second, and so on?

B: Yes, that's good, Mick. And don't forget the Internet – what if you could build your own pizza and order your take-out or delivery online?

J: Sounds like it might be expensive, Billie, but yeah, that's more the kind of thing I had in mind. Anyway, let's go on to points three and four on the agenda. I think we can take them together, because the box depends very much on the logo and the colour scheme. Billie, I think you feel strongly about this?

B: Yes, Jack, I do. We've had our current logo ever since your dad started the business. The Big Jack logo was perfect thirty years ago, but a lot of things have changed since Big Jack's time. Apart from anything else, the symbolism is all wrong, and remember, people are very sensitive to that kind of thing here.

J: What do you mean, the symbolism is all wrong? Green and red are the colours of Italy, it's what pizza is all about!

B: Maybe, but the green chequered table-cloth on the round table – it symbolizes old-world values that people in Hong Kong just don't identify with. And it's well-known that green isn't a good colour for packaging for the Chinese.

M: Oh, really? Why's that?

B: Oh, you know, it's that thing about green hats – it means your wife is, you know, seeing another man ...

J: Billie, this is all very interesting, but ...

M: No, hang on, Jack. I think Billie's right. We have to take this kind of thing into account. And the box; the box is really important. It's easily the best way we have to communicate with our customers. Couldn't we have a more exciting box, as well as new colours and graphics? I mean, every baker in the city sells pizza in the same standard box as us. We need to differentiate! An octagonal box would be good, maybe with a window so you can see the delicious hot pizza you're carrying?

J: Well, as long as it doesn't complicate storage or delivery, I don't see why not. But it seems to me we need to get more advice on this. I trust you'll agree that we need to have some brand-building and packaging consultants work on this ... We'll consider their proposals at our next meeting.

Listening for inference

4 Students could work with a partner to do this exercise. Play **1:42** again, two or more times if necessary, to allow students to get as many of the suggestions as possible. Make a list on the board.

Get students to choose the three best suggestions in their opinion. Ask them to give reasons for their answers. They could also say why they think some of the other ideas might not be successful.

ANSWERS:

1 new names
2 relaunch
3 specials
4 BOGOF
5 two-pizza box
6 gourmet club
7 feature national cuisines each month
8 compose and order by Internet
9 change logo and colours
10 more exciting box

Jack likes 8.

5 Point out that the phrases on the left are from the listening in Exercise 4. Give students a few minutes to do the matching task. Check answers with the whole class by getting one student to read out the phrase on the left and another student to read the corresponding phrase on the right.

You could then play the recording through so that students can hear the phrases again in context.

ANSWERS:

1 b) 2 d) 3 a) 4 g) 5 c)
6 h) 7 e) 8 f) 9 j) 10 i)

Brainstorming and presentation

6 Read the instructions through with the whole class. Remind them of the suggestions they heard at the marketing meeting in Exercise 3 – they could take some of these ideas and expand them. They could also think of completely new ideas. The important thing is to have some concrete ideas to present. Students could be encouraged to use realia in their presentation, e.g. some pieces of card or paper with the names of the new pizzas written in large bold letters; a mockup of a new logo or new shape of pizza box, etc. Alternatively, they could use PowerPoint for their presentations.

Before students start preparing for their presentation, remind them of the work they did earlier in the unit on how to structure a presentation and how to deliver it clearly. They could also look back at the work they did on describing specifications and features. All of this should feed into the presentations they are preparing now.

Give students a fixed time for their presentation, e.g. no more than 5–10 minutes. One student in each group could be nominated to give the presentation, or each student could present one recommendation.

While students are speaking, make a note of any common mistakes in the target language for remedial teaching.

After the presentations, get students to comment on their own performance – ask them what two things they liked and what two things they could have done better.

FURTHER PRACTICE

Get students to write a short report on their recommendations to Big Jack's Pizza. This could be done for homework.

4 Careers

Digital resources for Unit 4

eWorkbook

Language practice: interactive & printable grammar, vocabulary, listening & pronunciation practice activities, extra printable reading & writing worksheets
Listen: Student's Book audio, language practice audio
Watch: video & video worksheets
Tests: interactive multiple-choice test
Resources: word list, grammar help & writing tips

Teacher's Resource Disc

Video: video & video worksheets
Audio: Student's Book audio
Tests: progress test Unit 4, review test 1 (Units 1–4)
Resources: PowerPoint Unit 4, business document Unit 4, photocopiable worksheets, Student's Book answer key, Student's Book glossary

Subject background

This page gives a brief six-point job search plan aimed at students and other people early in their careers. You can photocopy this plan for your students if you think it will be a useful reference tool for them.

Job search plan

1 Decide on the 'big picture' issues.

- Determine the job you want.
  If you have no idea, make a list of the things you like to do. If you have an idea of the general field (e.g. marketing), but nothing more specific, then investigate various job titles in your area of interest.
- Determine where you want to live. Are you open to relocating? If you have a specific location in mind, then identify the companies that have offices / plants / locations in those areas.
- Determine the best companies for you. You need to make some decisions about the types of companies that fit your needs, style and personality.

2 Determine your search strategy.

On-campus recruiting? Career fairs? Networking through personal contacts and going to events such as conferences? Writing to specific companies with your résumé and a covering letter? Internet job sites? Company websites? Classified ads in newspapers and professional magazines? Local careers agencies?

3 Write a résumé (CV) and covering letter.

There are hundreds of Internet sites to help you write a résumé (CV in BrE) and a covering letter. Just type phrases like *résumé tips* or *CV tips* or *covering letter* into a search engine.

Obtain critiques of your résumé and covering letter from your family, friends, colleagues, professors, etc.

As well as any other ways you are thinking of using your résumé, post it on the Internet anyway.

4 Prepare for interviews.

Learn to research companies. One of the secrets of great interviewing is knowing something about the company where you are looking for a job.

Practise, practise, practise. For example, carry out mock interviews with other students / colleagues or a career counsellor. Also, if you are a student then have some on-campus interviews with companies who come to visit – just to gain confidence and experience.

Use an Internet search engine to research Frequently Asked Interview Questions.

5 Gain experience.

Employers value work experience as much as educational background.

- Internships – work part-time in your expected career field, either during one of the semesters or over the summer.
- Summer jobs – these jobs are not always in your field of interest, but having any kind of work experience is valuable and many offer transferable skills that carry over to other jobs.
- Self-employed jobs – a growing number of students start their own (very small) businesses in areas such as gardening or web design.
- Temporary work – do work for an agency while you are waiting for something better, and make sure to include any transferable skills on your résumé.
- Volunteer work – charity, community group, not-for-profit organization, etc.
- Campus activities – key positions on sports, social, cultural and other organizations.

6 Follow up.

Be proactive after an interview – don't just sit and wait for the phone to ring.

Write a brief 'thank you letter' restating why you would be the right person for the job.

Or make a follow-up call to ask how the decision process is going.

Useful websites

Typing key terms like CV or Job interview into a search engine will produce many useful sites. Here are three good ones:

http://www.quintcareers.com/jobseeker_glossary.html
http://www.businessballs.com/curriculum.htm
http://www.alec.co.uk

4.1 About business

Career choices

This module explores the ways in which working life has changed in recent years. It considers what motivates individuals in their choice of career and how to make more successful career decisions.

Internet research

An Internet search for 'personality profile test' will reveal details about the eight life interests (identified by career experts, James Waldroop and Timothy Butler from the Harvard School of Business) that can be linked to good career decisions. They are:

- Application of technology (connected with engineering, production, operations, and the general use of technology to accomplish business goals).
- Quantitative analysis (problem-solving that relies on mathematical analysis).
- Theory development and conceptual thinking (involves broadly conceptual approaches to business problems).
- Creative production (for example, the development of new products or marketing concepts, the generation of new business ideas, etc.).
- Counselling and mentoring (involves developing relationships, such as coaching, training and mentoring).
- Managing people and relationships (developing relationships, such as coaching, training and mentoring).
- Enterprise control (decision-making authority for complete operations).
- Influence through language and ideas (exercising influence through the skilful use of written and spoken language).

Job sculpting is a means of matching people to jobs in which they can express their true life interests.

Students could conduct this research before class and use it as part of the discussion activity in Exercise 5 or after the scan reading and summarizing activities in Exercises 6 and 7.

Alternatively, they could use it as the basis for further discussion when they have completed this module.

LEAD-IN ACTIVITY

With a partner or in small groups have students tell or remind each other what their jobs are and why they chose that career. For pre-work learners, get them to say what kind of career they would like to have and why. Take whole-class feedback. Write the reasons for career choices on the board.

Discussion

1 Get students to read each pair of statements aloud. Explain any new vocabulary, e.g.:
status (position of somebody or something in relation to others).
priorities (things that are regarded as more important than others).

After students have discussed their answers with a partner, get them to raise their hands to indicate which end of the scale they occupy for each pair of statements. Ask some students to share their choices and the reasons for them.

Predicting and listening

2 1:43 Discuss the possibilities with the whole class, making a list of their predictions on the board.

Students might have a number of suggestions relating to study and choice of future career, for example you need to make sure that you choose a career to match your chosen course of study (or vice versa). They might suggest that it is in fact a good thing to choose a career on the basis of your strengths or what you are good at. Even though the recording suggests somewhat differently, accept this comment for the moment and write it up on the board. Then play the recording and compare the predictions with the career coach's advice.

ANSWERS:

The two things you shouldn't do are firstly to let other people, such as parents, teachers or friends, choose for you. Your career choice must be a decision you make for yourself since it has such crucial importance for your whole life. Secondly, you shouldn't choose a career based on what you are good at in school. You need to be sure whether you actually enjoy that subject or activity rather than if you are good at it. Your career choice should be based on what you enjoy and find fulfilling. The two things you have to do are firstly to know yourself. You need to become objectively aware of your strengths and weaknesses and what things in life drive and motivate you. The speaker suggests that a good way of doing this is by taking a personality test such as Myers Brigss or Keirsey. Secondly, you need to really thoroughly research the different kinds of job and work available so that you have a clear idea of your options.

RECORDING SCRIPT

1:43

Basically there are just five things you need to know about choosing a career. Two of those are things you really shouldn't do; two of them are things you absolutely have to do, and then the last thing is something only you can do.
OK, let's start with the two things you really shouldn't do. The first sounds very simple, but can actually be very difficult to avoid: you shouldn't let other people decide. Don't choose a career just because your parents, or your teachers, or your friends want you to do it, or think you'd be good at it. Choosing the right career is one of the biggest decisions you'll ever have to make, so don't choose for other people, choose for yourself. You'll have lots of opportunities to make other people happy, but this one is for you; this is maybe the one time in your life when you need to be totally selfish and choose what feels right for you.
Secondly, you shouldn't choose a career just because it's something you're good at. Now don't get me wrong; if you're good at something, and you genuinely love doing it, well that's great, so go for it! But all too often I meet people who chose a career in science, for example, just because they were good at science in school. And although they're still good at it, actually they hate it. So please, don't choose something that you're good at but that isn't going to make you happy.
Now, what about the two things you really have to do? Well, the first one sounds like something from a Kung Fu movie, but it's true: before you can choose a career, you need to to know yourself. Now, you can go to the Himalayas and spend a couple of years learning martial arts if you like, but there are also a lot of simple, very practical personality tests you can use at home. Tests like Myers Briggs or Keirsey are not 100% reliable, but they really can help you identify what sort of person you are. You'll find lots of tests online, or you can ask your career advisor for help.
The second thing you have to do is to find out what sort of work is available, and what it involves. Your personality test results will guide you towards the kind of careers that should suit your profile; then, you need to find out as much as you can about them, preferably from people who are already working in the sector. Social media sites like Facebook and Google+ are a great way to contact people who can share their experience.

Listening for detail

3 Read the statements aloud or get students to read them aloud and to predict whether they are true or false. Then play the whole of **1:43** again and check the answers with the whole class. Ask students if they generally agree with Charlie's Schumann's advice and, if not, what would they do differently?

ANSWERS:

1 T
2 F – She says that these are possible ways to get to know yourself but recommends personality tests as a simpler approach.
3 F – They are personality tests.
4 T
5 T

4 **1:44** Read question with the students and check that they understand what all the factors in question 1 are. You could also ask the students to discuss briefly in pairs which are the top three factors they would consider the most important for career satisfaction. Play Part 2. With lower-level classes, pause at appropriate points so that they can answer each question individually. Play each section more than once, if necessary. Check answers with the whole class.

At this point, refer back to the list of reasons for career choices that you made during the lead-in activity. Are any of them the same or similar to those mentioned in the interview?

ANSWERS:

1 Variety, autonomy and recognition are the factors that Schumann claims can cause people to be happy in their jobs, along with contact with people (team spirit) and making the world a better place (a job helping people). According to research, money, fame and being beautiful do not in fact make people happier and, in fact, people who believe that these things are very important are much more likely to get depressed than the average person. Job security is mentioned but the interviewer suggests that is something people will forgo for a job that brings them more personal satisfaction, such as running their own company.
2 Flow activities are those that get a person so involved in what he or she is doing that they forget everything else, and time passes quickly.

RECORDING SCRIPT

1:44

That brings us to the last thing, the thing only you can do: understanding what makes you happy. Now, you're probably thinking, that's easy; money – the more, the better! Well, actually there's a great deal of research that shows that, although having enough money is very important, having more money doesn't actually make you any happier. In fact, people who believe that happiness depends on being rich, famous or beautiful are more likely to suffer from depression than the rest of us.

What does seem to make most people happy is surprisingly simple; things like contact with other people, variety, autonomy and recognition. Working with people you like and respect, having a wide range of different activities, and being able to decide what you do and when you do it are major sources of satisfaction. The feeling that you're doing something useful, that you're making the world a better place is also a big motivator. It's interesting that people who run their own businesses, or who work in small companies where they feel they are in control are usually happier than average, even though they probably earn lower salaries and have less job security than they would in a larger organization.

Now, just before I finish, let me ask you this: do you ever get so involved in what you're doing that you just forget everything else, and time just flies? Yeah? It's a feeling you often get when you do things like team sports, playing or listening to music, writing, painting, repairing or inventing things. These are times when most people say they are happiest, and they're called 'flow' activities. If you know what makes you happy, and if you can identify jobs that let you experience that 'flow', then you have almost certainly found the key to choosing your ideal career.

Discussion

5 First students discuss what they think these statements mean. Then they should decide if they agree or disagree with them. Students might also want to consider other, related questions, e.g. Does everyone make a conscious career choice or does it happen by accident? How easy is it to combine your interests with your choice of career? Take whole-class feedback.

Scan reading

6 Before students start reading the text, explain any of the colloquial expressions which may be new to them, e.g.
light someone's fire (make someone enthusiastic)
pick someone's brains (question someone who knows a lot about something in order to get information)
up in the air (uncertain, not yet decided)
earth-shattering (having a powerful effect).
Remind them to use the *Glossary* in their *Student's Books* on page 154.

With lower-level classes, you could break down the text into more manageable chunks to help them complete the task. First get students to simply read the headings for each section and predict what they think the section will be about. Then, get a student to read the two summarizing sentences aloud. Finally, read each section aloud and ask students to raise their hands if they think it matches the sentences they have just heard.

ANSWERS:

1 tip 4
2 tip 7

Summarizing

7 With lower-level classes, you could divide students into pairs or groups and get them to summarize just one or two tips.

Circulate while students are working and assist where necessary.

Get students to choose one or two tips that particularly impressed them.

SUGGESTED ANSWERS:

Tip 1 Take time to identify what motivates you.
Tip 2 Brainstorm ways to integrate what motivates you into your life.
Tip 3 Ask other people for advice about things you are interested in.
Tip 5 Identify your obstacles and the reasons why they prevent you from reaching your goals.
Tip 6 Surround yourself with people who can help and support you.
Tip 8 Make a practical, structured action plan.
Tip 9 Start taking action as soon as possible.
Tip 10 Make a visible commitment to achieving your goal.

4.2 Vocabulary

Careers, personal skills and qualities

This module focuses on vocabulary and expressions which enable students to discuss activities and performance in the workplace and the effect it has on career development.

Internet research

A search for 'mentoring' will reveal that a mentor is a person who guides and helps people in their careers. Mentoring can help people to explore their needs, motivation, desires, skills, and thought processes; it can help them to set goals, take action and make changes. Information from this search will be useful for Exercises 8–10.

Discussion

1 Students could do this activity with a partner or in small groups. Take whole-class feedback. You could also ask students to rank the benefits from the viewpoint of different kinds of people, e.g. a 25-year-old recent employee; an employee in their 40s with three children; a 55-year-old.

ANSWERS:

Answers depend on personal values. Suggested answers in terms of probable financial value:

1 free accommodation
2 company car
3 pension plan
4 free medical insurance
5 luncheon vouchers
6 profit-sharing
7 stock options
8 Christmas bonus
9 sports and social facilities

EXTENSION ACTIVITY

To personalize the activity, ask in-work students if they receive any of these benefits from their employer. Can they describe them and explain the pros and cons, e.g. *We get free membership of a sports club. They have good facilities, but it's a long way from where I live.*

2 Ask students to read through the sentences. Then, give them a few minutes to complete this activity with a partner. They could try to do this even if they don't know all of the words in bold. Check answers with the whole class.

ANSWERS:

Part 1

1 Before graduating, Josef Gutkind applied for jobs in 20 companies.
4 Wilson Brothers offered Josef a position as a management trainee.
3 His first interview was successful and he was short-listed for a second interview.
6 When Wilson's got into difficulties, Josef was made redundant.
5 Two years later he was appointed Logistics Manager.
2 He was invited for an interview at Wilson Brothers.

Part 2

10 In his early fifties he took a sabbatical to write a book.
7 Josef quickly found a new job, but was dismissed after arguing with his boss.
11 The book was a best-seller, and Josef resigned from the firm.
8 While he was unemployed Josef studied for a master's degree.
12 He retired from business and now lives in the south of France.
9 Thanks to the masters on his CV, Josef was hired by a firm of consultants.

If necessary, explain *sabbatical* (a period of leave, paid or unpaid, to allow an employee to do something which may or may not be related to their work; e.g. a company might offer one month off on full pay every four years; other companies might offer one month's unpaid leave after six years of service, and so on). Ask students if their company offers its employees sabbaticals and what the arrangements are. If they don't know, they could find out and report back. Pre-work students could investigate which local companies offer sabbaticals.

Focus on the words in bold and guide students towards an understanding of them and how they are used. For example, get students to pick out the expressions using the passive (*was offered a position, was dismissed, was appointed, was short-listed, was made redundant, was hired*). Ask students what the expressions have in common (they are all actions by a company towards an employee).

Ask students to pick out the expressions related to 'not being in work' (*dismissed, unemployed, made redundant, retired, resigned*).

Get students to pick out the verbs followed by *from* (*resign, retire*), *by* (*hire*) and *for* (*shortlist*).

3 and **4** Ask students do these exercises individually or with a partner. Circulate and assist where necessary. Check answers with the whole class.

ANSWERS:

Exercise 3

1 Could you tell me exactly why you were dismissed by OQP?
2 Were the departments merged before or after you were appointed Quality Manager?
3 After the factory closed, was it difficult to find a new job?
4 Have you applied for jobs in other companies in the area?
5 If you were invited for a second interview, would you be able to come to our head office in London?
6 How would you feel if we offered you a position as a product manager?

Exercise 4

1 short-listed
2 hired
3 on sabbatical
4 dismissed
5 resign
6 made redundant
7 unemployed
8 retire

FURTHER PRACTICE

To check that students have understood and can use the vocabulary correctly, get them to make sentences using the words in bold. The sentences could be about themselves or people they know or invent. They could do this orally and as a whole-class activity. Alternatively, they could work with a partner and write three sentences on a slip of paper. Students then exchange the slips of paper with another pair and check each other's sentences.

Collocations

5 Do this matching task as a whole-class activity. Explain any new vocabulary, e.g.:
initiative (willingness and ability to realize what needs to be done without being told).
negotiating skills (ability to reach an agreement through discussion).

ANSWERS:

2 a)	3 d)	4 e)	5 c)	6 h)
7 i)	8 f)	9 j)	10 g)	

6 and **7** Ask students to do these exercises with a partner. Check answers with the whole class. Then get students to discuss with their partner which of the four qualities mentioned in Exercise 7 they think they already have and which ones they need to develop.

ANSWERS:

Exercise 6

1 I enjoy taking initiative, and I keep my promises; when I make a commitment to a project, I always deliver.
2 I have a lot of experience in working closely with both product development and sales teams, and can adapt to their different working styles.
3 I have excellent organizational skills, and I hate being late – so I have no problem with working to strict deadlines.
4 I liaise with government officials: fortunately, I possess strong negotiating skills.
5 I'm used to managing a busy workload; I'm good at multitasking, and coping with pressure is no problem.
6 I often take on ownership of projects with multi-million dollar budgets.
7 I believe I can make a valuable contribution to any work group.
8 I'm a good listener, so I build good working relationships with colleagues.

Exercise 7

a) Are you able to take responsibility? 1, 6
b) Are you a good communicator? 4, 8
c) Are you a good time manager? 3, 5
d) Are you a good team worker? 2, 7

Listening for gist

8 1:45 Elicit from students what they understand by *high-flier* (a person with great potential for achievement) and *concerns* (people whose performance is causing worry or concern) and what the criteria might be for assessing individuals as one or the other. Then, play the recording through once.

With lower-level classes pause after the discussion of each person or play each section more than once.

ANSWERS:

Rachel Ratcliff +	Paul Stevens +
Michael Diegel -	Shane Garney -

RECORDING SCRIPT

1:45

B: All right. So that brings us to Rachel Ratcliff. You've flagged her as a high-flier. She's certainly very committed to her work.

A: Absolutely. Rachel is doing a terrific job for us. She's an excellent team-player, and she really enjoys taking initiative. The problem is that she's ambitious and we don't have any ways to satisfy her ambition for the moment. We planned to make her a department manager in a couple of years' time, but there are no openings right now. She's obviously had other offers, perhaps from a head hunter, and she's thinking about resigning.

B: Hmm ... It would be a shame to lose her. Solutions?

A: Well, we could offer her a two-year assignment in Germany. I know there's a vacancy over there for someone with her profile, and she'd certainly be able to make a valuable contribution. But I don't know whether she'd agree. She has a fiancé, so it may be difficult. Another possibility would be to send her on an MBA course, and start preparing her for senior management.

B: You really think she's that good? A potential MBA? Well, let me think about that one. I'll come back to you in a couple of days.

A: OK.

B: By the way, how is young Paul Stevens getting on? I believe he had a problem with his manager?

A: Yes, that's right. He was working to very strict deadlines, and just needed a break. I'm working closely with him now, and everything's fine. He's back on the high-fliers' list. He has strong negotiating skills, and I think he'll be an excellent engineer.

B: Good. OK, then, let's move on to Michael Diegel. He's a new hire too, isn't he?

A: Yes. Michael's been with us almost a year now, and we've marked him as a concern because he's not really delivering the goods. He arrived with a fantastic resumé, lots of skills and some good experience, but he's consistently underperformed, he just isn't able to manage the workload.

B: Hmm ... Any idea why?

A: Well, I'm not too sure ... Some people in the department feel that it's a problem of motivation; he doesn't like Seattle, and he wants to move east. But others of us feel that perhaps he just doesn't have the strengths that his resumé claimed. At the moment he seems to have more weaknesses than strengths.

B: So, what do we do, give him an official warning? Tell him we'll fire him if he doesn't deliver?

A: Maybe. But we've already invested too much time and money to just dismiss him. How about offering him an easier position in Chicago? Something that won't be so difficult. If he realizes that the job here in Seattle is too much for him, perhaps he'd be more motivated to perform at his real level. Moving to Chicago would be a good way to save face.

B: Yes, that's not a bad idea. Could you liaise with his manager, and see what's available in Chicago or Boston, then come back to me?

A: OK.

B: Good. Now then, we come to our old friend Shane Garney, Mr Wannabe himself. Is he still on the high-fliers list?

A: Not really. He's more of a concern now. He certainly has the skills, but he's getting greedy. We gave him a big raise six months ago when he was promoted, but now he says it's not enough. He says he's had a much better offer from the competition.

B: Well, I think it's time we had a serious talk with Mr Garney. He needs to understand that, although we appreciate ambition, our corporate policy is to reward achievement, not potential.

A: The problem is, of course, that he's very well-connected. You remember that his father's a senator. Wouldn't it be easier to give Shane a small raise to keep him happy?

B: Yes, I'm fully aware of that, and I'm aware that government contracts are very important to this company. But if Shane is only interested in money, he should join his father in Washington. The answer is 'no'. If he thinks he can get a better deal somewhere else, then fine, he can resign. We have a lot of good people like Rachel Ratcliff who would be happy to take his place.

Taking notes

9 **1:45** Remind students they are listening for words and expressions that describe the qualities of each person which are causing problems. Play **1:45** again. Check answers with the whole class.

ANSWERS:

	Rachel Ratcliff	Michael Diegel	Shane Garney
problem	thinking about resigning	new hire; under-performing	wants more money; has a better offer
causes	ambitious, no opportunities	motivation, or doesn't have potential	getting greedy; over-ambitious; father is a senator
possible solutions	transfer her to Germany; send her on an MBA	warning; move him east to an easier job	give him a small raise; say no

Discussion

10 Give students a few minutes to discuss their ideas. Remind them to use the vocabulary they have learnt in this module, and to consider the ideas explored in 4.1, to do with career choice and values.

Check answers with the whole class. Get students to give reasons for their solutions.

EXTENSION ACTIVITY

Ask students to consider how mentoring might help Rachel, Paul, Michael and Shane in their careers. Remind them of the information they gathered on the Internet about mentoring. Students write a list of questions for each person to try to find out more about what their values and interests are. They then roleplay mentor / mentee discussion using these questions.

Finish by asking students if they have any personal experience of mentoring. Ask if they found it useful. If they have no personal experience, ask if they would find it useful in their own careers.

4.3 Grammar

Present tenses

This module focuses on the use of the present simple and continuous and on the present perfect simple and continuous. It also practises the past simple.

Internet research

Students will find numerous websites offering grammar explanations if they search under 'English grammar practice'. Before students do this task, agree with them a list of questions to use when assessing each website, e.g.:

Are the grammar explanations clear and easy to understand?
Are the exercises useful?
Is the site easy to navigate?
Are the layout and presentation clear?

Get students to choose one or two of the tenses practised in this unit and work through the explanations and exercises on two or three websites so that they can compare how each one performs on the same task.

Students then present one or more of the websites they found to the whole class, commenting on the best and worst aspects of each one. You may find that several students liked or disliked the same website.

Students could do this task before you start this module or afterwards, as a follow-up to the work done in the unit.

The bluffing game

1 Start by reading the *Refresh your memory box* on present simple, present continuous, present perfect simple and present perfect continuous. If students seem unsure of how to use them, work through some or all of exercises in the *Grammar and practice* section (page 128 in the *Student's Book*, answers on page 114 in this book) before they do the exercise.

Check that students understand *bluffing* (trying to deceive someone about your true intentions). Get students started by producing two or three sentences about yourself using some of the prompts. Then ask students to prepare their own sentences.

SUGGESTED ANSWERS:

I often wear a tie at work.; I don't usually work at the weekend.; At the moment, I'm wearing yellow socks.; I've never been to the US.

2 Divide the class into groups of four or five. Students take turns to read out a sentence and face questions from other students in their group. The idea is that they should ask questions that will expose the bluff. After a few questions, the group guesses whether the speaker is bluffing or not. In feedback, ask groups to reveal their best bluffer.

FURTHER PRACTICE

As students are playing the game, walk round and note down any errors involving the use of present and present perfect tenses. At the end, write five or six sentences containing errors that you heard on the board. In their groups, students must correct them.

Do Exercises 1–14 in the *Grammar and practice* section (page 128 and 129 in the Student's Book, answers on page 114 in this book) for further practice on all of the tenses practised in this module.

Present perfect and past simple

3 Read the instructions with the whole class and give students a few minutes to skim read the table.

With lower-level classes, elicit the questions that students will need to ask, e.g.:
When does Mr/Ms ____ graduate?
What kind of work experience has he/she had?
What was his/her grade on the management potential test?

You could also complete the information for the first two candidates with one or more Student Bs to get lower-level classes started.

Circulate while students are completing the table and assist where necessary. Make a note of any incorrect use of tenses for remedial teaching when the activity is over.

Give students a few minutes to choose the most suitable candidate and then take whole-class feedback. Get students to give reasons for their choice.

SUGGESTED ANSWERS:

1 Ms Bianco or Mr Green, assuming he spoke Spanish in CA and FL. Mr Salmon hasn't graduated yet.
2 Miss Rose or Mrs Grey (but she hasn't worked in marketing).
3 Mr Schwarz. Mr Braun scored C-.
4 Miss Plum, assuming she spoke French in Quebec.
5 Miss Rose (if she wasn't chosen for 2) or Ms Violeta.
6 Ms Bianco (if she wasn't chosen for 1) or Mr Da Silva.

Listening: present perfect simple and continuous

4 1:46–1:55 Ask students to look at the ten pictures. Elicit what is happening in each. Then play the recording. Students listen and match the situations to the pictures.

ANSWERS:

1 h)	2 j)	3 i)	4 e)	5 c)
6 g)	7 d)	8 a)	9 f)	10 b)

5 Play **1:46–1:55** again, pausing after each situation to allow students time to write. Ask them to compare their answers with a partner. Take whole-class feedback.

Check that students are using the tenses appropriately and forming their sentences correctly.

SUGGESTED ANSWERS:

1 He's just been offered a job. / He's been having an interview.
2 They've just passed their exams. / They've just been looking at the exam results.
3 She's interviewed 17 candidates. / She's been interviewing since 8.00.
4 He's just run ten kilometres. / He's been doing recruitment tests.
5 Jon has failed his exams.
6 They haven't decided which candidate to choose. / They've been discussing candidates.
7 Nick hasn't finished his CV. / He's been working on his CV for a long time.
8 Paula has just been to an interview. / She's attended 27 interviews.
9 Mr Singh has spilt coffee over the interviewer's papers.
10 Sally has written 100 job applications. / She's been writing job applications since this morning.

RECORDING SCRIPT

1:46–1:55

1
A: Well, the job's yours if you want it.
B: Well, thank you very much, I'm delighted to accept.
2
C: Congratulations! Don't forget, the degree ceremony's next Friday!
D: Thank you, sir!
E: Thank you very much!
3
F: Nearly finished now.
G: Wow. Seventeen candidates in one day! And it's almost dinner time. What time did you start?
F: Eight o'clock this morning!
4
H: Ten kilometres! Phew! When they said 'recruitment tests', I thought they meant IQ and graphology, not an army assault course!
5
I: Have you seen the results, Jon?
J: Yeah.
I: Oh. Oh, I'm so sorry.
J: It's all right. It's not the end of the world.
6
K: I still think Ms Brown has more relevant experience than the others.
L: Look, we're not getting anywhere like this. Why don't we meet again tomorrow? And, remember, we can always ask all four candidates back for a second interview if we still can't decide.
7
M: Nick? Are you coming out for a drink?
N: Nah. Gotta finish my CV.
M: You still working on that CV?! I mean, how long can it take to say you've got no skills, no qualifications, and you've never done an honest day's work in your life?!
N: Very funny.
8
O: Hey, Paula, how did the interview go today?
P: Oh, so-so. Pretty much the same as the last twenty-six.
O: Ah. Well, I've got to hand it to you Paula, you certainly don't give up easily.
9
Q: Look out!
R: Oops, too late. Oh dear, it's all over your papers. Sorry about that. These cups are very easy to knock over, aren't they?
Q: Never mind.
R: Hope it wasn't anything important. Er, are you here for the interviews, then?
Q: Yes, as a matter of fact I am. I'm conducting the interviews, actually. It's Mr Singh, isn't it?
R: Oops!
10
S: Ninety-eight, ninety-nine, one hundred. There we are! Finished!
T: Finished what, Sally? You don't mean …?
S: Yep. Job applications. Started this morning.
T: One hundred job applications?! You're kidding!

Asking questions

6 Write *sports club* and *community arts centre* on the board and ask students to tell you what kinds of jobs might be available in each place (e.g. sports club: receptionist, tennis coach, swimming instructor, yoga teacher, etc. community arts centre: receptionist, marketing manager, exhibitions organizer, etc.).

Explain that students are going to interview each other for jobs at these places. Give them a few minutes to read the instructions and think about the questions they might ask. While they are speaking, circulate and check that they are forming the questions and using tenses correctly. Make a note of any mistakes for remedial teaching later.

EXTENSION ACTIVITY

This activity focuses on the four tenses practised in this module. Demonstrate what to do by preparing three or four sentences about yourself, one or more of which is false. Write the sentences on the board or read them aloud, e.g.:
I have been teaching for 10 years.
I am training to run a marathon.
I have never visited Australia.
When I left school I spent a gap year working at a hotel in Germany.

With a partner, students decide which sentence(s) is false. Then get students to raise their hands about each sentence, asking them to justify their choice if they can. Then invite learners to ask you questions to find out more about each statement.

Students then write their own similar sentences and, working in small groups, follow the same procedure as above.

4.4 Speaking
Job interviews

This module focuses on language and expressions useful for answering questions at a job interview. On the Teacher's Resource Disc, you will find more related practice material, including a video (with worksheets) featuring an example situation for students to analyse and discuss.

Internet research

A search for 'interview advice tips questions' will reveal a number of websites offering advice on how to prepare for an interview and how to answer specific questions. They will also include information on interview problems, body language, group interview tests, panel interviews, and questions to ask an interviewer.

Get students to search a number of websites and write down one or two pieces of advice that they find especially useful. They can then share these with the whole class in a feedback session.

This research could be done before the roleplay in Exercise 6 as it would be especially helpful for students roleplaying the candidate. Or it can be done at the end of the module as a follow-up activity.

Discussion

1 Ask students to work individually to answer these questions. Tell them to make notes on possible answers. Then get them to compare their answers with a partner. Take whole-class feedback and write any useful phrases or vocabulary on the board.

FURTHER PRACTICE

Get students to consider what an interviewer might be trying to find out by asking these questions, e.g.:
Are you ambitious? Are you making plans for your future career?
How do you deal with conflict / difficult situations? Will you make a good leader / manager?
Are you self-aware? Can you identify your own shortcomings?
How do you handle stress? Will you be effective under pressure?

Listening

2 **1:56–1:59** Play the recordings. Pause after each extract to allow students time to decide which question applies in each case. When they have finished, check answers. Ask students to tell you which words or phrases helped them to answer the questions.

ANSWERS:

1 B, C, D
2 D
3 B
4 C

RECORDING SCRIPT

1:56–1:59

1

Interviewer: Where do you see yourself in five years' time?
A: Well, that's a difficult question to answer; let's just say that I see myself as a top performing employee in a leading company, like this one. I plan to gain experience and learn new skills. Hopefully, in five years' time, I would be ready to move up to a position with more responsibility.

2
Interviewer: How do you motivate people to do their best?
B: Well, I think there are two important aspects to this question. The first is to create a positive atmosphere. If people feel happy about what they're doing, they're much more motivated to work towards a common goal. So making sure they understand the objectives, and the process, and that the atmosphere is pleasant and relaxed, those are really important. The second thing is to give feedback, especially when somebody does a good job, not just when they get something wrong. When I worked in a restaurant a couple of years ago, I realized that knowing how well you're doing is essential to staying motivated.

3
Interviewer: What are your weaknesses?
C: Well, of course, I'm aware that there are areas that I can improve on, but I have to say, as far as this job is concerned, I don't feel that I have any significant weaknesses. And if I do identify a problem, I take action to resolve it. Take time management, for instance. A couple of years ago, I realized I wasn't the most organized person in the world, so I followed a time management course. I applied what I learned, and now I would say that organization is one of my strengths.

4
Interviewer: Can you give an example of a situation you found stressful, and how you coped with the stress?
D: Yes. Last term, for example, I was on a work placement where my supervisor had to go off sick for three weeks, so the company asked me to take over responsibility for the project. It meant a huge workload, which was pretty stressful. Anyway, I sat down and planned out exactly what I had to do each day for those three weeks. I also planned an hour each evening in the gym. That really helped to ease the stress. I managed to finish the project on time, and in much better shape than when I started! Does that answer your question?

3 Before playing **1:56–1:59** again, see if students can complete the expressions. Then check answers with the whole class. Get students to repeat the expressions following the intonation and stress used by the speakers in the recording.

ANSWERS:

Asking for clarification or reformulating
Do you mean, ...?

Playing for time
That's a difficult question to answer; let's just say that ...

Structuring your answer
I think there are two important aspects to this question ...

Giving concrete examples
Take ..., for instance.

Talking about yourself
I applied what I learned.
I see myself as a top performing employee in a leading company.
I plan to gain experience and learn new skills.
I would be ready to move up to a position with more responsibility.
I realized that knowing how well you're doing is essential to staying motivated.
I'm aware that there are areas that I can improve on.
I don't feel that I have any significant weaknesses.
I would say that organization is one of my strengths.
I managed to finish the project on time.

Validating your answer
Does that answer your question?

4 Students work with a partner to put the words in the sentences in the correct order. They can then practise saying the sentences aloud, focusing on appropriate stress and intonation. Play **1:56–1:59** again so that students can hear the sentences in context.

ANSWERS:

1. I applied what I learned.
2. I'm able to cope with being unpopular.
3. I see myself as a top performing employee in a leading company.
4. I plan to gain experience and learn new skills.
5. I would be ready to move up to a position with more responsibility.
6. I realized that knowing how well you're doing is essential to staying motivated.
7. I'm aware that there are areas that I can improve on.
8. I don't feel that I have any significant weaknesses.
9. I would say that organization is one of my strengths.
10. I managed to finish the project on time.

5 Get a student to read the quotation aloud. Explain *enterprise* (a business company). Do the first part of the exercise as a whole-class activity. Read each question aloud and get students to decide whether it is type 1 or type 2. Check their understanding of:
to get something done (to achieve or complete something).

Circulate while students are asking and answering the questions and assist where necessary. Make a list of any useful vocabulary or expressions and teach them to the whole class after the activity is over. They could be used in the roleplay which follows.

ANSWERS:

a) What are your strengths and weaknesses? 1
b) Why do you want to work for us? 2
c) What is your greatest achievement? 1
d) How do you make sure things get done? 1
e) Why do you want to leave your present job? 2
f) Tell me about a time when you successfully handled a difficult situation. 1
g) What sort of environment would you prefer not to work in? 2
h) What are the most difficult kinds of decisions for you to make? 1

FURTHER PRACTICE

Point out that in an interview situation different questions can be answered in the same way. For example, in the listening task, *How you do motivate people to do their best?* and *How do you make sure things get done?* are different questions, but could both be answered in the same way. Similarly, *Can you give an example of a situation you found stressful?* and *Tell me about a time when you successfully handled a difficult situation?* could be answered by using the same information and examples.

Get students to think of alternative ways of asking the other questions in Exercise 5.

Roleplay

6 Read the instructions and the job ads with the whole class and explain any new vocabulary or allow students to look them up in a dictionary.

Candidates should refer to the Internet research they did on interview tips and advice. If they have not done this, elicit from the whole class a list of topics that they could ask questions about (e.g. details about the job itself; information about the company and department; opportunities for training and developments; benefits, etc.).

Remind the interviewers to look back at the previous exercises in this module for help and ideas when they are preparing their questions.

Circulate and check that all students are using expressions and tenses correctly in their questions.

When the activity is over, get students to give each other feedback, either with a partner or as a whole-class activity. The interviewers can say which answers were most satisfactory and which were less satisfactory; the candidates can say which questions they found easy to answer and which ones were difficult.

4.5 Writing
A CV

This module focuses on the content, organization and style of CVs.

Internet research

An Internet search for 'résumé style' will reveal information about a number of possible approaches to presenting information in a CV. For example, a chronological CV starts with your most current position and progresses back in time; a functional CV lists your major areas of experience and/or accomplishments; a skills CV emphasizes what you can do. Different styles will be appropriate for different individuals and different situations.

Students will find many sample CVs on the Internet. They could download some and evaluate which style would best suit their individual circumstances and the profession or industry they are interested in.

Discussion

1 Start by reminding students that *CV* stands for 'curriculum vitae', a Latin term meaning 'course of life'. *Résumé* has a similar meaning; it is more commonly used in American English.

Students discuss the questions in small groups. As the answer to most of these questions is likely to be 'it depends', encourage students to give reasons for their answers. Take whole-class feedback.

SUGGESTED ANSWERS:

The 'correct' answers to all of these are 'it depends'. There are valid arguments for both sides of each case.

1 In general, one page is enough, especially for new graduates; but if you need more space, it's better to use two pages rather than try to squeeze everything onto one page.
2 Decide which is more relevant. If your experience is more relevant to the job than your qualifications, put it first. However, many employers like to have a summary of your qualifications at the top of the page.
3 Some experts recommend not giving references until they are requested, so that you have time to contact the people concerned and inform them about the context, your objectives, etc. Others advise supplying genuine references rather than stating 'references available on request'. Practice also varies from country to country; find out what is normal in the country where you are applying for a job.
4 If you feel that a photograph gives you an advantage, include one. If not, then don't feel obliged to include one unless the employer specifically requests one. In some countries, companies may require an anonymous CV in order to eliminate ethnic or gender prejudice.

Model

2 Give students a few minutes to put these categories in order individually or with a partner.

Students check their answers against the sample CV. To check answers with the whole class, read out sections from the CV and get students to give the category it falls under, e.g. *British* (personal details), *clean driving licence* (general / additional skills), *I coordinated an office reorganization project* (work experience).

ANSWERS:

1 personal details
2 qualifications
3 work experience
4 voluntary roles / positions of responsibility
5 general / additional skills
6 references

Analysis

3 Students underline all the verbs in the CV. Let them compare their answers in pairs. Then have a whole-class discussion and discuss what the students notice about the verbs.

ANSWERS:

Verbs in past: played, required, involved, coordinated, was, ran, represented, chaired
Verbs in present: run, am
Verbs in English CVs are usually active and in the simple past (as opposed to some languages where the historic present is used, or where verbs are avoided in favour of nouns and adjectives.)

Language focus

4 This exercise highlights the degree of formality usually found in CVs. Get individual students to read each of the sentences aloud, while the rest of the class finds the matching sentence in the CV.

Focus on the useful verbs and verb phrases, e.g. *liaise, coordinate, run, represent, play an integral part in, be responsible for* which students can use in Exercises 4 and 5.

ANSWERS:

1 ... involved liaising with a client's parent company in Germany.
2 Advanced computer literacy
3 I coordinated an office reorganization project.
4 I ran a language training programme for members of the department.
5 I represented over 400 members in faculty meetings.
6 I played an integral part in a team of consultants working on IS projects.
7 I was responsible for managing the outdoor exhibition of camping equipment.
8 This position required familiarity with networking solutions.
9 I am responsible for motivating the team.
10 I chaired conferences with visiting speakers.

FURTHER PRACTICE

Use the sample CVs which students downloaded from the Internet and/or real job ads taken from newspapers to compile a list of useful 'action words' – i.e. verbs that that students could use in their own CVs to describe their achievements. Examples of the kinds of words that might be included in this kind of list are *administer, analyse, assess, build, create, design, develop, devise, direct, ensure, implement, improve, increase, instigate, introduce, manage, monitor, organize, produce, re-organize, solve, support, test.*

Output

5 Students could do this task with a partner. Circulate while they are working and assist where necessary. Then get students to exchange their CV with another pair, who check the organization and choice of language.

SUGGESTED ANSWER:

Justine Dominga Collier
Date of birth: 4 November, 1989, Auckland, NZ
Nationality: New Zealand
Address: 14 Green Street, Newcastle NE13 8BH
Telephone: 01879 122 7789

Education
2007–2010 BA in Economics at Newcastle University (Expected final grade 2:1)
2005–2007 Northern High School: 3 'A' levels – Mathematics (A), Economics (B), French (B)

Work history
Oct–Mar 2005 *Internship with Arbol Oil*
I played an integral part in the finance department. This position required familiarity with accounts software, and involved liaising with colleagues in S America.
June–Sept 2004 *Information officer with Newcastle Social Security*
I was responsible for managing a confidential personnel database. I coordinated a three-day visit for a representative of the Spanish government.

Positions of responsibility
2009 *Secretary of Newcastle Junior Chamber of Commerce*
I was responsible for communications and edited a monthly newsletter. I also liaised with guest speakers and the local authorities.
2008 to present Voluntary work for the charity OUTLOOK: I devise and organize events for disabled children.
Social secretary for the University Basketball team.

Other
Bilingual Spanish
First violin in a string quartet
Typing speed 90 wpm

References
Mr Bowers, tutor, Newcastle University
Mrs Broadbent, Principal, Northern High School

6 Students could use the results of the Internet research task to help them write or update their own CV. Otherwise, they could use the model in Exercise 2 as the basis for their CV. Circulate while students are working and make a note of any useful new vocabulary or phrases that could be shared with the whole class.

4.6 Case study
Gap years and career breaks

This module focuses on the reasons for and experience of taking time off from your career to do something different.

Internet research

A search for 'gap year' will reveal a wide range of websites suggesting ways of spending a gap year, including travel, adventure holidays, and voluntary work.

Carrying out this research before they start this module will be useful for students who do not have any knowledge or experience of gap years or career breaks.

Brainstorming

1 Explain that *gap year* usually refers to the time taken off at the beginning of a career, while *career break* refers to the time taken off at a later stage of life.

Do this as a whole-class activity. If students have difficulty getting started, give them the brief outline of a story to comment on, e.g.: *A friend of mine had been working for seven years in a big company. He enjoyed the work, but the job was stressful and he wanted a break from the pressure and the routine. So he left his job and decided to take some time off and do something different …*

SUGGESTED ANSWERS:

Gap year: travelling, working, doing voluntary work, writing a book, building a house, studying, meditating, etc. Advantages: gain experience and maturity, see the world, do something you can't do professionally, do something for people in need, give yourself time to make important choices, escape pressure or difficulty, save money for studies, etc. Disadvantages: get out of step / lose touch with friends / colleagues, financial cost, acquire 'bad' habits, be perceived as less serious / ambitious, lose job or miss opportunities, etc.
Ask students if gap years and career breaks are common in their country. Do they know anyone who has taken a gap year or career break? What were their experiences? Would they consider taking one themselves?

Listening

2 2:01–2:06 Play the recordings. Pause after each speaker to allow students time to answer the questions. Then get students to comment – which of these gap year options would they have chosen to do themselves and why?

ANSWERS:

	When	Where	Experience	Why
1	between 2nd and 3rd year at university	Nepal	positive	learned more than in three years at university
2	between school and degree course	Dublin	mixed	good for English and culture, but boring at school
3	in work	around the world	mixed	clearer idea of goals, regrets not helping people
4	before business school	car factory	negative	bored, wasted a year
5	after 20 years in same job	India	positive	changed outlook on life
6	before studying Medicine	East Africa	mixed	very hard, but made a difference

RECORDING SCRIPT

2:01–2:06

1 My gap year? Oh, yes, it was a fantastic experience. It was between my second and third years at university. I went to Nepal to teach English. I think I learned more in that year than in three years at university. It was incredible. Everybody should do it.

2 I went to live with a family in Dublin for a year before starting my degree course. Of course, it was really good for my English, and interesting from a cultural point of view. But it was pretty boring going back to school for another year, even if it was in English.

3 I've had a great year. I've been around the world, working for two or three weeks, then moving on to the next place. I've just gone back to my job, and now I have a much clearer idea of where I'm going and what I want to achieve. My only regret is not doing something to help people. If I could do it again, I'd definitely volunteer for charity work, probably in Africa.

4 Yeah, I had a gap year before starting business school. I needed to earn some money, so I worked in a car factory. It was hell. I've never been so bored in my life. I suppose I learned some valuable lessons, but now I wish I'd done something more exciting, gone somewhere exotic. I feel I wasted a year of my life.

5 I'd been in the same job for about twenty years, and I decided I needed to step back and think about what I wanted to do with the rest of my life. So I took a sabbatical. Fortunately my company was very understanding. I travelled in India for six months, then I wrote a book about my experiences. It completely changed my outlook on life. I'd recommend it to anybody.

6 I've just started studying medicine. I wanted to get away from my parents and see the world, so I've just come back from nine months in East Africa. It was really hard. I almost came home after the first week. I'm glad I stayed, because I felt I made a difference to people's lives – a very small difference, but a difference all the same. But if I'd known what it would be like, I'm sure I wouldn't have gone.

Scan reading

3 Read the title of the article with the whole class and get them to explain what they understand by the two expressions *change the world* (make a difference to other people's lives) and *want a change* (do something different, for yourself).

You could do this task by reading the first question aloud and giving students a few minutes to find the answer in the text. They should then raise their hands when they have found the answer. Wait until most of the class have raised their hands and then call on a student to give you the answer. Continue in this way until students have answered all the questions.

ANSWERS:

1 People over 17 years of age, before, during or after a degree course, or in work.
2 Broaden your horizons, enhance your CV, step back from your studies to decide what you want to do with your life, do something concrete and tangible to help people in need in underprivileged areas of the world.
3 Education, conservation, medical support and care work.
4 Participants work as volunteers. Food and accommodation are provided, but participants pay their own travel costs.
5 Send in the application form together with your CV.

Reading and discussion

4 Get students to read the four descriptions of gap-year placements silently. Then ask them some questions to get them thinking about what is involved in each placement, e.g.:
What kinds of things do you think a classroom assistant in South Africa or Costa Rica would do on a daily basis? (help the teacher with lessons; spend time with individual children; help with break times and lunch breaks)
What kind of physical work might a conservation volunteer do in Malaysia? (digging, cutting back vegetation, clearing land, caring for animals)
What do you think it would be like to teach in a school in Tanzania? (classes may be large; facilities and resources may be limited; teachers have to teach all subjects so would need a wide range of knowledge and skills).

While students are discussing with a partner circulate and assist where necessary. Make a note of any new vocabulary or expressions and write them on the board at the end of the discussion. Take whole-class feedback on students' choice of placement. Ask them to explain the reasons for their choices.

Writing and roleplay

5 This activity could take place over two lessons – completing the application form in one lesson, and conducting the interviews in another lesson. Alternatively, the application forms could be completed for homework before the class.

With lower-level classes, work through the questions on the application form, eliciting possible answers and making a list of useful words and expressions on the board. Remind them of the information provided in the previous exercises in this module which will help them to complete the answers.

With higher-level classes, before students do the interviewing part of the activity, brainstorm a short list of 'success criteria' to use when assessing each candidate. Possible criteria might be: previous experience of community or care work (for the placements in South Africa and Costa Rica); involvement in sports and extra-curricular activities (Tanzania); health and physical wellbeing (Malaysia), etc. Students could also refer to the vocabulary for personal skills and qualities in module 4.2 to help them, e.g. is the candidate a good communicator (Tanzania), a good team worker (Costa Rica), etc.

Remind students about the work they did on interviewing skills and techniques in module 4.4. Interviewers and interviewees should refer back to the questions and expressions practised there.

Circulate while students are speaking and make a note of any mistakes in the target language for remedial teaching later. You could also make a note of any particularly good questions or responses to share with the rest of the class when the activity is over.

Review 3 and 4 Answer key

Review 3

(page 60 in the *Student's Book*)

Products and packaging

1

1 competitive
2 attractive, effective, distinctive
3 critical, efficient, limited
4 original, impractical, technical

2

1 chance
2 view
3 sale
4 communication, process
5 field
6 needs
7 issues
8 solution

3

1 generate new ideas in focus groups
2 screen out unfeasible or unprofitable ideas
3 launch the product onto the market
4 draw up specifications for the product
5 conduct market studies
6 draw sketches and build mockups
7 go into production on a large scale after tests
8 test the product by using it in typical situations

4

1 length
2 width
3 height
4 weight

5

1 USP (unique selling point)
2 feature
3 specification
4 benefit
5 function

6

2 Here's the email that arrived this morning.
3 The team leader is an interesting man who comes from Spain.
4 The team leader who I met yesterday is an interesting man.
5 The team leader is an interesting man whose background is in IT.

7

1 Here's the email (that) I got this morning.
4 The team leader (who) I met yesterday is an interesting man.

8

2 travel insurance document
3 packaging design concept
4 household-cleaning product

9

1 go on
2 answer
3 objective
4 Finally
5 I'll
6 listening
7 into
8 feel
9 reasons

10

Possible order:
Beginning of presentation 3, 7, 5, 1, 4, 8
End of presentation 9, 6, 2

11

1 Can we come back to that later?
2 I'm not sure that's a direction we want to go in.
3 That's more the kind of thing I had in mind.

Review 4

(page 61 in the *Student's Book*)

Careers

1

1 make a career choice
2 reach your long-term goal
3 prefer money rather than job satisfaction
4 learn new skills
5 gain experience
6 get a performance-related bonus
7 send off a job application
8 apply for a gap-year placement

2

1 targets
2 objectives
3 aim

3

1 know-how
2 knowledge
3 skill
4 experience
5 background
6 aptitude

4

1 be dismissed, be fired, be sacked
2 be dismissed
3 be laid off, be made redundant
4 be made redundant

5

1 short-listed
2 resign
3 attend
4 promoted
5 hired
6 apply

6

1 'm / am interviewing
2 interviewed
3 've / have interviewed
4 interview
5 need
6 Has anyone seen
7 put
8 'm / am talking

7

1 have been writing, have finished
2 have written, have been trying

8

1 strength
2 weakness
3 responsibility
4 performance
5 commitment
6 achievement

9

1 responsibilities
2 performance
3 strengths
4 weaknesses
5 achievement
6 commitment

5 Making deals

Digital resources for Unit 5

eWorkbook

Language practice: interactive & printable grammar, vocabulary, listening & pronunciation practice activities, extra printable reading & writing worksheets
Listen: Student's Book audio, language practice audio
Watch: video & video worksheets
Tests: interactive multiple-choice test
Resources: word list, grammar help & writing tips

Teacher's Resource Disc

Video: video & video worksheets
Audio: Student's Book audio
Tests: Progress test Unit 5
Resources: PowerPoint Unit 5, business document Unit 5, photocopiable worksheets, Student's Book answer key, Student's Book glossary

Subject background

There are often two misconceptions about negotiating. The first is: 'Negotiating is all about making offers and finding compromises.' The typical image is buying a carpet in the bazaar. But, in fact, this is really the stage of 'bargaining', and negotiating also includes the earlier stages of establishing rapport, information gathering, stating needs, etc. Even in the bazaar the serving of mint tea is an essential part of the process – a chance to get a sense of the other person as an individual before the hard bargaining begins. The second is: 'Negotiating is all about supplier-customer situations.' But, in fact, the textbook negotiation of a purchasing manager buying materials from a supplier is a specialized situation in business. The same language may be used when negotiating with colleagues and bosses about day-to-day work procedures.

In negotiation roleplays in the classroom, another common mistake that is made, especially amongst those with little or no work experience, is trading concessions and finding compromises issue by issue. In real business, negotiators often leave everything open right up to the end, at which point everything falls into place as a whole.

Issues that might be subject to negotiation include: price, minimum order, discount, delivery, quality standards, payment terms, extras, penalty clauses, other contract details, procedures, documentation, after-sales service, timing, guarantees, etc.

There is always a good deal of preparation before a negotiation. This might consist of:
- Setting broad objectives for what you want to achieve. What are your main priorities?
- Identifying the other person's needs. Initial contact by phone and email will allow you to do this – ask lots of questions.
- Listing all possible variables. Divide them into quantifiable (price) and unquantifiable (design). For each variable, write down i) your best possible outcome, ii) a realistic outcome and iii) the worst position you will accept (beyond this point you walk away).
- Deciding on possible concessions. What are you prepared to give?

Some of the above can be simulated in the classroom by students with the same role preparing together first, or at least reading (and adding to) a role card for homework.

In the negotiation itself, there is a psychological element to the trading of concessions.
1 Maximize your concessions:
- stress the costs to you (*Well, I could do that, but it would involve …*).
- refer to a major problem your concession will solve (*Well, if I agreed to that it would remove the need for you to …*).
- imply that the concession is exceptional (*I really don't know what my boss would say.*).

2 Minimize their concessions:
- acknowledge a concession briefly without putting any value on it (*Right, let's do it that way.*).
- devalue their concession (*Right, that's a small step forward I guess.*).
- amortize their concession into smaller units (*Well, at least that saves me X per month.*) rather than quoting the total figure.

Other key techniques during the negotiation include:
3 Summarize frequently.
4 Take notes.
5 Use silence. It gives you time to think and – you never know – the other person might fill it with a concession.
6 Where agreement is easy, use this to promote good feeling (*That's a good suggestion. / Yes, let's do it that way.*).

Useful websites

Here are three Internet sites that have articles on a whole variety of business topics, including negotiating:
http://www.salesvault.com/artman/publish/index.shtml
http://www.expertmagazine.com/artman/publish/index.shtml
http://www.mindtools.com
(For this last one go to the 'Communication Skills' area of the site.)

5.1 About business

Retailing

This module focuses on the ways in which companies are trying to increase sales in real 'bricks-and-mortar' stores by using smartphone technology to reach out to their customers.

Internet research

These websites allow users to note their locations with a smartphone and to find out where their friends are. They also allow users to pass on information, such as good shops or other venues to go to. Get students to try out two or three different examples and say which ones appeal and why. In class, get students to work in small groups to exchange their findings and note down the main points. Then take whole-class feedback.

Students could do this research before they start this module or before they do the discussion activity in Exercise 6.

LEAD-IN ACTIVITY

To start students thinking about the topic, ask them the following questions:
What was the last thing you bought online?
What was the last thing you bought in a bricks-and-mortar store? (explain that bricks-and-mortar here refers to a real, physical building)
Which products do you tend to buy online? Which ones do you buy in the real world?

Discussion

1 Question 1: Give students a few minutes to discuss this question. Then take whole-class feedback and make a list of the pros and cons of website and store shopping on the board.

Questions 2 to 4: Ask students to share their views and experiences in groups. Take whole-class feedback and find out whether there are differences of opinion on this subject in the class.

Scan reading

2 Start by reading through the summaries as a class. Ask students to predict what might be in the article from the summaries.

Students read the article quickly and choose the best summary. Let them compare their answer in pairs before discussing as a class.

ANSWER:

d

Reading for detail

3 Give students time to read the statements through carefully and check any unknown words. Ask them to decide whether the statements are true or false. Students then read the article again to confirm their answers or to find answers to statements they aren't sure of. Let them compare their answers in pairs before discussing as a class.

ANSWERS:

1 F 2 F 3 T 4 T 5 F 6 T

To help students engage with the topic, ask them the following questions:
In what ways has it not been a 'fair fight' between online and offline retailers up to now? (Up to now online retailers have been able to personalize shopping for customers in ways that offline retailers haven't been able to do.)
What role have services like Foursquare helped retailers get in touch with their customers? (They have enticed users to check in to real-world locations.)
What benefits do consumers get when they check in to stores? (They get points, badges and 'heroic' titles as well as gift certificates and prizes.)

Discussion

4 Ask students to work in pairs to explain the significance of the phrases. Follow up with whole-class feedback and elicit ideas.

ANSWERS:

e-commerce doesn't let go easily (line 4) Online businesses store and use data about their customers to make regular offers by email, text or phone to try to make further sales.
app-mania came flying to bricks-and-mortar's rescue (line 11) New services using smartphone technologies have made it possible for offline stores to benefit from collecting and exploiting the same customer data as e-commerce.
all-important foot traffic (line 19) For bricks-and-mortar stores, persuading customers to come through the door is essential as a high percentage of visits result in sales.
if that seems somehow less than essential (line 27) The article suggests that many customers will not be particularly interested in letting their friends know they are in a particular store, so they will need to be offered stronger incentives to use these social media apps.
powerfully addictive experiences (line 58) Social media use, competitive games and shopping have all proven they have the potential to become an addiction. Retailers hope that users will acquire the habit of making repeated visits to their outlets (and, they hope, regular purchases).
to hook users into a self-perpetuating race to ... their individual identity (line 60) Social media use is seen as an unending circle of making new friends, which creates a need to be special or influential, which in turn creates a need to link to more new friends, and so on. Retailers push users to start using apps which become an indispensable part of their lifestyles.

Listening

5 2:07 Before playing the recording, read through the options in the questionnaire and check any unknown words. Write <u>UPC</u> on the board and elicit what it is (the universal product code, which has 12 numerical digits and is commonly used in the US, UK, Australia and New Zealand for tracking trade items in stores).

Play the recording. Students listen and complete the questionnaire. Let them compare their answers in pairs before discussing as a class.

ANSWERS:

1 checking in to shopping venues so your friends know where you are 5
2 winning gift certificates or prizes after a certain number of check-ins 5
3 receiving information on special deals from stores 3
4 checking in to a product by scanning a UPC 0
5 becoming the mayor of your favourite coffee-shop or the queen of lipstick 4

RECORDING SCRIPT

2:07

Interviewer: Excuse me, madam, could I ask you a few questions?

Shopper: It's miss actually, but all right then, if it doesn't take too long.

I: Thank you, miss, only a couple of minutes. I'd like you to tell me how interested you are in some of the opportunities offered by internet services like Facebook and Foursquare.

S: Oh, I'm on Facebook, of course! Jessica Johnson, Miss Basildon twenty-twelve!

I: Really? Actually, I don't need your name, just a rating between zero and five. Zero means you're not interested at all, five means you're very interested.

S: OK.

I: So, how interested are you in checking into shopping venues and letting your friends know where you are?

S: Oh, can you do that? So, you can meet up for coffee, or go and try on some shoes together? Oh, yes, that sounds cool!

I: So, that's a five then? Right. And what about winning gift certificates or prizes after a certain number of check-ins?

S: Ooh, wow! I love free stuff, don't you?

I: Uh-huh. Now, how about receiving information on special deals from stores?

S: Well, yes, I s'pose so. But not too many, you know what I mean? I can never resist a special offer! I end up spending more than I can afford!

I: OK. And how interested are you in checking in to a product by scanning a UPC?

S: Scanning a what?

I: A UPC. You know, a bar code.

S: What, on my iPhone?

I: Yes.

S: Why would I want to do that? Anyway, I wouldn't know how. I'm not really into technical stuff.

I: All right. Last question then; how interested are you in becoming the mayor of your favourite coffee-shop, or the queen of lipstick?

S: A lipstick expert? Nah, not really my thing. But wait a minute, what about shoes? Jessica Johnson, queen of shoes? Oh, yes, I can see it now!

Discussion

6 Divide the class into pairs to take turns interviewing each other and completing the questionnaire. Once students have completed their interviews, put each pair with another pair and ask them compare and discuss their findings. In feedback, ask one student from each group to summarize findings for the class.

FURTHER PRACTICE

You could turn this into a class survey. Divide the class into pairs (or, with a larger class, into threes or fours). Ask students to stand up and walk round the class, interviewing three or four different students. Tell pairs or groups to make sure that each member of the group interviews different students and notes names.

After a few minutes, ask students to sit down in their pairs or groups and compare their findings. Tell them to turn the findings into a report which they should then present to the class.

5.2 Vocabulary
Negotiating and retailing

This module focuses on key expressions for negotiating and describing the process of a retail transaction.

Internet research

'Principled negotiation' is the name given to the approach to negotiation described in the book, *Getting to Yes*, first published in 1981 by Roger Fisher and William Ury. The book advocates four basic principles of negotiation:

- separate the people from the problem.
- focus on interests, not positions.
- devise a variety of options that will benefit everyone concerned.
- insist that the agreement is based on objective criteria.

Principled negotiation is a win-win approach, with the aim of reaching a lasting agreement.

Students will find several websites which explore these principles in more detail. They could do this research before they start module 5.2 or at the end of the module, to supplement the work done here. This research will also be useful for the negotiating activities and exercises which appear in later modules of the unit.

Discussion

1 Do this as a whole-class activity. Get students to brainstorm ideas and write them on the board. Encourage students to think of positive and negative aspects to shopping in an e-store and shopping in a high-street store.

SUGGESTED ANSWERS:

In an e-store you can't (usually) negotiate the price.
In a high street store you can't (usually) read what other people think about the product, know how many items the store has in stock, easily compare prices in other stores, find out what other products people who bought this one also bought, set the product aside for a later purchase, or make a wish list for your friends to choose a present for you.

Collocations

2 Students could complete these exercises individually or with a partner. Allow them to use dictionaries, if they wish. Circulate while they are working and assist where necessary. Check answers with the whole class. Then ask students to pick out any collocations that are new to them or that they are unsure of, and review their meaning and use.

ANSWERS:

1 an order 2 a price 3 a discount 4 the benefits
5 the details 6 a proposal 7 negotiation 8 a deposit
9 fee 10 costs 11 a deadline 12 a compromise

Listening

3 2:08–2:15 Students work with a partner. Play the extracts from negotiations one at a time and give students a few minutes to note down their answers. Check answers with the whole class and get students to tell you the words or phrases they heard which helped them to get the answer.

With lower-level classes, do the first one or two extracts with the whole class. Elicit answers from the whole class and write them on the board. Accept all possible answers.

With lower-level classes, write the possible answers in random order on the board, numbered 1–8. Students then listen and choose the best answer from those on the board.

Circulate while students are writing their own extracts. Then circulate again while they are working with a partner and assist where necessary. Get some students to read their extracts aloud for the whole class to identify the collocations.

SUGGESTED ANSWERS:

1 A supplier is *taking* an order.
2 A buyer is trying to *bring* down the price.
3 A buyer is *asking for* a bigger discount.
4 A seller is *rejecting* a proposal.
5 A negotiator is saying that availability is open to / subject to *negotiation*.
6 A seller is asking the buyer to *pay / to put down* a deposit.
7 A customer is complaining that a supplier has *missed a* deadline.
8 A negotiator is *seeking / offering* a compromise.

RECORDING SCRIPT

2:08–2:15

1 So that's five hundred at 12 euros a box, then. And you need them by Wednesday, you say?
2 Considering this would be a regular order, I think two and a half thousand is still a bit expensive.
3 How about if we paid cash? Could you give us an extra 2%?
4 No, I'm sorry, that's my final offer. I can't go any lower than that.
5 And then we'd need you to be available five or six weeks a year. Or maybe a bit less. Anyway, we can talk about it. Nothing's decided yet.
6 Yes, we usually ask for 20% now and the balance on delivery.
7 Look, this just isn't good enough! If you don't deliver until tomorrow morning, it'll be too late!
8 Well, there's not much between us now. What do you say we split the difference?

FURTHER PRACTICE

Get students to close their books. Using the nouns in the boxes in Exercise 2, write a list of scrambled words on the board and get students to unscramble them, e.g.:

mpemrcoiso	(compromise)
giiatnotnoe	(negotiation)
eieddnla	(deadline)
topeisd	(deposit)
nbeiftes	(benefits)
ldsiaet	(details)
dostnuci	(discount)
orpplaso	(proposal)
ipcer	(price)
sotsc	(costs)
efe	(fee)
errod	(order)

When they have unscrambled the letters, students should give one or more of the verbs that collocate with them.

Pronunciation

4 **2:16–2:20** Play the recordings and get students to underline the schwas in each case. Then get them to compare their answers with a partner. Write the phrases on the board and get individual students to underline the correct words on the board. Then practise saying the phrases aloud with the whole class.

Play **2:16–2:20** again. Pause after each phrase so that students can repeat it quietly to themselves, either with their eyes closed or by reading the words from the book.

Play the whole extract **2:08–2:15** again (extracts 1, 2, 3 and 5 in Exercise 3) so that students can hear the complete sentence in context.

For homework, students could record themselves saying the extracts aloud (using the recording script which can be found at the back of the *Student's Book*). They could then play this back and assess their own delivery.

ANSWERS:

1 five hundred at 12 euros a box
2 two and a half thousand
3 an extra 2%
4 five or six weeks a year
5 We usually ask for 20% now.

RECORDING SCRIPT

2:16–2.20

1 five hundred at 12 euros a box
2 two and a half thousand
3 an extra 2%
4 five or six weeks a year
5 We usually ask for 20% now.

5 If necessary, explain *browse* (to examine something in a casual way). Students work with a partner to put these sentences in the correct order. Check answers with the whole class by calling on students to read the sentences aloud. Remind them to use schwas, where appropriate.

ANSWERS:

8 The product is shipped to the customer's address by mail or express carrier.
10 The seller exchanges the product or gives a refund.
4 The customer goes to the check-out and pays by credit card.
6 The website records the transaction and generates an invoice.
3 The customer selects the product and places it in a cart.
9 The customer sends the faulty product back under guarantee.
5 The customer's credit card account is debited.
1 The customer clicks on the link to the seller's site.
2 The customer browses the site and identifies the product which interests him.
7 The website sends an instruction to the warehouse to ship the product.

6 Students complete this exercise with a partner. Check answers with the whole class.

Alternatively, do this activity as a listening task. Students close their books. Write the words in bold on the board. Tell students you are going to read two separate emails aloud and that they should choose the best word to fill the gap when you pause.

With higher-level classes you could present all the words together. With lower-level classes, keep the two lists separate. Then get students to open their books and read the two emails.

ANSWERS:

1 a) product b) site c) product d) credit
2 a) transaction b) invoices c) refunds d) product e) link

Discussion

7 Give students time to read through the task and the phrases in the box first. Ask for a few suggestions about how students could use the phrases when describing a difficult negotiation.

In-work students could talk about a situation at work, if this is appropriate. Pre-work students could talk about an agreement with a family member or friend, in a holiday job, or during a work placement.

Circulate while students are working and check that they are using the target language correctly. Make a note of any difficulties for remedial teaching later.

EXTENSION ACTIVITY

To follow up this discussion, get students to write some minutes in which they report the agreement their partner described to them. Write the following sentence starters on the board to help students write the minutes:
[Paul] said / pointed out / suggested / proposed that ...
[Sophie] asked him to ... / asked for ... / offered to ...
[Paul] summarized the position by saying that ...

5.3 Grammar

Conditionals and recommendations

This modules focuses on the uses of the first, second and zero conditionals and on verb patterns with *recommend, suggest* and *advise*.

Internet research

Students will find numerous quotations about negotiating if they search the Internet. Below are a few examples.

'In business, you don't get what you deserve, you get what you negotiate.'
(Chester L. Karrass)
'Never cut what you can untie.'
(Joseph Joubert)
'The most important trip you may take in life is meeting people half way.'
(Henry Boyle)
'Negotiating is finding out what the other person needs and working out the best way to give it to them.'
(Philip Laut)

You could use these as discussion points in class if students do not have time to conduct a search themselves. Get students to think about what they mean and how they could use them in real situations. You could do this as preparation for or follow-up to Exercise 5, when students work with a partner to negotiate an agreement.

Start by reading the *Refresh your memory* box with the class. Check that students can recognize the form of both the first and second conditionals. Remind them that we use both of the forms to talk about future events. The difference between them is whether the condition is seen as likely or unlikely by the speaker. Check the form (*If* + present simple, (*then*) + present simple) and use of the zero conditional too.

If students seem unsure of the conditionals or would like further practice in them, work through some or all of Exercises 1–14 in the *Grammar and practice* section (pages 130–131 in the *Student's Book*, answers on page 115 in this book) with them.

Discussion

1 Students read through the questionnaire and prepare answers using conditional forms or forms using *recommend, suggest* or *advise*. Start them off by providing one or two examples for the first question. With weaker classes, you could ask them to write their answers in full sentences before talking with their partner.

Once students have thought about answers, ask them to compare them with a partner. In feedback, elicit interesting answers and comment on errors made using conditional forms.

SUGGESTED ANSWERS:

1 If they can't decide, I recommend buying the expensive one.
2 If they ask for a discount, I usually offer one.
3 If a customer is angry, I recommend being polite but firm.
4 If she injured her foot, I'd call an ambulance.
5 If they break equipment, I will ask them to pay for it.
6 I would point out that I have a lot of qualifications if they said that.
7 I suggest refusing to give it.
8 If a customer complained, I would tell them to speak to the manager.
9 If I short-change a customer, I will call them and return the money.
10 If they made such remarks, I would ask them to leave.
11 I recommend giving / refusing the refund.
12 If I saw someone steal something, I would call the security guard or police.
13 If the item is out of stock, I order a new one.
14 If a customer asks this question, I will point out that you get better service in a store.
15 If they left their credit card, I would keep it safely and inform the customer or their bank.

FURTHER PRACTICE

Ask students to prepare five pieces of advice for someone who is about to start a job very similar to their own.

Reformulating

2 Higher-level classes could do this exercise orally. Lower-level classes might need to write the sentences down first. Students can turn to the *Grammar and practice* section (pages 130–131 in the *Student's Book*, answers on page 115 in this book) for further practice of *unless, if, providing* and *as long as*.

ANSWERS:

2 Our production manager is willing to make the changes, providing you supply a prototype.
3 We are reluctant to consider a larger discount, unless you pay in advance.
4 We would be prepared to sponsor the exhibition, but only if we had a large stand in the entrance hall.
5 Unless we can get the sub-components in time, it will be impossible to meet the deadline.
6 As long as several other top CEOs were present, our president would be available.

Discussion

3 While students are speaking, circulate and check that they are using the target language correctly. Make a note of any errors for remedial teaching when the discussion is over.

Students who finish early could formulate one or two questions of their own to ask and answer.

Listening

4 2:21 Play the recording through once and get students to do the exercise. Ask how many things Petra has agreed to do (two) and how many things Jan has agreed to do (three). If students have the correct numbers, get them to tell you the answers. If not, play the recording again so that they can check their answers.

To focus on the language and expressions used, get students to listen to the recording and read the recording script (*Student's Book*, page 145) at the same time. Get them to underline examples of the target language (conditionals and recommendations).

ANSWERS:

[P] – tennis tournament with customer
[J] – run exhibition stand in Kazakhstan
[J] – conference in Madagascar
team-building course in Siberia
relocate call centre manager to India
[P] – take holiday in August
[J] – take holiday in January
open office at 6am
close office at 10pm
supervise intern for six months
share office with PR Manager

RECORDING SCRIPT

2:21

Petra: OK, we have to decide how to divide this list of responsibilities between us. What are your priorities?
Jan: Well, I'd really like to go the conference in Madagascar. Could I suggest that you go to Siberia? If you agreed, I'd be willing to take my holidays in January and let you take yours in August.
P: I'm sorry, but I'd really like to go to Madagascar too. I couldn't agree to your proposal, unless you were prepared to take your holidays in January and go to the exhibition in Kazakhstan.
J: Hmm ... Well, I might consider going to Kazakhstan. I've got an uncle who lives there ...
P: Great!
J: Providing you looked after the foreign customer at the tennis tournament – I know nothing about tennis!
P: OK, we're making progress. So, can I just summarize the position so far? You can go to Madagascar, as long as you also go to Kazakhstan, and you let me take my holidays in August. OK?
J: OK. But only if you do the tennis weekend.
P: All right, no problem. I'll handle the tennis, if you take your holiday in January.
J: And you go to Siberia.
P: Oh, now wait a minute, I never agreed to that! I couldn't possibly go to Siberia unless you were able to ...

Negotiating

5 Remind students of the work they did in module 5.2 on negotiating and about the idea of principled negotiation. Circulate while students are speaking and assist where necessary.

FURTHER PRACTICE

For further writing practice, get students to write a short summary of the agreement they reached in Exercise 5 along the lines of the summary in module 5.2, Exercise 7.

5.4 Speaking
Negotiations – bargaining

This module focuses on the language and skills needed for successful negotiating. On the Teacher's Resource Disc, you will find more related practice material, including a video (with worksheets) featuring an example situation for students to analyse and discuss.

Internet research

A search under 'cross cultural negotiation' will reveal a wide range of articles and information. The kinds of factors that need to be considered in cross-cultural negotiation include cultural differences in eye contact, personal space and touch, time, meeting and greeting, gift-giving, negotiating styles, and the nature of business relationships.

Get students to focus on one or two topics and gather as much information as they can on them. They then prepare a brief summary for oral or written presentation to the class. Then compile the material into a folder which is made available to the whole class or give each student a copy.

This research could be done as a follow-up to the work in this module.

Discussion

1 Students should first decide what their 'bottom line' is, i.e. what they want to achieve, what they want to get out of the sale, e.g. a minimum price they will accept or a concession that they are prepared to make, such as having the bicycle serviced before selling it or delivering the item to the buyer's house.

When the time is up, get students to say if they think they won or lost the negotiation. How much did they deviate from their initial plan?

Discuss the notions of *win-lose*, *lose-lose*, and *win-win* in negotiations and get students to explain what they understand by these terms (reminding them that they explored win-win in module 5.2). How would they describe their own negotiation? How did each person feel at the end of the process – satisfied or dissatisfied?

ANSWER:

Negotiations can generally be categorized as win-lose, lose-lose, or win-win.

Listening

2 2:22 Read the questions with students and play the conversation through. Explain any new vocabulary, e.g. *logistics* (the organization of supplies and services for an operation). Play the recording. Pause the recording if necessary to allow students to note down their answers. Get students to compare their answers with a partner and then take whole-class feedback.

ANSWERS:

1 Harry Petersen's company sells sheet music.
2 The package includes website design, building and management, processing sales, dealing with payments and logistics.
3 Harry intends to deliver products electronically as PDF files.
4 Holman will charge a monthly fee.
5 Harry will have no capital investment to make, no new staff to hire, no overheads, and a small monthly fee to pay compared to the money coming in.
6 The next step is to define exactly what Harry wants the site to do.

RECORDING SCRIPT

2:22

Part 1

Ingrid: So, Harry, you want to set up an e-business to sell music – MP3s and so on?

Harry: No, not MP3s – sheet music. You know, printed music for musicians to play, like song books, orchestral parts, and so on. At the moment we sell through our network of shops in Denmark, but I'd like to set up an e-business.

I: To reach customers worldwide?

H: Exactly. But the problem is, we don't have the skills, the staff, or the money to do it ourselves.

I: Well, Harry, Holman Multimedia can offer a complete package solution. We design, build and manage your website, and process your sales. We deal with the payments, we can even handle the logistics for you if you want. Although I suppose you'll send most of the music electronically, right?

H: Yes – as PDF files. It's much easier for us, and the customer gets immediate delivery.

I: Exactly. So, all you have to do is make sure you have the product in stock, and count your profits!

H: And pay you a monthly fee, is that right?

I: That's right, Harry. No capital investment, no new staff, no overheads. And once you start selling music all over the world, that monthly fee is going to look very small.

H: All right then, Ingrid, I think we're in business. So, what's next?

I: That's terrific, Harry! OK, well, can you tell me exactly what you want the site to do? You see, it all depends ...

3 2:23 While listening to this version of Part 2 of the negotiation, ask students to note down the things Harry says which help them identify his failure to negotiate. (*No, there's no way I could pay that. No, I can't agree to that. And I can't commit myself to three years.*)

Play the recording and check answers with the whole class. Ask students to comment on why Harry's choice of words were not helpful in the negotiation (words like *No, no way,* can't sound very 'final' and don't offer room for discussion). Point out that Harry's failure to negotiate also means that Ingrid is less open to negotiating her own terms, i.e. she does not offer any alternatives.

ANSWER:

Harry says no. He rejects all Ingrid's proposals and doesn't try to negotiate.

RECORDING SCRIPT

2:23

Part 2, Version 1

H: So, how soon can you deliver, and how much is it going to cost?

I: OK, look. I'm going to write down a figure per month here, just so it's clear, then you can tell me what you think. There, how do you feel about that?

H: Wow! No, there's no way I could pay that!

I: Well, I might possibly be able to bring it down a little, but only if we had a three-year contract.

H: A three-year contract! No, I can't agree to that.

I: Well, in that case, I can't bring the monthly fee down, I'm afraid.

H: And I can't commit myself to three years.

I: Well, Harry, you have my phone number. If you change your mind, just give me a call.

4 2:24 Ask students to listen and answer the questions. Get them to compare their answers with a partner.

Higher-level classes could comment on the tone of this version, in comparison with Version 1. For example: the discussion is longer because both Harry and Ingrid question, bargain, and make offers; their language is more tentative as they discuss the options, e.g. *Hmm, Well, I'd be reluctant to, I don't really want to ...*, etc.; both of them seem satisfied with the outcome.

ANSWERS:

1 Harry negotiates and offers a compromise.
2 Ingrid will bring down the monthly fee if Harry signs a three-year contract.
She will guarantee a maximum down time of 24 hours per month if Harry chooses the platinum service level.
She will have the site up and running by next month if Harry pays a year's fees in advance.
3 Harry agrees to pay six months in advance and to sign a three-year contract.
Ingrid agrees to have the site online in two months, bring the monthly fee down 5% and include the platinum service.

RECORDING SCRIPT

2:24

Part 2, Version 2

H: So, how soon can you deliver, and how much is it going to cost?

I: OK, look. I'm going to write down a figure per month here, just so it's clear, then you can tell me what you think. There, how do you feel about that?

H: Wow! Is there any way we could bring it down, say 10%?

I: Well, I might possibly be able to bring it down a little, but only if we had a three-year contract.

H: Well, I'd be reluctant to agree to a three-year contract unless you could guarantee a maximum down time of 24 hours per month. Could you do that?

I: Let me reassure you on that point, Harry. Our sites and servers are very, very stable, and average down time is less than 24 hours per year. So we're happy to guarantee less than 24 hours per month, as long as you choose our platinum service level – but of course, it's more expensive.

H: Well, I don't really want to increase the budget. Hmm ... What about lead time? Can you have the site up and running by next month?

I: Not unless we hire another developer. I suppose we could do it, providing you paid a year's fees in advance.

H: Hmm ...

I: Normally, development time is around three months.

H: Look, let's split the difference. I can pay six months in advance, on condition that you have the site online in two months. And if you can bring the monthly fee down 5% and include the platinum service, I'll agree to the three-year contract.

I: You're a tough negotiator, Harry. But, OK, I think we can agree to that.

H: Excellent!

5 Elicit from students or explain the meaning of any unknown terms in the table, e.g.:
tentative (something which is not definite or final).
counteroffer (an offer which opposes or challenges the first offer).
compromising (giving up a particular demand so that an agreement can be reached which satisfies both parties to some extent).

Divide the class into pairs to try to complete the expressions. Then play **2.24** (Part 2 Version 2) again. Students listen and check their answers.

Pause at appropriate places to allow students time to complete the sentences. Check answers with the whole class. Draw attention to the use of conditionals and get them to identify likely and unlikely future events and how modals are used.

ANSWERS:

Tentative offers
I might <u>possibly</u> be able to bring it down a little, but <u>only</u> if we had a three-year contract.

Compromising
let's <u>split</u> the difference.

Firm offers
... so we're happy to guarantee less than 24 hours per month, as <u>long</u> as you choose our platinum service level.
I can pay six months in advance on <u>condition</u> that you have the site online in two months.

Counter-offers
I'd be <u>reluctant</u> to agree to a three-year contract, <u>unless</u> you could guarantee a maximum down time of 24 hours per month.
I suppose we <u>could</u> do it, providing you <u>paid</u> a year's fees in advance.

Students discuss their answers to the question about the conditional tenses with a partner. If necessary, refer students to the notes and exercises in the *Grammar and practice* section (pages 130–131 in the *Student's Book*, answers on page 115 in this book) to remind them of the use of these tenses.

ANSWERS:

Past forms are used in the *if* clause of tentative offers (*had, increased*).
Past forms are used in the *if* clause of counter offers (*could, paid, guaranteed*).
Present forms are used in counter offers and firm offers (*can, choose, have*).
The second conditional (*if* + past ... *would*) is used in tentative offers and counteroffers to make a hypothetical, exploratory offer with no commitment.
The first conditional (*if* + present ... *will*) is used in firm offers to express a definite commitment.

Bargaining

6 With lower-level classes, read the instructions with the whole class and elicit from them the kinds of things they might say at each stage of the negotiation. Remind them of the value of trying to reach a win-win conclusion.

While students are speaking, circulate and assist where necessary. Check that they are using the conditional tenses correctly and stressing the key words appropriately.

Pronunciation

7 Encourage students to say the sentences aloud as they decide which words are stressed. Tell them to underline the key words.

8 2:25–2:27 Play the recordings. Students listen and check their answers. Circulate while students practise the sentences with a partner.

Get students to close their books and repeat each sentence after you, putting the stress in the appropriate place. As these are long sentences, read out chunks, e.g. *I might possibly be able / to bring it down a little / but only if / we had a three-year contract.*

ANSWERS:

1 I might <u>possibly</u> be able to bring it down a little, but <u>only</u> if we had a three-year contract.
2 I <u>might</u> consider reducing the price, <u>if</u> you increased your order.
3 I'd be <u>reluctant</u> to agree to a three-year contract, <u>unless</u> you could guarantee a maximum down time of 24 hours per month.

RECORDING SCRIPT

2:25–2:27

1 I might possibly be able to bring it down a little, but only if we had a three-year contract.
2 I might consider reducing the price, if you increased your order.
3 I'd be reluctant to agree to a three-year contract, unless you could guarantee a maximum down time of 24 hours per month.

FURTHER PRACTICE

Write the sentence stems on the board and some word prompts and get students to make their own sentences using them, e.g.
Sentence stems:
I might possibly … but only if we …
I might consider … if you …
I'd be reluctant to … unless you could …
Word prompts:
homework, car, lunch, laptop, concert, tennis racket, etc.

Example: *I'd be reluctant to lend you my laptop unless you could help me with my English homework.*

Negotiating

9 Allow students time to prepare and practise their conversation. When they have finished get students to raise their hands to indicate how many ideal, acceptable and unacceptable options they managed to get. Then get one or more confident pairs to present their conversation to the rest of the class.

Alternatively, with higher-level classes, get one or two pairs to do their negotiating in real time, i.e. without preparing it beforehand. The rest of the class listens and comments on the performance, giving two things that worked successfully and two things that could be improved.

EXTENSION ACTIVITY

Sometimes in negotiations it is necessary to 'read between the lines', i.e. to look for or discover a meaning that is not openly stated. By paying attention to what might be implied, students can pick up on signals from others and use them to further the negotiation. Below are some example statements, with possible answers in brackets.

It would be difficult for us to meet that demand.
(… but we might be able to compromise on other demands.)
It is not our normal practice to give discounts.
(… but on this occasion / under certain circumstances we might be able to give a discount.)
Our price for that quantity is X.
(… but we might be able to give you a lower price for a bigger quantity.)
We never negotiate on price.
(… but we could negotiate on other things.)
These are our standard contract terms.
(… but we might be able to change some of them.)
We are not prepared to discuss that at this stage.
(... but we could discuss it later.)

Write the sentences on the board (the underlined text). Students work with a partner or in small groups and write down what they think is really being said (the text in brackets). Take whole-class feedback. Accept all possible answers.

5.5 Writing
A proposal

This module explores the structure and content of a business proposal and requires students to write their own proposal.

Internet research

Searching under 'how to write direct mail' will produce several websites which list tips and techniques for writing effective direct mail. Some of the tips include the following: get to the point; be clear and concise; sell benefits not features; use a conversational style; keep the language simple; include a guarantee; include testimonials.

Students may find that some websites appear to give contradictory advice, e.g. 'keep to one page' in one place, but 'write a long letter' in another.

Get students to compile a list of useful tips. This could be a short list of five to eight key or fundamental points. If students have more time, they could compile a more complete list. If they find contradictory advice, get them to review this and reach their own conclusion.

This research could be done before students do this module or at the end, as part of the extension activity.

Discussion

1 Get students to explain the similarities and differences between *mailshots* and *spam* (both are advertising material; both are unsolicited; mailshots are sent by post, spam is sent electronically). Ask if students know another common term for this kind of advertising (junk mail).

Students discuss the question in small groups for a few minutes. Take whole-class feedback. Get students to give reasons for their answers.

EXTENSION ACTIVITY

To personalize the activity, ask students these questions:
Do you receive mailshots or spam?
How do you feel about them?
Have you ever bought anything as a result of a mailshot or spam email?

Model

2 Read each question aloud and get students to scan the letter for the answer. When they have found the answer, they should raise their hands. When most of the class has raised their hands, ask one student to give you the answer, and then ask two or three other students if they agree or would like to add anything. Repeat this procedure with the rest of the questions.

ANSWERS:

1 The proposal is for a merchant account for an e-business.
2 Prestige and respect for Mr Bellows' e-business; transparent control of sales, cash-flow and administration fees; independent power of decision on refunds; low charges.
3 $12 per month, minimum transaction fees of $10.
4 Because PZpay has more than 1,800 satisfied members in 26 countries.

Analysis

3 Read the section headings and descriptions with the whole class. Ask students to tell you which are likely to be the first and last sections (Introduction, Conclusion). Without looking at the article, get them to try to put the remaining sections in the correct order.

Then give students a few minutes to read the article and check their answers.

ANSWERS:

[3] Solution
[4] Benefits
[1] Introduction
[8] Conclusion
[6] Qualifications & references
[5] Process & schedule
[2] Needs/Background
[7] Costs

Language focus

4 Get students to read the sentences quickly and identify the tenses used to express the options and contingencies (conditionals). If necessary, they could review module 5.3 or the relevant *Grammar and practice* section (pages 130–131 in the *Student's Book*, answers on page 115 in this book).

Point out the use of *should* in sentence 3. This could also be *If you should* ... and is used to suggest that something is unlikely or not particularly probable.

Students can refer to the proposal on page 70 to help them with words and expressions that they could use to complete the sentences.

Get two or three different groups to read each completed sentence aloud.

SUGGESTED ANSWERS:

1 If you would like to see similar projects we have managed, we would be pleased to put you in touch with some of our customers.
2 In the unlikely event that you were less than 100% satisfied with the result, we would offer a full refund.
3 Should you require on-site support, our engineers are available seven days a week.
4 If you would like to see some examples of our work, I would be delighted to organize a demonstration on your premises.
5 In the unlikely event of a breakdown, we would provide a replacement while your server was repaired.
6 Should you require greater capacity, our engineers can perform an upgrade on-site.
7 If you wish to place an order, we require a deposit of 25%.

Output

5 Read the notes with the whole class. To help students get started, brainstorm some ideas about what they might do to improve the website.

Ask students to work with a partner to write the proposal. Circulate while they are writing and assist where necessary. Get them to write a first draft, making use of the headings listed in Exercise 3. They then exchange their texts with another pair for feedback.

When they are reading each other's texts, students should check that the proposal is well structured, and should also look for the appropriate use of language.

Then ask students to revise their texts. Display the finished texts on a table or on the wall so that students can read them all. If you wish, get them to choose the best proposal, i.e. the one they think would be accepted by Poster Passion.

MODEL ANSWER:

Dear Ms Nash-Williams,

Thank you for taking the time to talk to me by telephone today. As agreed, please find below a proposal for a 'MaxiMedia' website, which I believe will increase your traffic and sales dramatically.

Your current website is out of date and unable to compete with your competitors' sites. You are looking for an exciting, interactive site which will attract teenagers and improve sales of your posters.

We recommend our 'MaxiMedia Experience' range of interactive sites, which incorporate music and video presentations. If you subsequently required online games, you would be able to upgrade to the 'MaxiMedia Gamer' range with no additional set-up fee.

A 'MaxiMedia' site will increase traffic to your e-business, since teenage customers will enjoy exciting music and video on your website. In addition, they will be able to download thumbnails of your posters and free ringtones. In the unlikely event of a technical difficulty, MaxiMedia guarantee to solve the problem within two hours. Our charges are amongst the lowest on the market, meaning that your business will be more profitable from day one. We provide a complete, ready-to-use website installed on your server. Please allow 30 days for development and installation. Should you encounter any difficulties, our helpline is available 24 hours a day, seven days a week to assist you.

With more than 400 satisfied customers and several design awards, MaxiMedia is one of the top site designers in the country. I will be happy to put you in contact with other MaxiMedia customers in your area.

The design fee for a 'MaxiMedia Experience' site is just €3,000, with monthly technical support fees of only €15. You will find full details of our terms and conditions in the attached quotation.

We look forward to meeting you to discuss design options: I will call you next week to fix a date. Should you have further questions, please feel free to call me on 0800 113 647.

Sincerely yours,

EXTENSION ACTIVITY

If possible, bring to class a selection of English-language mailshots. Get students to analyse the structure, language, style, etc. and to say how effective they think the mailshots are. This activity could be done in conjunction with the Internet research – students use the list of techniques they compiled on how to write effective direct mail as a checklist to evaluate the authentic examples.

5.6 Case study

St John's Beach Club

Students negotiate a deal between a company and a buyer to get the best price for a company incentive trip.

Internet research

Students will find a wide range of employee incentive programmes, with examples including birthday gifts, day trips, parties, tickets for sporting events, theatre and concerts, days out, weekend trips, etc.

This research could be done before class, so that the information feeds into the Discussion activity.

Discussion

1 Do this as a whole-class activity, getting students to brainstorm ideas. Write a list of advantages and disadvantages on the board.

> **EXTENSION ACTIVITY**
>
> To personalize the activity, ask students to tell you about any incentives they themselves or anyone they know have received.

Reading

2 Give students a few minutes to read the memo and look at the brochure. Then, get them to close their books. Ask the four questions. Students open their books and check their answers.

To develop the theme of incentives, get students to brainstorm some examples of what kinds of team-building events and competitions might be offered in a resort of this kind.

ANSWERS:

1 The top ten performing sales reps and their partners.
2 No. ('As usual ...')
3 The memo was sent in the third quarter to encourage sales reps to make an extra effort in Q4.
4 Suggested answer: corporate clients, young, active professional people with available income and a taste for luxury.

Listening for detail

3 2:28 Read the statements aloud before you play the recording. Pause at appropriate places to allow students time to note down the reasons for their answers.

ANSWERS:

1 F *'Shall we use my office?' 'No, here is fine.'*
2 F Loretta doesn't have the time.
3 T Loretta has asked him (i.e. told him) to allocate the budget.
4 T $26,500 + 5% is almost $28,000.
5 F He is going to get one of their best negotiators to negotiate with a couple of travel agents.
6 T Ten reps + partners + Malcolm and his wife, + maybe two more reps + partners.
7 F A week, plus perhaps a couple more nights.

RECORDING SCRIPT

2:28

Loretta: Oh, Malcolm, there you are. I just wanted a quick word.
Malcolm: Sure. Shall we use my office?
L: No, here is fine. I think I'll have a coffee too.
M: Black, no sugar?
L: Yes. Thanks, Malcolm. I saw your memo about the incentive trip – it sounds great. I wish I was going!
M: Well, why don't you? It would be an excellent opportunity to get to know the sales team better.
L: Yes, it would, wouldn't it? But I just don't have the time, I'm afraid. Anyway, the reason I wanted to catch you was to confirm the budget.
M: Ah, yes.
L: Mm. I spoke to Charles. I've asked him to allocate a global budget of $28,000. That's for everything except travel, which is a separate budget. That's up about 5% on last year. How does that sound?
M: That sounds great. Thanks, Loretta. I'm going to get one of our best negotiators to talk to a couple of travel agents, see what sort of deal we can get. The hotels usually work with several agents, and some of them are prepared to negotiate better terms than others.
L: Uh-huh. Try to persuade them to throw in some extra benefits too. After all, if we use the full budget, we're giving them a lot of business. Sometimes you can get a free upgrade to an executive suite, that kind of thing. How many people are you taking?
M: Well, the top ten sales people, plus myself, and partners – that makes 22. But if we can negotiate a really good package, I'd like to take one or two more sales reps along. They've all worked fantastically hard this year.
L: Yes, I agree. It would encourage the reps who almost made it into the top ten. I always think it's hard on number 11! It'll be about a week, like last year, I suppose?
M: Well, again, if we can squeeze a couple more nights out of the budget, that would be great. But we'll see.
L: OK, Malcolm. Let me know what you decide.
M: Sure. Thanks, Loretta.

4 Students could make a guess at how the sentences end, on the basis of the first listening. They may be able to suggest one or two words for each one. Write them on the board as prompts. Play **2:28** again. Check answers with the whole class.

SUGGESTED ANSWERS:

1 Loretta would get to know the sales team better <u>if she went on the trip.</u>
2 If they only talked to one travel agent, <u>they might not get such a good deal.</u>
3 Loretta thinks the agents may give a free upgrade <u>if they use the full budget.</u>
4 If they can negotiate a really good package, Malcolm <u>would like to take one or two more sales reps along.</u>
5 They'll stay longer than a week <u>if they can squeeze more nights out of the budget.</u>

Negotiating

5 Give students a few minutes to read the instructions. Circulate and assist where necessary. Get students to review the work they have done in this module and in the rest of the unit which will help them with this task, e.g. conditionals and recommendations (5.3), making offers, counteroffers, firm offers, and compromising (5.4).

While students are speaking, circulate and monitor their use of language, pronunciation and stress, and how the negotiation is developing. Make notes to use for feedback at the end.

When students have finished the task, get them to evaluate their performance in terms of language use and negotiating skills, e.g. by answering the following questions:
Which part(s) of the negotiation are you happy with?
Which part(s) could you have done better?

6 Company and community

Digital resources for Unit 6

eWorkbook

Language practice: interactive & printable grammar, vocabulary, listening & pronunciation practice activities, extra printable reading & writing worksheets
Listen: Student's Book audio, language practice audio
Watch: video & video worksheets
Tests: interactive multiple-choice test
Resources: word list, grammar help & writing tips

Teacher's Resource Disc

Video: video & video worksheets
Audio: Student's Book audio
Tests: progress test Unit 6
Resources: PowerPoint Unit 6, business document Unit 6, photocopiable worksheets, Student's Book answer key, Student's Book glossary

Subject background

This unit deals with the topic of what is commonly referred to as Corporate Social Responsibility (CSR). This is an expression used to describe two related features of business practice.

1 A company's obligation to be sensitive to the needs of all of its stakeholders (so not just shareholders, but also employees, customers, suppliers, community organizations, subsidiaries, local neighbourhoods, etc.).

2 The principle of 'sustainable development', which says that businesses should make decisions based not only on financial / economic factors, but also on the social and environmental consequences of their activities.

So CSR covers:

- business and the environment (reporting and regulation of waste, sustainable production, recycling).
- people in the workplace (equal opportunities, encouraging employee involvement, promoting diversity, health and safety, labour standards, family-friendly policies).
- community affairs (developing programmes for effective engagement with local communities).
- reputation management (using good practice as part of the marketing message of the company, as well as PR when things go wrong).

There is a lot of activity in the field of CSR.

- At the European level there is the European Alliance for CSR, launched by the EU in 2006 (link given below).
- At the national level there is a UK government body for CSR (link below).
- There is a private sector initiative in the UK called 'Business in the Community' (link below).
- At the individual company level, there are many big names proudly stating their activities in this field on their websites.
- There are many university courses devoted to the subject.

It is clear that CSR has become an established and important area in the business world. Indeed, good practice in CSR is now a key part of many companies' marketing strategy. Businesses stress their green and community credentials in their advertisements, and most annual reports these days would be incomplete without the CEO making reference to their company's beneficial effects on society and the environment.

But not everyone is happy with the idea that business has a role to play in CSR. Some people would argue that this is the proper responsibility of government, not business. Where are the limits? Consider these areas:

- human rights.
- fair trade.
- sustainable consumption.

These areas are on the borderline between social policy (the responsibility of government) and business policy.

In general, companies are usually happy to comply with social and environmental legislation. But they want to see a 'level playing field' with other companies also having to comply. Acting alone, a business has few guidelines on how to proceed (it is not their job to set social policy) and by raising standards they run the risk of increasing costs (and thereby losing profitability, causing layoffs, etc.).

A few companies are happy to take the lead and be pioneers in this field. The Body Shop is perhaps the best-known example, but BP is at the forefront of developing green energy and Marks & Spencer is famous for its diversity, employee involvement and CSR policies generally.

Useful websites

The EU organization referred to above has a website with a useful glossary:
http://www.csreurope.org/
The UK government body is:
http://www.csr.gov.uk/
And the UK private sector initiative is:
http://www.bitc.org.uk/index.html

6.1 About business
Corporate social responsibility

This module focuses on the issues around corporate social responsibility and examines the approach taken by one multinational in particular.

Internet research

Students could conduct these Internet searches before they start this module. For example, searching for 'CSR' will provide them with information which will feed into Discussion (Exercise 1) and Reading and discussion (Exercises 3–4); searching for 'Starbucks bean stock' and 'Starbucks standards business conduct' will provide them with extra information for Part 1 of Listening (Exercise 5).

Before the class, assign groups of students to conduct one of the searches. Each group can then report their findings to the class at the appropriate point in the exercises.

LEAD-IN ACTIVITY

Ask students some questions about their everyday lives, e.g.:
What did you have for breakfast and where did it come from? (e.g. coffee – Brazil, orange juice – Florida)
What are you wearing and where it was made? (e.g. shirt – China)
How did you get to work? (e.g. by Japanese car), etc.

Get students to comment on the fact that many of these things come from other countries. Ask these questions:
Why are these things produced in other countries?
What impact does this have on their own local / national economy?
What impact does it have on the countries in which they were produced?
How does it affect the environment?

Discussion

1 Do this as a whole-class activity, writing students' ideas on the board. If necessary, explain *conflicts of interest* (when two or more things are in opposition to each other).

SUGGESTED ANSWERS:

Employees, customers, shareholders, the community
Shareholders generally want profitability, which is usually in conflict with employees' and sometimes customers' and the community's interests.
Employees and the community want jobs, which may conflict with the customer's wish for low prices.
The community would like companies to be socially responsible and ecologically neutral, which may conflict with growth, job creation and mass production to achieve low prices and profitability.

EXTENSION ACTIVITY

To personalize the activity, ask students to tell you:
a) about the different groups their own company has a responsibility towards.
b) any personal experience they have of conflicts of interest(either in their working life or in their life outside work).

Scan reading

2 Get students to read the text quickly to find the answers. Give them just one minute to do this as there will be more detailed analysis of the text in later exercises.

Then give students a few more minutes to read the text again more carefully. Remind them to check any new words in the *Glossary* on page 156 in the *Student's Book* or in their dictionaries. Circulate and assist where necessary.

ANSWERS:

customers and end-users (doctors, nurses and patients)
employees
the community
stockholders

Reading and discussion

3 If students need help getting started, brainstorm with the whole class possible decision-makers, e.g. national government, local government, EU, courts, stockholders. Students work in small groups. Take whole-class feedback.

Focus on the meaning of *fair* (treating each person equally and according to the rules or the law), and on *reasonable* and *just*, which have similar meanings. These adjectives describe a wide range of the activities revolving around corporate social responsibility.

ANSWERS:

This is a matter of personal opinion and political sympathies. The following points may arise in discussion:
1 Today, prices for health care products are regulated by government in many countries.
2 Companies whose profits are perceived as being excessive attract criticism, principally from the media.
3 Many western governments have implemented minimum wage legislation, and labour tribunals decide disputes over compensation.
4 Perhaps a distinction should be made between justice, as defined by the judiciary, and ethics, as defined by philosophers and the community.
5 Using tax specialists to find the most favourable way to apply tax laws defined by government is generally considered 'fair'; exploiting tax loopholes might be judged 'unfair' by the media and the community.
6 This seems to be decided by stockholders themselves, and can cause the problems discussed by Marc Gunther below.

4 Students work in small groups. You could assign questions 1–3 to half of the class and questions 4–6 to the other half.

Questions 1–3: Students should list examples of the three aspects of corporate social responsibility. Take whole-class feedback and write students' ideas on the board.

Questions 4–6: If necessary, explain *PR* (Public Relations – the company department which works to present a good image of the organization to the public). Students should be prepared to give reasons for their answers.

Take whole-class feedback. If you divided the questions between the class, students who did not prepare answers to the questions, should listen carefully and add any further ideas of their own.

SUGGESTED ANSWERS:

The core dilemma in points 1–3 is where to draw the line.
1 disaster relief, the Red Cross, Aids research, soup kitchens, holidays for underprivileged children, churches, museums, orchestras, sports clubs
2 hospitals, orphanages, shelters for the homeless, parks and gardens, zoos, tennis courts, art galleries
3 eliminate pollution from manufacturing, use only recyclable materials, use clean vehicles and machinery, encourage employees to use public transport
4–6 are completely subjective and all views are valid.

Listening

5 2:29, 2:30 Lead in by asking students to predict ways in which beach cafés might be 'ethical'. For example, you could elicit: keeping the beaches clean; recycling waste; not using local resources such as water and electricity; employing local people

Give students a moment to read through the true or false statements in Part 1 and check any unknown words, e.g. *priorities* (the things you consider most important). Then play the recording. Students listen and write *T* or *F* next to each statement. Let students compare their answers in pairs before discussing as a class.

ANSWERS:

1 F – for their ethical principles
2 F – Profit and social responsibility are absolutely compatible.
3 T
4 F – Happy employees look after their customers.

Give students a moment to read through the statements in Part 2 and check any unknown words, e.g. *biodegradable* (will naturally degrade without causing pollution), *hybrid vehicles* (vehicles that use electricity and petrol), *altruistic* (caring and generous to others even at your own expense). Then play the recording. Students listen and delete the incorrect item in each statement. Let students compare their answers in pairs before discussing as a class.

ANSWERS:

1 hybrid vehicles
2 keep prices low
3 low taxes
4 shareholders

Ask students in pairs to read through the summary and guess what type of words (nouns, verbs, adjectives, etc.) might go in each gap. In feedback, ask students if they can guess any of the words. Check any unknown words, e.g. *boosted* (promoted in a positive way). Then play the recording. Students listen and complete the summary. Let students compare their answers in pairs before taking whole-class feedback.

ANSWERS:

1 beaches 2 schoolchildren 3 awards 4 website
5 packaging 6 loyal 7 competitive
8 long-term 9 sustainable 10 short-term

RECORDING SCRIPT

2:29

Part 1

Interviewer: My guest today is Estela Maldonaldo who is the co-founder and Chief Executive of 'Beach Hut', Argentina's most successful chain of beach cafés. Estela, Beach Hut is not only a very profitable business, but it's also famous for its ethical principles. Are profits and social responsibility really compatible?

Estela: Absolutely. I opened the first Beach Hut in Pinamar in 1998 with a close friend who, like me, had just lost her job. We both felt we'd been badly treated, and we wanted to prove a point. Unlike the multinationals we used to work for, we set out to treat our employees well, to look after the environment, and to support the local community. And of course we also wanted to make a little money!

I: And today you have, how many, thirty seven cafés?

E: Yeah, number thirty eight opens next month.

I: OK, so you've grown incredibly quickly, and you've won a number of awards along the way. How exactly have you managed that?

E: We've always felt that our employees should come first. Of course we love our customers, and we're very grateful to our shareholders. But our philosophy is this: if you make your staff your first priority, if you make sure they're happy and motivated, then they're going to look after your customers and so the business is going to do well. And when the business does well, shareholders are rewarded too.

2:30

Part 2

I: So, Estela, tell us something about your environmental policies, how have they helped you?

E: Right from the start, we wanted to be the greenest café in town. We do everything we can to reduce our carbon footprint: we have solar panels on the roof, we recycle, we use biodegradable packaging ...

I: And all your food and drink is locally sourced?

E: Yes. We work with local businesses as much as possible; we want to be part of the local community, not a big brand that just takes people's money without giving anything back. But it makes good business sense too because it means we get quality produce and minimise our transport and logistics costs.

I: Right, so this is not just about altruism, then? The bottom-line is just as important?

E: Everything is linked. We can only give something back to the community if we make a profit, but taking care of the environment and the local community is very good PR – that makes it easier to attract customers and to recruit good staff. It's a virtuous circle!

Part 3

I: I understand you also run educational programmes for children in schools. How does that help your business?

E: Argentina's beaches are an incredibly beautiful and precious resource – but they're also very fragile. We send volunteer staff members to teach schoolchildren how to protect our natural environment. Of course, it doesn't have an immediate impact, and it doesn't bring customers through the door the next day. But in the medium and long term, having the environmental awards, and displaying the logos on our website and on our packaging really helps to build a positive image. The market is extremely competitive, but our customers are very loyal because they know we share the same values. They know we're not short-term driven; we have to think more long-term about building sustainable businesses, and it's the same for society in general. If you want a society that cleans up the beaches and plants trees and uses hybrid vehicles, you have to think long-term. The short-term model just doesn't work – not for business, and not for society.

Discussion

6 Divide the class into pairs to play the roles and discuss the quotes. In feedback, ask different pairs to summarize their opinions about any key points.

EXTENSION ACTIVITY

Get students to investigate the activities of their own company or local companies in the areas of good works and charities, civic improvement, and protection of the environment and natural resources from company websites or printed materials. Alternatively, collect some relevant brochures and reports from local companies, and distribute them in class. Students should extract relevant information from them, then make a short presentation to the class describing the activities of the company in these areas.

6.2 Vocabulary

Meetings, ethical behaviour and social performance

This module presents and practises vocabulary in three areas and develops the themes of corporate social responsibility.

Internet research

A search for 'ethical and unethical business practices' will generate links to a wide range of articles related to current issues in business ethics as well as various case studies and examples, some of them developed for business students.

You could either ask the students to find a story or an angle that interests them and report back to the class or, alternatively ask them to research a specific question such as 'is ethical behaviour good or bad for business?'

Get the students to do this activity as an introduction to the module or as background research for the Exercise 5 discussion about the specific ways in which different departments in a company can develop and implement corporate social responsibility programmes and demonstrate a commitment to ethical business.

Meetings

1 Ask students to do this exercise with a partner. To check answers, get students to read the complete sentences aloud. Monitor stress and pronunciation.

ANSWERS:

2 a) 3 e) 4 b) 5 f) 6 d) 7 j)
8 l) 9 k) 10 g) 11 i) 12 h)

2 Again, ask students to work on this with a partner. Check answers with the whole class. Then get students to tell you what might be happening at a meeting which would give rise to the rest of the phrases, e.g.:

Phrase 3: at the end of a discussion which does not reach an agreement / decision.
Phrase 5: in the middle of a meeting; perhaps when participants are starting to look tired.
Phrases 6 and 10: if a participant starts to talk at length about something unimportant.
Phrase 9: at the end of a discussion when everyone agrees.
Phrase 11: when there is some additional information to feed into the meeting.

ANSWERS:

at the beginning of a meeting: 1, 2, 7, 8
at the end of a meeting: 4, 12

Adjectives

3 Students do this exercise individually or with a partner. Allow them to use dictionaries, if you wish. To check answers, read the text aloud and pause at each word in **bold**. Call on students to give you the correct definition for the word before continuing.

To focus on meaning, get students to divide the adjectives into two groups:

1 positive qualities (*reliable, trustworthy, accurate, prompt, altruistic*).
2 negative qualities (*deceptive, confusing, misleading, dishonest, false*).

ANSWERS:

1 prompt
2 dishonest
3 misleading
4 deceptive
5 trustworthy
6 reliable
7 confusing
8 false
9 altruistic
10 accurate

Collocations

4 Students could complete these exercises individually or with a partner. Circulate while they are working and assist where necessary. Check answers with the whole class by getting students to read the whole extract aloud.

When students have finished, get them to pick out any words or phrases which are new to them or that they are unsure of, and review their meaning and use.

ANSWERS:

1 supporting (a charity)
2 think (long-term)
3 identify with (an issue)
4 contribute (funds)
5 obey (the law)
6 uphold (standards)
7 respecting (human dignity)
8 recognizing (merit)
9 limit (the impact)
10 acknowledge (the problem)
11 negotiate (a settlement)
12 compensate (the victims)

FURTHER PRACTICE

Some of these collocations are used in the Johnson & Johnson credo on page 74, in either the same or similar ways. Get students to scan the credo for these collocations so that they can see them in another context.

Discussion

5 Divide the class into pairs or small groups.

Decide whether you want the students to discuss possible corporate responsibility practices for an entire company, covering all the departments, or whether you are going to assign a department or departments to each pair or group. Find out if there are students in the group who work or have work experience in any of the company departments mentioned, so they can share their experiences of any corporate responsibility initiatives they have witnessed or been part of.

If students need help in getting started, refer them back to the credo on page 74 to spark off ideas.

Circulate while students are discussing and assist with ideas and vocabulary where necessary. Take whole-class feedback and write up interesting ideas on the board.

SUGGESTED ANSWERS:

- R&D: using recyclable, non-toxic, sustainable materials, designing eco-friendly products
- Production and Quality: respecting health and safety legislation and best practice, avoiding waste and pollution
- Marketing & Sales: respecting advertising standards, not taking advantage of customers, giving fair deals, being honest
- HR: avoiding discrimination of any kind, protecting the local community from redundancy, encouraging education and training
- Purchasing: not applying unfair pressure on suppliers, paying a fair market price, encouraging local suppliers
- Finance: paying taxes, ploughing back profits into the business, supporting community projects, honesty

Once students have a good set of notes on specific practices and policies, ask groups to prepare their list of guidelines. You could ask them to write these up as a guide, similar to the extracts in Exercise 4, then ask one person from each group to read out their guidelines. Alternatively, you could ask students to prepare notes for a short talk about the guidelines. Again, ask one person from each group to give the talk at the end.

Support students in preparing guidelines by writing the following useful phrases on the board before they begin:
A company's first duty is to ...
We strongly believe that ...
Being socially responsible helps a company to ...
Being socially resonsible means that ...

FURTHER PRACTICE

Prepare a quiz which tests the vocabulary practised in this module. You could divide students into two teams and award points for correct answers or simply do this as a quick-fire practice session to review the vocabulary at the end of this lesson or the beginning of the next one. Some example questions are given below. Answers are in brackets.

This word means the same as:
on time (prompt).
correct (accurate).
not simple or easy to understand (complicated).
not true (false).

Form the opposite of these words:
honest (dishonest).
reliable (unreliable).
short-term (long-term).

Complete these collocations:
obey ... (the law).
recognize ... (merit).
compensate ... (the victims).
negotiate ... (a settlement).

Make sentences using these words or phrases:
side-tracked
misleading
unanimous decision
handout
competitive edge

6.3 Grammar
The passive and reported speech

This module focuses on the meaning and use of the passive and reported speech within contexts related to corporate social responsibility.

Internet research

Students might search a number of newspapers and news magazines online, e.g. *Financial Times, International Herald Tribune, Wall St Journal, South China Morning Post, Japan Times, Time,* or *Newsweek* to find interesting comments and quotes from people and companies in the news. To focus on the topic of this unit, get students to search for stories related to corporate social responsibility. Students could also look out for the vocabulary and grammatical structures they have practised here in the articles they read.

This research could be done at the end of this module as a follow-up activity.

The passive

1 Start by reading the first part of the *Refresh your memory* box with the class. If students seem unsure of the passive or would like further practice, work through some or all of the Exercises 1–6 in the *Grammar and practice* section (page 132 in the *Student's Book*, answers on page 115 in this book).

Divide the class into groups of four. Introduce the situation and tell each group to decide which student will play the company spokesperson. Remind students that the stakeholders are angry and the spokesperson is trying to take the heat out of the situation.

Model the activity first with the examples so that students see that they should make an active sentence first then wait for the spokesperson to respond with a passive sentence. When students are clear about the task, ask them to roleplay the situation. After two or three sentences, tell the groups to change spokesperson. Circulate and listen carefully for accurate uses of active and passive sentences.

In feedback, at the end, ask students to say whether they were reassured by the spokesperson, and then comment on the use of passive forms. Write up errors that you heard on the board for students to correct.

ANSWERS:

Stakeholders

2 Your factory manufactures products which are a risk to workers' health.
3 Your company has promised salary increases but you still haven't paid them!.
4 Do you anticipate redundancies, and do you have any plans for compensation?
5 Your company pay local suppliers late, and sometimes you never pay them!
6 Your company pays enormous salaries to managers, but you don't invest in the local community.
7 Your suppliers use child labour.
8 You haven't paid local company taxes.
9 Your company used our pension fund to buy a Chines competitor, so you have no money left to pay retirees.
10 You could relocate to Eastern Europe to cut costs.

Spokesperson

2 Some restricted products are manufactured but all government safety procedures are respected.
3 Salary increases were discussed by the HR manager, but they haven't been confirmed yet.
4 Some redundancies will have to be made, but workers will be compensated.
5 Payments have occasionally been delayed, but our suppliers have always been paid.
6 Top salaries have to be offered to keep the best managers. A lot of money is invested in the local economy.
7 Young adults are employed by our suppliers, but children have not been employed since 2010.
8 Most of last year's tax bill was paid. It has been agreed that we will postpone payment of the rest.
9 A Chinese company was bought last year but it is to be sold at a profit.
10 A possible relocation is being discussed, but a decision won't be taken until next year.

2 Read the second part of the *Refresh your memory* box with the class. If students seem unsure of the uses of the reported speech or would like further practice, work through some or all of the Exercises 7–11 in the *Grammar and practice* section (page 133 in the *Student's Book*, answers on page 115 in this book).

Ask the groups to close their books and tell other what they remember of their roleplay, using reported speech. Provide two or three examples to get students started.

SOME SUGGESTED ANSWERS:

He said that salary increses had been discussed.
She said that some redundancies would have to be made.
He said that young adults were employed by their suppiers.

3 Read each of the four extracts aloud or get students to read them silently. Then, one by one, read the statements 1–12 aloud. After each one, ask students to say who made the statement and to say what the phrase is that helped them work out the answer.

ANSWERS:

1 CEO Klaas Roos – labour costs in Europe could not be justified
2 Employees at Plazachem's Tashkent plant – they claimed that several fatal accidents had occurred
3 Ms Gronko – discussions were being held with local representatives
Mr Sanchez – no decision had yet been reached
4 Mr Sanchez – negotiations may be protracted
5 Ms Gronko – she was unable to give a figure
6 Mr Sanchez – the complexity of the legal situation
7 Mr Sanchez – no decision had yet been reached
8 Ms Gronko – all villagers forced to leave their homes by the new road would be compensated
9 CEO Klaas Roos – announced an end to manufacturing in Europe
10 Plazachem management – journalists are reported to have been refused entry
11 CEO Klaas Roos – Asian textile imports could no longer be matched for price
12 Plazachem's receptionist – Plazachem management declined to comment

Listening and reporting

4 2:31–2:36 Play all six extracts so that students get an overview of the conversation. Ask the following questions to check comprehension:

Why are 100 people being made redundant? (new automated machinery means that operators are no longer needed)

What three things is the company doing to help the redundant workers? (setting up an outplacement service; making redundancy payments; helping people who want to start up their own businesses).

Play the recordings again. Pause after each extract to allow students time to note down their answers.

With lower-level classes, brainstorm with the whole class which reporting verb(s) they could use. Point out that there may be more than one possible answer. Check answers with the whole class.

SUGGESTED ANSWERS:

2 Mr Bullard explained that new technologies had revolutionized the industry. He emphasized that the company would no longer need so many operators.
3 I agreed that it was difficult to remain competitive, but I enquired what Mr Bullard was intending to do to help people.
4 Mr Bullard told me that the company was setting up an outplacement service, and said that he was sure most people would find work very quickly.
5 I asked how those people who didn't find jobs would survive. I commented that they didn't have a lot of savings, and asked whether the company was offering financial help.
6 Mr Bullard reassured me that each person had received a generous redundancy payment, and he added that the company was making interest-free loans and advice available for people wanting to start their own businesses.

RECORDING SCRIPT

2:31–2:36

1

Leila Belabed: Mr Bullard, the mayor is very upset. You've just dismissed 500 people from the factory! Have you forgotten that when your company arrived, you promised to create jobs for our town?

2
Geoffrey Bullard: Well, of course I understand that you are upset, Ms Belabed. Unfortunately, new technologies have revolutionized our industry. You must understand that with new automated machinery, we will no longer need so many operators.
3
LB: I know that it is difficult to remain competitive, but what about these people and their families? It's a disaster for them. What are you intending to do to help them, Mr Bullard?
4
GB: Please call me Geoffrey. Of course we share your concerns. We are setting up an outplacement service to help people find new jobs, and I'm confident that most of them will find work very quickly.
5
LB: But what about those who don't, Mr Bullard? How will they survive? These people don't have a lot of savings, you know! Are you offering them financial help?
6
GB: Yes, of course, Ms Belabed, you don't need to worry about that. Each person has already received a generous redundancy payment. And we're also making interest-free loans and advice available for those who want to start their own businesses.

5 Students work with a partner to rewrite these announcements in informal language. Read the sentences aloud with the whole class. Before they start, elicit or explain some of the features of informal language they might use here, e.g. active voice, imperatives, contractions, etc. Check answers by getting students to read their revised announcements aloud.

SUGGESTED ANSWERS:

2 Could you please use the stairs while the lift is being repaired?
3 We are sorry, but we can't give you your money back unless you have the receipt.
4 We can only give you your deposit back when you've brought all the equipment back to reception.
5 They're holding all the meetings in the training centre until they've finished redecorating the conference room.
6 I'm afraid we can't reimburse your expenses unless your manager has approved them.

FURTHER PRACTICE

Divide the class into pairs to act out a roleplay between a dissatisfied customer and a salesperson. Tell students to decide what the customer bought and make a list of promises that the salesperson made. To help students get started, brainstorm some products or services with the whole class, e.g. an item of clothing, a computer, a night at a luxury hotel. If possible, bring some pictures to class to stimulate ideas. Ask in what ways they might be dissatisfied with the products and services they have listed (e.g. the item of clothing has shrunk in the wash).

Write the following list of phrases on the board to help students express their dissatisfaction:
You told me that …
You promised / assured me that …
You guaranteed that …
You calimed / implied / stated that …

While students are working, circulate and make a list of any common mistakes in the target language for remedial teaching later.

6.4 Speaking
Meetings – teamwork

This module explores appropriate language and behaviour at meetings and provides contexts for students to discuss issues of ethical behaviour. On the Teacher's Resource Disc, you will find more related practice material, including a video (with worksheets) featuring an example situation for students to analyse and discuss.

Internet research

A search using 'golden rules of meetings' will find a number of websites which explore how to run effective meetings. Typically these will include the following advice:
- Be clear about the purpose of the meeting.
- Invite the right people.
- Start and finish on time.
- Be prepared.
- Don't get sidetracked.
- Don't hold unnecessary meetings.
- Finish meetings with a clear statement of the next steps and who will take them.

Students could do this research before they do the work on meetings in this module. They could then aim to implement some of these rules in Exercises 4 and 5, e.g. the third and fifth rules.

Alternatively, they could do this research as a follow-up to the work done in this module.

Discussion

1 Students discuss this question in groups. Take feedback from the whole class, getting students to give reasons for their answers.

Useful words and expressions that may arise from this discussion are:
bribe / bribery (money, services, etc. offered to someone in return for (often) dishonest help).
backhander (an informal word for a bribe).
corruption (dishonest behaviour).

In-work students may be able to share information about their company's corporate gift policy, which sets out what kinds of gifts are acceptable. Pre-work students could comment on what kinds of gifts might be acceptable or unacceptable. If necessary, provide some prompts, e.g.: a corporate pen; dinner at a top-class restaurant; a gold watch; cash; tickets to a sporting event, concert or play; a weekend at a beach resort.

ANSWERS:

It will often depend on the relationship with the customer, but in most cases everything except cash and employing a relative would be acceptable.

Listening

2 2:37 Read the questions with the class. Then play the recording. Students note their answers and compare them with a partner before discussing them as a class.

ANSWERS:

1 Mr Vieri not only accepted a case of champagne, but also actively encouraged the supplier to send more.
2 The purpose of the discussion is to decide on a clear company policy on gifts for the future.
3 Stan and Jon disagree about whether Mr Vieri should be dismissed or given a second chance.
4 Anna decides to break for coffee and to come back to the issue later.

RECORDING SCRIPT

2:37

Anna: Do we all agree on that, then? All right. The next point on the agenda is company policy on gifts. What's your feeling? Personally, I tend to think that we need …
Stan: Sorry to interrupt, but …
A: Yes, Stan. Go on.
S: Well, in my opinion, accepting any kind of gift from a supplier is unwise. Would you agree, Anna?
A: Well, Stan, on the whole, yes, I would. Now, recently we had a major problem with our packaging suppliers. They were sending 'thank-yous' to our buyer's home.
S: Sorry, Anna. I don't see what you mean.
Jon: Gifts, Stan. Cases of champagne, I believe.
S: Champagne? Oh, that was nice of them!
A: Well, I agree up to a point, but unfortunately our buyer, Mr Vieri, not only accepted the gifts, but also actively encouraged the supplier to send more.
S: Well, I feel strongly that we should dismiss Mr Vieri! It's bad for the company's image.
J: Stan, I see your point, but you can't just dismiss someone for making one mistake!
S: So are you saying that we should keep him? I'm afraid I can't agree, Jon! It's not right, and he should leave the company.
J: But Stan, don't you think that everyone should have a second chance? I mean …
A: Jon, Stan, can we stick to the agenda? We're not here to talk about Mr Vieri; we're here to decide on a clear company policy for the future.
S: Yes, but wouldn't you agree that his behaviour was unethical? So he should be dismissed.
Magali: Could I just come in here?
A: Yes, Magali, do you have any views on this issue?
M: I'm sorry, Anna. When you say this issue, do you mean just our policy on gifts, or the wider issue of corporate ethics? It seems to me that we need to go further than just …
A: Sorry Magali, but perhaps we should break for coffee. I think we're all a bit tired. Could we come back to this later?

3 Divide the class into pairs to look through the expressions and remember or guess the missing words.

Play **2:37** again so that students can check the expressions. Check answers by getting students to read the complete sentences aloud, using appropriate intonation.

ANSWERS:

Asking for opinions
What's your feeling?
Would you agree?
Do you have any views on …?

Giving an opinion
I tend to think that …
In my opinion, …
It seems to me that …
I feel strongly that …

Disagreeing tactfully
I see your point, but …
I agree up to a point, but …
I'm afraid I can't agree.

Interrupting
Sorry to interrupt, but …
Could I just come in here?

Asking for clarification
Sorry, I don't see what you mean.
So are you saying that …?
When you say …, do you mean …?

Persuading
Don't you think that …?
Wouldn't you agree that …?

Managing the discussion
Do we all agree on that, then?
The next point on the agenda is …
Can we stick to the agenda?
Perhaps we should break for coffee.
Could we come back to this later?

4 Read the four issues aloud with the class. With lower-level classes, brainstorm some opinions on each issue with the whole class and write them on the board. Students can use these in their conversations.

Circulate while students are speaking and assist where necessary. Check that students are using the target language appropriately. When they have finished, get some pairs of students to present their conversation to the class.

5 Each group should choose one person to chair the meeting. Give students a few minutes to read the instructions and think about what they might say. Remind them to review the language and expressions in this module and in earlier modules which might help them with this task.

While students are speaking, circulate and assist where necessary. When they have finished, get the chairperson in each group to report to the whole class what was decided in each case.

To follow up, students could write a brief summary of their decision in each case.

EXTENSION ACTIVITY

Students discuss how they would deal with the following behaviour at meetings:

- someone who never speaks.
- someone who dominates the meeting by talking too much.
- someone who always arrives late.
- someone who can't stick to the point.
- someone who constantly interrupts.
- someone who often does not come to meetings and does not inform you in advance.

Students work in groups or pairs and note down what they would say or do in these situations. Check answers with the whole class.

6.5 Writing

Reports and minutes

This module provides practice in using the appropriate grammar and vocabulary for writing reports and minutes of a meeting.

Internet research

A search for 'email ethics' will reveal a wide range of information on the use and abuse of email within companies, including real-life stories about employees losing their jobs because of inappropriate use of email; suggestions for a code of ethics for email use; tips for avoiding problems with email at work, etc.

This research could be done as a follow-up activity after students have completed Exercises 5 and 6.

Discussion

1 Get students to explain the meaning of *community projects* (schemes or activities which improve the quality of life for people living in a certain area) or explain it yourself, and make a list of some examples of community projects, e.g. building a children's playground, establishing a community garden, planting trees, providing books for schools, etc.

Get students to work in groups to brainstorm ideas. Take whole-class feedback.

SUGGESTED ANSWER:

Companies often rely on the local workforce, so it's in their best interests to invest in the community so that they have a happy, committed and loyal workforce. It will also raise their profile with local councilors and government which could be useful for them.

EXTENSION ACTIVITY

To personalize the activity, get students to add to the list any community projects they know of in their own locality.

Model

2 Question 1: Students read the report silently, underlining the answers to the first question. With lower-level classes, you could tell students in advance how many arguments there are for and against. Check answers with the whole class.

Question 2: Get students to close their books and listen for the answers to question 2 while you read the minutes aloud. Check answers with whole class. Students then open their books and read the minutes silently to double-check their answers.

ANSWERS:

1 Arguments for:
Benefits to the company's image justified more active and extensive support, in particular after the recent difficult negotiations.
Substantial benefits in terms of motivation and job satisfaction.
A positive effect on expansion of our manufacturing facilities and recruitment of our workforce locally.
Need for good relations with local communities.
Benefits in developing team spirit.
Arguments against:
Group policy is to give encouragement, but only limited financial support.
Concerns about the size of the investment and the project's impact on productivity.
Risks involved for production, for example, absenteeism and quality issues.
The project could become an excuse to take time off work.

2 a) Head Office decided to support Mirratec's decision.
b) Mirratec decided to approve the project.

EXTENSION ACTIVITY

Put students into groups of three and get them to roleplay the meeting that was reported in the minutes on page 82 in the *Student's Book*. Before they start, each student should re-read the minutes to check what was said by the person they will be roleplaying. They can also review the language practised in module 6.4. Circulate while students are speaking and monitor the use of language, pronunciation, and how effectively the meeting is run.

Analysis

3 Divide the class into pairs to read through the quotes and discuss the questions. They will have to refer back to the report and minutes to find and underline structures. In feedback, discuss question 3 and elicit explanations from the class.

ANSWERS:

1
it was felt that
it is recommended that
it is hoped that
it is believed that
It is expected that

2
stressed, agreed, felt, emphasised, claimed, reminded, suggested

3
Impersonal reporting verbs are used to avoid mentioning the person who made the statement. Active reporting verbs are preferred in the minutes because we wish to record who said what.

Language focus

4 Read through the list of titles in the left-hand column with the whole class. See if students can guess what the missing words are. Then give them a few minutes to read the report and the minutes and complete the answers.

ANSWERS:

Function	Linking words
Addition	besides, moreover, in addition, furthermore
Conclusion	lastly, in conclusion, finally
Consequence	so, therefore, consequently
Contrast	but, however, even so
Equivalence	that is to say, namely, in other words
Example	for instance, such as, for example
Generalization	in most cases, as a rule, on the whole
Highlighting	mainly, chiefly, in particular, especially
Stating the obvious	of course, naturally, obviously, clearly
Summary	to sum up, overall, in brief

5 Lead in by providing some brief information about Josiah Wedgwood. (He was an influential 18th century businessman who founded the world-famous Wedgwood china company. He pioneered innovative products, efficient production methods, and effective marketing strategies for his products.)

Students do this exercise with a partner. Check answers with the whole class by getting students to read the sentences aloud with the appropriate linking word in place.

SUGGESTED ANSWERS:

Josiah Wedgwood was a pioneer in social responsibility, building a village for his workforce. In addition, his products combined technology with classical culture.
More than a century later, George Cadbury developed social housing for his chocolate factory workers. Consequently, Cadbury's became one of Britain's most respected companies. Both men were pioneers of corporate social responsibility. However, they were also accused of paternalism.

Today, sustainable development policies aim to manage the effects of business on employees, the community, and especially on the environment. Multinationals like Shell are focusing on the idea of being good neighbours, in particular, by consulting local stakeholders before beginning new projects which may affect them.

Output

6 2:38 Play Jan's first speech and pause the recording. Ask students what they think *diversity* in the workplace means (employing people from different parts of society and ensuring a representative mix of ages, gender, mobility, ethnic background, etc.).

Play the rest of the recording and get students first to listen, without making notes, so that they can get an overview of the whole discussion. Then play the recording again, pausing at appropriate moments while students take notes. They then compare answers with a partner. Circulate and assist where necessary. Check answers with the whole class to ensure that everyone has the correct information.

Students then write their summary. When they have finished, they should exchange their summaries with another pair and check each other's work. They should underline or circle any mistakes or things which are unclear and pass the summary back for correction and improvement.

When students have finished, display the summaries on a desk or wall and allow students to read them all.

RECORDING SCRIPT

2:38

Jan: All right, then. Let's move on to point two on the agenda: diversity. As you know, our workforce is still 80% male. What's more, we have very few employees from ethnic minorities. The general feeling within the group is that we need to take measures in order to reflect the increasing diversity …

Ines: Sorry to interrupt, Jan, but when you say 'measures', do you mean positive discrimination? Hiring women in preference to men, for instance? Because that's all very well in sales and admin, but I really, really can't see women doing the heavy jobs in production. And anyway, I'm not sure that positive discrimination is the right way to approach the problem.

Christopher: No, I don't think it is either. It seems to me that we would just go from one extreme to another – you know, all our employees would be middle-aged female.

J: Point taken, Christopher. But, seriously, that's what we want to avoid – extremes. In fact, what we need are measures to ensure that we don't discriminate against anyone on whatever criteria, whether it's their age, their race, their gender, their religion, or anything else.

C: But Jan, don't you think that's just an HR problem? I mean, they're the people who interview the candidates, not us. Nine times out of ten, we only see a short-list of people they've already approved. It's even worse when we recruit from the agencies. And that's another problem, by the way: half of the people they send us are absolutely hopeless. I don't know how they select them, but honestly …

J: Yes, Christopher. I know the agencies are a problem, but I think we're getting sidetracked here. Could we agree that we'll talk about the agencies next Monday?

C: OK.

J: Good. So, getting back to diversity. Ines, what can we do to attract more applications from women?

I: Well, for a start, we should offer more part-time positions. Flexible hours, longer holidays when the schools are closed, a four-day week. You know, jobs that women with families can manage. That's really obvious. I've been saying this for years! I mean, why don't we start by allowing our present staff to go part-time if they want to? I can think of at least four women who'd be delighted to work part-time! That would mean we could offer more part-time jobs to new candidates.

J: Yes, Ines, thank you. That's an excellent idea. Shall we get HR to work on it? Christopher?

C: That's fine by me.

J: All right, that's decided then. All right, shall we break for coffee now, or take point three first?

6.6 Case study

Phoenix

This case study brings together the themes and language practised in the unit requiring students to roleplay interest groups at a public meeting about the site of a new vehicle recycling centre.

Internet research

Students will find detailed information about what is involved in automobile recycling contamination (only 82% of a car is recycled which means 18% of them go into landfill).

This search could supplement the information in Exercises 2, 3 and 4. It would be useful to do this research before you start this module. However, it is not essential, and could be done as a follow-up to this module.

Discussion

1 Students work in groups to answer this question. First elicit from the whole class or explain the meaning of *recycling centre* (a place where used or waste materials are processed and converted into reusable material) and ask what kinds of things might be recycled (fridges, building materials, garden waste, cars). To focus on the topic of the case study, ask students to answer the question about a car recycling centre. Take feedback from the whole class.

Reading

2 Read the text aloud or get a student to do it. To help them answer the questions students can refer back to the vocabulary and expressions they practised earlier in the unit.

SUGGESTED ANSWERS:

1 The company tries to present itself as a responsible member of the community, protecting the environment by providing a valuable service, and applying an ethical code of fair practice in its dealings with all its partners.

2 Depending on how high-tech their equipment is, it may be very clinical and relatively clean, or very dirty, dusty, heavy, noisy, unpleasant and dangerous.

Roleplay preparation

Read the roleplay preparation notes with the whole class and divide the class into three groups. Students should work in their groups for the remaining exercises in this module.

Listening

3 2.39 This exercise provides the background information for the meeting in Exercise 6.

Question 1: Read this question aloud and play the first part of the meeting up to '... attract new business and jobs to the area'. Check answers with the whole class.

Question 2: Play the rest of the meeting. First get students to tell you where sites A, B and C are and write notes about the locations on the board. If necessary, play the second part of the recording again so that students can answer question 2.

Question 3: Explain *charm* (the power to please or attract people) and *diplomacy* (art or skill of dealing with people by gentle or tactful means) and get the whole class to brainstorm what 'Operation Charm and Diplomacy' might involve in this context.

ANSWERS:

1 Port Katherine is a good choice for Phoenix because:
   a) it's close to Perth.
   b) it's far enough away not to attract too much attention from the environmentalists.
   c) the population is only about 3,500, so there shouldn't be too much local resistance.
   d) the local authorities are desperate to attract new business and jobs to the area.

2 For the Planning Department, site A is likely to be politically sensitive, but is conveniently close to the highway on the edge of town.
Site B will probably produce the most income for the community and seems to have no major disadvantages.
Site C would involve major demolition and road-building work, so is less suitable.
For the Residents' Association, site A is a problem because it's close to a school.
Site B seems to be a good choice as it will not disturb residents.
Site C may involve a lot of demolition and building, which could disrupt residents' lives in the town centre.
For Phoenix, site A is the best: it's close to the highway, the price for the land is reasonable and it's a nice flat site to build on. The disadvantage is that it's right next to the local school.
Site B is on a business park, but it's a bit expensive, and taxes will be higher.
Site C is an old factory site near the harbour in the town centre. Access would be a problem, unless they built a new road, and they'd have to demolish the old building.

3 'Operation Charm and Diplomacy' is an attempt to establish good relations with the local community by stressing the company's environmentally friendly ethics and mission statement in order to outweigh the disadvantages and break down resistance in people's minds.

RECORDING SCRIPT

2:39

Justin: ... so we all agree that we need to keep an eye on that one. All right, that just leaves point six on the agenda: the new site for the South West. Helen, can you bring us up to date?

Helen: Yes, Justin. There's good news: we've identified three possible sites in a place called Port Katherine.

Glenn: Never heard of it!

H: Well, it's a small town about 30 miles south of Perth. It's exactly what we were looking for: close to Perth, but far enough away not to attract too much attention from the environmentalists.

G: Well, that's good news! We don't want another disaster like Cairns. Those Greens have absolutely no idea what this country would look like if we didn't recycle cars!

J: Yes, all right, Glenn. Shall we let Helen finish?

G: Oh, yes. Sorry, mate.

J: Helen?

H: Thank you. Port Katherine's population is only about three and half thousand, so Glenn will be happy to know there shouldn't be too much local resistance. And the local authorities are desperate to attract new business and jobs to the area.

J: Sounds good. You said there were three possible sites?

H: Yes, that's right. I've put all the details in this handout. There you are, Glenn.

G: Oh, yeah. Thanks.

H: Now, site A is a good one. It's a greenfield site just on the edge of town. There are several plus points. Firstly, it's close to the highway, so access for our trucks is easy. Secondly, the price of land is reasonable. And thirdly, it's a nice flat site to build on.

J: Any negatives?
H: Well, just one. It's right next to the local school.
G: Uh-oh!
H: But I don't think it's going to be a problem. I spoke to someone at the planning department, and they were very enthusiastic. Sites B and C are also possible, but they have other problems. Site B is on a business park, so no problems with residents, but it's a bit expensive and taxes will be higher. Site C is actually in the town centre.
G: Oh yeah, perfect! Twenty-ton trucks in the high street!
H: Actually, Glenn, it's not that bad. It's on a big old factory site near the harbour. We'd have to demolish the old building, and access would be a bit of a problem, but they could build a new road. It's possible.
J: OK, thanks, Helen. Excellent work. I'll send somebody out there to start talking to the locals.
G: 'Operation Charm and Diplomacy', eh?
J: Yes.
H: Hmm ... Better not send Glenn, then!

Reading and discussion

This section provides key information that each of the three interests groups will need to present its case in Exercise 6.

4 and **5** Circulate while students are doing these exercises and assist where necessary. You could set a time limit for the opening presentations, e.g. five minutes per group. Encourage students to refer to the previous modules in the unit to help them in their preparation, e.g. modules 6.2 and 6.4. Students could write notes on cards to help them with their presentations.

ANSWERS:

Group A: Port Katherine Planning Department
1 The email is from Duncan Gillespie, one of the Mayor's staff.
2 Your role is to organize and chair the meeting, and to try to find an agreement which suits everyone.
3 It's important to keep the residents happy because the elections are coming up soon. If they are unhappy, the Mayor may not be re-elected.
4 The project is important because the town desperately needs new jobs and investment.
5 Site B is the best choice for financial reasons.

Group B: Port Katherine Residents' Association
1 Members feel strongly about preserving the environment and the safety of their children.
2 Demonstrations, protests, lobbying, sabotage?
3 Because the elections are approaching and the mayor wants to be popular.
4 Ideally, you would prefer the centre not to be in Port Katherine at all. The industrial environment of site C seems to be the best choice.
5 Make sure site A is not chosen.

Group C: Phoenix
1 Make friends and sell the benefits of the recycling centre.
2 Improving facilities at the school, redeveloping the port area in the town centre, attracting new businesses to the business park?
3 To develop the largest recycling centre on the continent.
4 Site A is the best if the residents' resistance can be overcome. Site B is possible, but more expensive. Site C depends on the town agreeing to build a new road.
5 The cost argument against site B may not receive much sympathy from the residents and the authorities; the contamination argument is delicate and may increase resistance to the project. The cost for the town of a new road is probably a good argument to use against site C. The disruption to the city centre is more delicate, as this argument can also be used against site A.

Roleplay

6 Play the part of chairperson of the meeting yourself – welcome the participants and introduce the three presenters; summarize the discussion at the end.

Hold the meeting, following the agenda. While students are speaking, make notes of any common errors for remedial teaching later. You could also make a note of any particularly good uses of the target language to share with the rest of the class when the activity is over.

When they have finished, students could also assess their own performance, commenting on one thing they think they did well and one thing that could be improved.

Writing

7 Students should refer to earlier work in the unit on the passive and reported speech (module 6.3) and writing reports (module 6.5). Students could exchange their first drafts with another group for feedback before finalizing it.

Review 5 and 6 Answer key

Review 5

(page 86 in the *Student's Book*)

Making deals

1

1 website 2 eyeballs
3 search ads 4 web chats
5 purchase 6 databank
7 browsers 8 expectation
9 merchandising 10 approach

2

1 tracking
2 consent
3 violation
4 privacy

3

1 c) 2 d) 3 b) 4 a)
5 g) 6 e) 7 h) 8 f)

4

1 offer
2 find
3 put on
4 put back
5 take
6 meet

5

1 miss the deadline
2 place an order
3 reach a compromise
4 are entitled to a discount

6

will increase / would increase, do you give

7

If we increased our order, would you give us a discount?

8

If we increase our order, will you give us a discount?

9

1 if + increased
2 unless + guaranteed
3 providing + agree

10

1 recommend me
2 advise me to do
3 suggest
4 advise you
5 suggested to him

11

1 agreed, below
2 Should, available
3 unlikely, replacement
4 charges, lowest
5 wish, require

Review 6

(page 87 in the *Student's Book*)

Company and community

1

1 shareholder value
2 compensation
3 facilities
4 charities
5 environment
6 exploiting
7 sustainable
8 equal opportunity
9 complaints
10 align, with

2

1 acknowledge any problem that exists
2 act with integrity towards employees
3 compensate victims for any damage caused
4 limit the impact of any problem
5 negotiate settlements which satisfy everyone
6 obey the law or face a lawsuit or fine
7 recognize merit when staff perform well
8 uphold standards of common decency

3

1 apology for absence
2 approving the minutes
3 stick to the agenda
4 introduce the first item
5 getting side-tracked
6 come back to this
7 have any views
8 see your point
9 Wouldn't you agree
10 take a vote
11 break for coffee
12 unanimous decision
13 any other business
14 close the meeting

4

1 tries
2 are made
3 was lost
4 took
5 was found
6 dismissed

5

as a rule = on the whole
clearly = obviously
consequently = therefore
especially = in particular
finally = in conclusion
in addition = moreover
in brief = to sum up
in other words = that is to say

6

1 in addition, moreover
2 especially, in particular
3 as a rule, on the whole

7 Mergers and acquisitions

Digital resources for Unit 7

eWorkbook

Language practice: interactive & printable grammar, vocabulary, listening& pronunciation practice activities, extra printable reading & writing worksheets
Listen: Student's Book audio, language practice audio
Watch: video & video worksheets
Tests: interactive multiple-choice test
Resources: word list, grammar help & writing tips

Teacher's Resource Disc

Video: video & video worksheets
Audio: Student's Book audio
Tests: progress test Unit 6
Resources: PowerPoint Unit 7, business document Unit 7, photocopiable worksheets, Student's Book answer key, Student's Book glossary

Subject background

A *merger* is when two companies join together as equals to form one, and the process is mutually consensual, whereas an *acquisition* (or *takeover*) is when a larger company buys a smaller one, and the smaller company may not be happy because its identity will be lost. In practice the differences are not so great, firstly because nearly always one partner will be more powerful, and secondly because the legal and practical arrangements are very similar.

The term *M&A* is common in place of *mergers* and *acquisitions*, and it is used a lot in the context of investment banking, where advising on and organizing M&A activity is a very lucrative part of their business.

What is involved in deciding on a merger or acquisition? The initial idea will come from the board of directors – it is a very long-term strategic decision and operational managers are unlikely to put forward the idea of joining together with a company who they see as a competitor in their day-to-day work.

So, the board has to make a decision that for reasons of growth, or increased competitive advantage, or extending their product line into other related areas, they will look for a target company to merge with or buy. The next step is to analyse the potential target. This means not only understanding its products and its customers, but also its cost structure,
a) because the aim is to make substantial savings when the two companies join together and
b) any future investments that might be necessary if it were bought.

Eventually you arrive at two figures – the first is what the company is worth to the current owners, and the second is what it is worth to the company making the acquisition. The difference between the two arises because of the benefits (added value) that the acquisition will bring. If those benefits are clear and substantial, the takeover will go smoothly – the acquiring company will start to accumulate shares in its target until it has a controlling stake. Existing shareholders of the target company are likely to be happy – the price of their own shares will be rising because of the increased demand as shares are being bought, and because of the future prospects for synergy between the two companies.

People inside the target company will be less happy – they will be worried about their jobs. The larger company who is buying them is unlikely to need two marketing directors, two finance directors, and all the extra middle managers. Indeed, one of the main arguments in favour of the acquisition will have been precisely this – to make cost savings by merging budgets and running the same business with fewer employees. In relation to the board of the target company – they may be prepared to fight for their independence if the takeover is hostile, or they may be pleased (perhaps they had decided to sell off this part of the business in order to focus on their core activities).

After the acquisition has happened, success is by no means certain. The first problem is cultural – the two organizations may have a different way of doing things, and there may be personality clashes between the two groups of managers. The second is poor implementation – reorganization, new job descriptions, unfamiliarity with the customers and markets of the other company will all lead to a period of confusion, and any expected cost savings may not materialize.

Useful websites

For more details on M&A, look at the 'investopedia' website – this is generally one of the best sources of financial information for language teachers on the net:
http:llinvestopedia.comluniversitylmergersl

7.1 About business

Risks and opportunities in M&A

This module explores issues around mergers and acquisitions; students examine the pros and cons of taking over a business and practise making effective presentations using visuals.

Internet research

A search under 'surviving a merger' will bring up numerous articles offering advice on what employees can do when their company is taken over, including the following:

- develop a plan of action in case you are made redundant.
- re-assess your position in the company and take advantage of any opportunities for promotion.
- be willing to accept change.
- work out ways of managing the effects, e.g. confusion, increased workload, low morale, by trying to remain positive.
- being supportive of colleagues' who lose their jobs or suffer in some way as a result of the takeover, etc.

This research could be done after the extension activity at the end of Exercise 5 or after students have finished the module, as a follow-up activity.

Discussion

1 Getting married could be seen as a kind of merger or acquisition! Get students to make a list of the kinds of things that happen to two people's separate lives when they get married and in what ways these are similar to two companies merging.

SUGGESTED ANSWERS:

How a marriage is similar or different to a merger:
Usually, both people in a marriage bring assets (car, stereo, house, an income) into the marriage so their combined wealth is greater than their individual wealth. In the same way a merged company will have more assets than the individual companies had had.
A newly-married couple have to learn to live with each other and work out the best way to do things as a couple. One person might be good at housework while the other might be better at doing the household accounts. In the same way employees in a merged company have to learn to live with each other and accept that there may be different ways of doing things in the newly-merged company.
Married people have to pull together and work hard to make the marriage a success – the same can be said of a newly-merged company.

Skim reading

2 Read the four questions aloud. Give students a few minutes to read the article and find the answers. Check answers with the whole class. Remind students not to worry at this stage about any unknown words.

With lower-level classes, split the text into four parts and get students to look for answers to the questions section by section, i.e. read paragraphs 1 and 2 and look for the answer to question 1; read paragraph 3 and look for the answer to question 2; read paragraph 4 and look for the answer to question 3; read paragraph 5 and look for the answer to question 4.

ANSWERS:

1 American executives. Because merger and acquisition deals are worth astronomical sums, and many mergers result in a net loss of value.
2 Techniques based on best practice in the conception, planning, due diligence, negotiation and integration stages, and common acquirer errors.
3 Improving earnings, asset growth, developing synergies, making economies of scale, increasing market share; cross-selling, diversification, or taking on debt to make the acquirer a less attractive target.
4 Reasons which involve excessive pride or arrogance on the part of management, e.g. wanting to build too big an empire, too quickly.

Reading for detail

3 Circulate while students are discussing the true / false statements. Get them to underline the parts of the text that helped them find the answers.

ANSWERS:

1 T 70% of half the 1,500–2,000 mergers in the world: 1,500 I 2 x 0.7 = 525
2 T American executives are queuing up to go back to school for M&A classes.
3 F Classes are 'open enrolment' – the only condition of attendance is your, or rather your company's, ability to pay the fees.
4 F Guest speakers illustrate some of the most common acquirer errors.
5 F You might think that B-school professors would discourage their students from taking on mergers. But you'd be wrong.
6 T Developing synergies and making economies of scale are conveniently long-term goals.
7 T Empire-building is a wrong reason, but diversification and increasing debt can be good reasons.
8 T CEOs need to be brought back down to earth and follow their heads rather than their hearts.

EXTENSION ACTIVITY

Ask students to look at the 'jigsaw' picture on page 89 in their *Student's Books*. Ask them to discuss in small groups or with a partner what they represent in relation to the subject of mergers (the idea that the two companies with very different natures have to fit together).

You could ask students to think of other metaphors for mergers (e.g. two animals – an elephant and a mouse = big and small; owl and kitten = old, wise, serious and young, immature, fun / playful; etc.).

Listening for gist

4 2:40 Get students to predict what the 'five Gs' might be. Write their answers on the board. Play the whole interview through and get students to put up their hands when they hear a 'G'. Pause the recording and check answers. Write the words on the board. Get students to give you the correct spellings in each case, if they can.

ANSWERS:

Goals, Gains, Genes, Geography and Growth

RECORDING SCRIPT

2:40

Interviewer: If mergers are so difficult to do well, why bother with external growth at all? Why not just grow internally?

Bernard Degoulange: Well, the most common reason, and probably the best reason for a merger, is that your customers are asking you for something you can't deliver. Let's say you sell champagne. If people are satisfied with your champagne, they're going to start asking you for whisky, simply because everybody would like to be able to get the solution to all of life's problems from the same place. Now, if you can't give your customers the whisky they're asking for, you have a problem. Because however satisfied they are with your champagne, they're going to go somewhere else for whisky, and that's when you risk losing those customers.

I: What advice would you give on finding the right company to acquire?

BD: Personally, I have five points that I want to examine when looking at a possible acquisition: the five Gs. If I don't get good answers to at least four of them, I don't do the deal. The first of the five Gs is Goals. Are our goals compatible? Are both companies trying to achieve something similar? If not, keep looking. Secondly, Gains. I want to know if there will be real gains in terms of economies of scale. And will these gains compensate for perhaps not being able to react as quickly to new trends in the market because of the size of the organization? Being bigger is not always better. The third point is Genes. And by that I mean company culture. There's no point in trying to merge a traditional, hierarchical family business with a fast-moving start-up with a relaxed management style.
It just won't work, the cultural genes are too different. It's not enough to find a partner whose strengths compensate for your weaknesses, and vice versa; there has to be a real synergy in culture and personality.

I: Yes, if that synergy isn't present, there's a risk that neither company's customers recognize the firm that they used to trust.

BD: Exactly.

I: OK, so, Goals, Gains and Genes. What are the other two Gs?

BD: Geography and Growth. Are the companies based in the same city or geographical area? If not, communication between headquarters is much more difficult, and the Gains are harder to achieve.

I: And Growth?

BD: Will the merger provide technology or skills that you don't have now, which would take too long to develop yourself, and which will unquestionably allow your company to grow? If the merger will open new markets, which would otherwise be inaccessible, then it makes sense.

I: When you've identified the right partner, how can you make sure the merger goes smoothly?

BD: The most important thing is to look after your people: employees, management and of course customers, but especially employees. First of all, you have to keep them focused and productive. A merger is a wonderful opportunity for everybody to take their eye off the ball – and so it's a great opportunity for the competition to jump in and take market share from both companies in the merger. Secondly you have to help employees get over their feelings of loss and perhaps anger as quickly as possible, and accept the new situation. Whenever there is a merger, two companies die and a new company is born. It's essential to help people get through that traumatic period, to explain how things will change and what their new roles will be, and to get them to accept the new organization and their new identity. It's essentially about communication, sometimes counselling, and compensating those who leave the company, whether by choice or not.

Listening for detail

5 2:40 Students work with a partner to note down the answers to the questions. Play the recording as many times as students need to hear it. With lower-level classes, pause the recording after the answer to each question to give students more time to write. Check answers with the whole class.

Make a note of the answers to question 3 on the board to make sure everyone has the same information. This will be a useful reference for Exercise 6.

SUGGESTED ANSWERS:

1 Probably the best reason for a merger is that your customers are asking you for something you can't deliver.
2 If people like your champagne, they're going to start asking you for whisky. If you can't give your customers whisky, they're going to buy it from someone else, and then you risk losing your champagne customers too.
3 Goals: the goals of both companies must be compatible.
Gains: there must be real gains in terms of economies of scale, big enough to compensate for becoming less reactive.
Genes: company cultures must be compatible.
Geography: head offices of the two companies should be geographically close.
Growth: the merger must unquestionably allow the company to grow.
4 The opportunity for the competition to jump in and take market share from both companies, because people are distracted by the merger.
5 Because two companies die and a new company is born.
6 By communicating and counselling, explaining how things will change and what their new roles will be, and getting them to accept the new organization and their new identity.

EXTENSION ACTIVITY

Ask if students have any personal experience of mergers and acquisitions.

For pre-work students, get students to think about the impact of a takeover on the employees. Ask, e.g.:
What would be traumatic about it?
How might employees feel?
Why might some people be made redundant?
Why might some employees want to leave voluntarily?

Discussion

6 Students work in small groups to make a list of pros and cons, using the five Gs as a starting point, but adding any other ideas of their own. Get students to make a decision about whether they will take over Kadris' Kebabs. Circulate while they are working and assist where necessary.

When they have finished, get each group to say whether they would proceed to a takeover or not and give reasons for their decision, incorporating the five Gs into their answers.

7.2 Vocabulary
Business performance

This module practises a range of words and phrases for describing business performance, talking about cause and effect, and describing information in graphs.

Internet research

An Internet search of 'bulls' and 'bears' will reveal that bulls buy shares hoping to sell them at a higher price later, while bears sell shares hoping to buy them back later at a lower price. Bulls may be seen as optimistic because they hope the market will improve. Bears may be seen as pessimists because they are hoping for a fall in the market price. Other 'animals' that students may find mentioned in connection with the stock markets are chickens, pigs (or hogs), and sheep.

Students could do this research as a follow-up to this module to find out further information about stock markets.

Discussion

1 Ask students to work with a partner. Remind them to use clues in the extracts to help them match the headlines to the sentences and to work out whether good or bad news is being reported. Check answers with the whole class, getting students to tell you how they arrived at their answers.

To focus on the meaning and use of the phrases in the headlines, get students to tell you:

- which two phrases are opposites (*in the black / in the red*).
- which phrase means that a company has failed (*go under*).
- which two phrases mean that the company didn't make a profit (*cover costs / break even*).

ANSWERS:

1 Titanic Enterprises go under f) – bad news
2 Air New Zealand in the black e) – good news
3 Oldies Records cover costs b) – good news
4 Liverpool F.C. in the red a) – bad news
5 Brizal Coffee break even c) – good news
6 Predictions Inc. make a profit d) – good news

EXTENSION ACTIVITY

When asking students to explain how they arrived at answers, ask them to explain the humour and cultural references in the headlines:
Titanic Enterprises go under / tip of the iceberg – a reference to the sinking of the ship the Titanic when it hit an iceberg in the Atlantic in 1912.
Air New Zealand in the black – the New Zealand rugby team famously play in a 'all black' strip
Liverpool FC in the red – the famous English football club play in a red strip

Giving financial information

2 Ask students to mark the sentences alone and then compare their answers with a partner. Check answers with the whole class by getting students to read the sentence aloud. Ask them to say whether it describes an increase, a decrease, or stability. Monitor pronunciation.

ANSWERS:

1 ↗
2 ↙
3 →
4 ↙
5 This phrase means up ↗ and down ↙ over a period of time
6 ↗

3 Ask students to match the sentences alone and then compare their answers with a partner. Check answers by reading sentence 1 aloud yourself, and getting students to read the correct matching sentence from a–f.

To focus on meaning, get students to divide the verbs into three lists headed *Increase, Decrease, Stable* and *Other* (i.e. words which don't fit into the other three categories), e.g. Increase: *rise, double, peak, reach a high*; Decrease: *fall, slide, slump, drop*; Stable: *stabilize, level off*; Other: *fluctuate, vary*.

ANSWERS:

1 c) 2 f) 3 a) 4 b) 5 d) 6 e)

4 Do this as a whole-class activity. Get students to read out the correct sentence to match each of the four graphs.

To check students' understanding of the differences in meaning between *by / to, of / to, of / from* in this context, get them to draw graphs showing the correct meaning of the other sentence in each case.

ANSWERS:

1 b) Sales increased to $3M.
2 a) There was a decrease of 10%.
3 a) Prices fell by €15.
4 b) There was a rise from 30%.

5 Students work with a partner. They take turns to read the first part of the sentence, while their partner reads the matching second half.

Ask students which group in Exercise 4 (*Increase / Decrease / Stable / Other*) the following verbs would go into: *improve, go up, grow, shoot up* (*Increase*).

ANSWERS:

1 d) 2 a) 3 b) 4 c) 5 h) 6 e) 7 f) 8 g)

6 With lower-level classes, first get students to sort out the verbs + adverbs from the adjectives + nouns. Check answers with the whole class.

ANSWERS:

verb + adverb (smallest to largest)
grow slightly → improve significantly → go up sharply → shoot up dramatically
adjective + noun (smallest to largest)
a slight increase → moderate growth → a considerable improvement → a sudden surge

7 Students work with a partner. Check answers by getting students to read the completed sentences aloud.

Although several of these phrases can be used interchangeably, the second part of the exercise demonstrates the differences between some of them.

ANSWERS:

1 due to, as a consequence of, as a result of, because of
2 resulted in
3 as a result, as a consequence
4 thanks to, due to, as a consequence of, as a result of, because of
5 resulted in
6 As a result, as a consequence

due to, as a consequence of, as a result of, because of, thanks to explain causes.
resulted in, as a result, as a consequence introduce effects.

FURTHER PRACTICE

To check that they can use the phrases correctly, give students a number of sentence starters to complete, using the phrases in Exercise 7, e.g.:

I didn't finish the report on time; as a result ...
Thanks to ..., I got the promotion I wanted.
As a consequence of the takeover, my department ...
Due to ..., I had to relocate to London.
Because of ..., I decided to look for another job.

Check answers with the whole class, accepting any reasonable answers.

Listening for detail

8 2:41 Before students listen, get them to look at the axes on the blank graph so that they know what will be discussed (time, money) and to look back at the vocabulary they have practised in Exercises 1–4.

With lower-level classes, draw a simple graph on the board, e.g. showing a fluctuation in number of students at a school / doing a particular course, etc. The vertical axis could represent the number of students in units of 10. The horizontal axis should represent a range of years, e.g. 2001 to 2012. As a whole class get students to describe the graph. Encourage them to use as much language as possible from the module, e.g. *There was a sudden surge in students numbers in 2010 with 100 students compared to 80 the year before.*

Play the recording as many times as students need to hear it to complete the graph. To check answers, get individual students to tell you about sections of the graph, using the phrases used in the recording or their own words, e.g. *In 1993 the share price was $15. In 1994 it dropped suddenly to $12. Then it reached $50 in 1996*, etc.

ANSWERS:

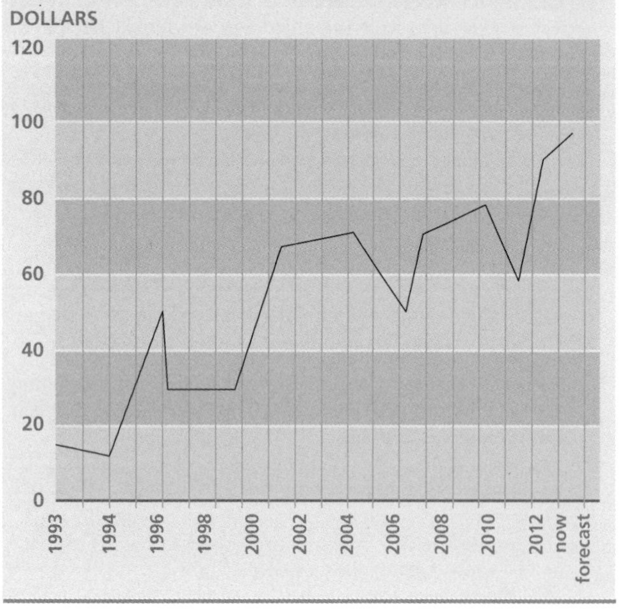

RECORDING SCRIPT

2:41

Anchor: Oxter Holdings today confirmed that they have increased their bid for Fraxis Corp. to $98 per share. Fraxis Corp. was floated in 1993 at just $15 per share. After a sudden drop of $3 in 1994, the stock rose gradually over the next two years to reach $50 in early 1996, when Fraxis acquired one of their smaller competitors, Nimmco. The market was not enthusiastic about the takeover, and Fraxis fell sharply by over 40%. It then recovered slightly and levelled off around the $30 dollar mark for the next three years. In 2000, Fraxis CEO Alex Firman announced an alliance with the European market leader Haffmann; the reaction was immediate. The stock price climbed to $65 as institutional investors rushed to share in the profits. The alliance has been a great success; with the exception of temporary falls to $50 in 2006 and $59 in 2011, Fraxis has climbed steadily to peak at $95, shortly after Oxter's first offer of $90 a share was rejected last week. Analysts believe thatFraxis are unlikely to accept anything less than $110, so expect to see the price jump to $100 plus when trading opens on Monday.

Presenting

9 Circulate while students are speaking and check that they are using the target language correctly. Make a note of any mistakes for remedial teaching later. Get students to check their answers by comparing their completed graphs with their partner's original graph.

FURTHER PRACTICE

Get students to write a short summary of the information in one or both of the graphs in Exercise 9.

7.3 Grammar

Future forms and expressing likelihood

This module focuses on ways of talking about the future and discussing forecasts and predictions.

Internet research

A search for 'Alvin Toffler' will reveal that he is an American writer and futurist. He is well known for his ideas on, among other things, technology, communications, the digital revolution and corporate and political affairs, and their impact on society. He is the author of the best-selling *Future Shock and The Third Wave*, and many other books.

Students could research aspects of Alvin Toffler's work and ideas and make either oral or written presentations on them. This research could be done before or after Exercises 4–6.

Arrangements, plans and contingencies

1 Start by reading the notes on future forms in the *Refresh your memory* box with the class. If students seem unsure of the future forms or would like further practice, work through some or all of Exercises 1–9 in the *Grammar and practice* section (pages 134–135 in the *Student's Book*, answers on page 116 in this book).

Read through the example as a class and point out the use of three future forms and the modal verb *might* to express possibility in the sentences. Then divide the class into pairs to make sentences about Tom's diary. In feedback, ask different pairs to describe different days and correct or improve any misuses of future forms or modal verbs.

SOME SUGGESTED ANSWERS:

On Monday afternoon, Tom is going to the eye doctor at 3.45. He may go swimming later. He's going to order a pizza and watch the big match on TV. He might invite Martin.
He's having dinner with Ashley on Wednesday evening. He's going to book a nice restaurant and buy flowers.
He may stay in bed and sleep on Sunday morning, or he might play squash. He's going to read the newspaper. He must phone his mum.

2 Give students a few minute to prepare things to say then ask them to tell their partner about plans for the coming week. Let students refer to their PDA or smartphone to prepare the task.

Expressing likelihood

3 Ask students to look at the table and check that students understand the degree of likelihood involved in using the phrases. Point out that some phrases are a bit more informal (*there's no way; there's not much chance; it's bound to happen*).

Read through the example as a class and point out the use of future forms, modal verbs and expressions to express likelihood in the sentences. Then divide the class into groups of three, four or five to make predictions about the situations. In feedback, ask different groups to tell the class about their predictions.

For further practice, students could complete Exercises 10–12 in the *Grammar and practice* section (pages 135 in the *Student's Book*, answers on page 116 in this book).

Discussion

4 Read the events in columns A, B and C with the whole class.

With lower-level classes, write the phrases in bold from Exercise 3 on the board so that students have easy reference to them, and brainstorm phrases students could use in defending their views, e.g. *We think …; In our opinion …; We reached this conclusion because* ... Students could also use some of the phrases they practised in module 7.2, e.g. *as a result, due to, as a consequence,* etc.

To get students started, demonstrate what to do with one of the events. Discuss students' views on the topic with the whole class. Make notes on the board and use them to prepare a very short presentation.

Circulate while students are speaking and assist where necessary. Get students to make their presentations. Students in the other groups should ask at least one question per group about what they hear. Make a note of any mistakes in the target language that you hear for remedial teaching later.

Listening

5 2:42 Play the recording through once and get students to complete the exercise. Check answers with the whole class. Then play the recording again. This time, get students to note down the words and phrases that helped them arrive at their answers. Check answers with the whole class.

ANSWERS:

go freelance (U)
start evening classes (P)
stay at Artip (U)
find a new job (P)
Artip take-over (P)
read the job ads (P)
give up smoking and drinking (P)
retrain as a marketing assistant (P)
Ashley has forgotten to mention her engagement / wedding.

RECORDING SCRIPT

2:42

Ashley: Emma, Happy New Year!
Emma: Happy New Year!
A: What are you doing all alone over here? I haven't had a chance to talk to you all evening. Have some more champagne!
E: No, I shouldn't. I'm going to give up smoking and drinking this year. It's my New Year's resolution.
A: Really?! Well, you can start tomorrow. Come on, Em, it's New Year!
E: Oh, all right, just a drop. Thanks. Anyway, what about you, Ashley? What's the New Year going to be like for you? Have you made any resolutions?
A: No, not really. But I'm definitely going to find a new job. There's no way I'm staying at that company for another year.
E: Right. Have you got anything in mind?
A: No, but I'm going to read the job ads until I find something good. I'm bound to find something better than what I do now.
E: Oh, I'm sure you'll find something easily. Or you could go freelance, with the talent you've got ...
A: Freelance?! Well, I suppose I could, but I think it's unlikely. It's far too complicated. No, I'm just going to choose about ten or twelve jobs to apply for, go along to the interviews, and we'll see what happens. I'm going to take my time, not rush into anything.
E: Right. I think that's very sensible.
A: So, what about you? Are you going to stay at Artip?
E: I doubt it.
A: Really?! Are you going to leave, or are they going to throw you out?
E: Well, both of those are quite likely, actually. The company's being taken over in February, so we don't know what will happen. I mean, they're bound to make redundancies, we just don't know how many. Anyway, I'm starting evening classes next week. I'm going to retrain as a marketing assistant.
A: Excellent! Well, here's to a successful New Year for both of us!
E: Yes, cheers! But, um, Ashley, isn't there another New Year's resolution you've forgotten to tell me about? Is that a real diamond? Who's the lucky man, then?

Discussion

6 As an alternative to pairwork, students could do this as a whole-class activity, milling about as if at a party, talking to several different people. Read through the question and the list together. Ask students what kind of questions they might ask each other.

With lower-level classes you could write the questions or question prompts on the board, e.g.:
What are you planning to do with the rest of the day?
What are you doing at the weekend?
What (subjects, course, etc.) do you think you might do next term / year?
When do you think you'll retire?

Tell students that they should remember or take simple notes on some of the answers for feedback at the end. Give students time to mingle and talk, participating in the activity yourself. When they have finished, get some students to report back, e.g. *I spoke to Klaus about his plans for next year. There's a good chance he will do an MBA in the States.*

FURTHER PRACTICE

Students discuss or write about plans, intentions and hopes for their town or city. Topics could include, shopping, leisure facilities, roads, public transport, taxes, government.

7.4 Speaking
Presentations – visuals

This module explores ways of presenting information through the use of visuals and practises expressions for explaining the information in them. On the Teacher's Resource Disc, you will find more related practice material, including a video (with worksheets) featuring an example situation for students to analyse and discuss.

Internet research

'Vertical integration' means that a company expands its business into areas that are at different points of the same production path, e.g. a car company expands into tyre manufacturing.

'Horizontal integration' refers to the activity of a company when it expands its business into different products that are similar to its current products, e.g. a hot dog seller expands into hamburgers.

Students could choose one of the three industries mentioned – music, drinks, or TV – and gather information and examples about vertical integration.

This research could be done before the presentation activity in Exercise 6 or as a follow-up to it.

Discussion

1 Read through the list of presentation tools and make sure that students know what they are. Encourage them to think about the pros and cons of each tool. Give students a few minutes to write their own answers and compare them with a partner. Take whole-class feedback.

Students could also consider which tool(s) might be appropriate for different types of presentations and audiences, e.g. an audience of more than 100 people in a large room; a small group of people around a table; a formal sales conference, etc.

Some students may decide that none of these tools is essential to a good presentation, and that other things are more important, e.g. tone of voice, body language, preparation, knowing your audience, etc. At this point you could remind students of the discussion they had in Unit 3 on the qualities of a good presentation.

ANSWERS:

Answers will vary. It usually depends on the formality of the presentation, where it takes place, whether it involves any audience participation, the size of your audience (an interactive whiteboard – IWB – will be better than a flip chart for larger audiences), what the presentation's about and what your audience expects.

Listening for gist

2 2:43–2:46 Before students look at this exercise, get them to brainstorm the ways in which visuals can be used badly or ineffectively in presentations. Get them to think about their own experience – presentations they have seen (or have done themselves!) which have not worked well.

Read the sentences aloud or get students to read them. Compare these points with the ones students made themselves. Then play the recordings through once while students listen and match. Get them to compare their answers with a partner.

Play the recordings again so that students can check their answers. Check answers with the whole class by getting students to read the sentences aloud. Ask them to add some information about what each presenter did which failed to meet these guidelines, e.g. *Presenter 1 showed three slides one after the other very quickly. The audience may not have had enough time to look at them properly and there was probably too much information to take in.*

ANSWERS:

a) 2 b) 1 c) 3 d) 4

RECORDING SCRIPT

2:43–2:46

Presenter 1

Now, my next slide shows how the number of takeovers is likely to increase over the next decade. This one gives a breakdown by sector. This next slide highlights the probable effect on company performance. And this one, this one and now this third slide show how share prices will fall.

Presenter 2

Now, the next slide shows some very interesting data. As you can see – oh, perhaps you can't see – I'm sorry, the figures are rather small. Anyway, the forecast is particularly good, in contrast to the data for the last three years, which is in the, ah, smaller table, over here, which you, ah, can't read either.

Presenter 3

If you look at the next slide, you'll see that we collected data using a Grossman scheduled EMTI questionnaire modified from the standard CDF rapid assessment surveys procedure, and compensated for statistical significance using an unbiased reflex standard deviation algorithm.

Presenter 4

OK, customer reactions to price and service levels after mergers: 30% of customers noticed an improvement; 49 said things had got worse. Erm, customer satisfaction by sector: almost 9% down in retail; stable in the service and financial sector; and 5% up for manufacturing companies.

Listening for detail

3 2:47 Play the recording while students listen and choose the slide that is being described. Play the recording again. Get students to listen for the ways in which the presentation has improved, e.g. the speaker shows one slide and explains it clearly; he doesn't just read the contents aloud, he gives further information and interpretation of it.

ANSWERS:

Slide C

RECORDING SCRIPT

2:47

Presenter

How will our customers react to a merger? My next slide shows two charts which illustrate the problem. Recently, customers of large Spanish companies were asked if they felt that prices and service had improved, remained the same or deteriorated as a result of a merger. As you will notice in the pie-chart, only a third of customers noticed an improvement, compared to almost half who said that things had got worse.

Let's look at the bar chart, which shows customer satisfaction by sector. As you can see, after a merger, customer satisfaction falls by an average of almost 9% in the retail sector, whereas it remains about the same in the service and financial sector, and rises by 5% on average for manufacturing companies.

The figures seem to suggest that, on the whole, customers are always likely to react negatively to mergers. This is due to a perceived drop in levels of service after a merger. The results indicate that retailers, where service is crucial to customer satisfaction, are particularly affected, as opposed to manufacturers, who benefit from mergers. Of course, this is the result of improved product quality and design, which are the most important factors for their customers.

4 Divide the class into pairs to choose the correct options.

Play **2:47** again. Pause if necessary to allow students time to check their answers. Check answers with the whole class. Get students to repeat the phrases, using the appropriate pronunciation, stress and intonation.

ANSWERS:

Introducing a slide or visual

My next slide shows two charts

Let's look at the second chart.

Highlighting

As you will notice in the pie-chart ...

As you can see, after a merger ...

Contrasting

compared with almost half who said ...

whereas it remains about the same in ...

Explaining and interpreting

The figures seem to suggest that ...

This is due to a perceived drop ...

The results indicate that retailers ...

as opposed to manufacturers ...

This is the result of improved product quality ...

Presenting visuals

5 Spend a few minutes discussing the pie chart, especially with lower-level classes. For example, you could ask students to give you some examples of what might be included under each heading:

housing (mortgage repayments, rent, utilities bills)
transportation (bus, train, petrol, car insurance, road tax)
food (meat, vegetables, fruit, fish, household requirements such as washing powder, etc.)
disposable (gym club membership, mobile phone costs, cinema or theatre tickets, weekends away, etc.)

While students are drawing their own pie charts, circulate and assist where necessary. Give them time to practise their presentation, using the words and phrases in Exercise 4, before putting them into groups.

Circulate again while students are giving their presentations in small groups, monitoring use of the target language and making notes of any mistakes for remedial teaching later. Check also that students are following the four-point framework given in the exercise.

When students have finished, get some of them to repeat their presentations for the whole class.

Presentation

6 Read the instructions with the whole class. Check that students understand *diversify* (vary your range of products/ service in order to be more competitive) and *accelerate* (make something happen faster).

Brainstorm with the whole class the kind of businesses a manufacturer of tennis racquets might be interested in, bearing in mind the five Gs discussed in module 1.

Give students a few minutes to read their instructions. Circulate and assist where necessary. Remind students to use the *Glossary* on page 157 at the back of their books and their dictionaries, if necessary. Students could add some ideas of their own to the presentation, if they wish.

When the groups have decided which is the best candidate for acquisition, they should present their decision to the whole class, explaining the reasons for their choice.

As a follow-up activity, get students to write a short summary based on their oral presentation.

EXTENSION ACTIVITY

Get students to consider other kinds of visuals they could use in a presentation, e.g. flow chart, bar chart, mind map, diagram, organigram, clip art, pictures. Students should think about the best ways to use them and ways in which they might be used ineffectively.

Bring examples of alternative visuals to class or get students to bring them. They can frequently be found in brochures, annual reports, conference papers, sales and marketing reports. Students can then evaluate their effectiveness, taking into account design, layout, usefulness, etc.

7.5 Writing
Presentation slides

This module explores how to use PowerPoint slides and provides practice through reading and listening in preparing slides for presentations.

Internet research

'Death by PowerPoint' refers to the poor use of PowerPoint for presentations and the effect this produces on audiences. Used ineffectively, presentation slides can make a presentation boring, for example if they are overused or are difficult to read or uninteresting.

Students will find websites offering advice on how to avoid 'death by PowerPoint', such as limiting the number of words on each slide, using simple, large fonts, using transitions wisely, customizing templates, and using pictures and graphs.

Students could do this research before they do this module, as a lead-in or after they have completed this module, to supplement the information given here.

Discussion

1 Do this as a whole-class activity, working through each item and getting students to comment on its suitability or unsuitability for a presentation slide. Get students to tell you where you might expect to find the two unsuitable items, e.g. footnotes might be found in an academic book or article; paragraphs are more suitable for a longer written text.

SUGGESTED ANSWERS:

no footnotes – they won't be legible
no paragraphs – just single lines of text

Model

2 Ask students to work in small groups. After they have chosen the best way of presenting the information, get them to comment on the weaknesses of the two ways they rejected.

ANSWERS:

Slide B is the best: it highlights the key ideas the presenter wants to communicate. Each point can be understood without any commentary, but leaves room for the presenter to add interesting details.
Slide A has too much text and will be illegible. In fact, this is the oral commentary that the presenter might make on slide B.
Slide C is too succinct: there is not enough information for the key points to be understood without the presenter's explanations.

Analysis

3 Ask students in pairs to compare the slides A and B and discuss the question.

ANSWERS:

Only the key-words have been retained; most of the words that have been deleted mainly have a grammatical function, which is not required on a slide – verbs, pronouns, articles, etc.

Language focus

4 Students work alone, then compare their answers with a partner. Check answers with the whole class.

With lower-level classes, you could do this as a whole-class activity, writing the key-words on the board.

If you wish, draw students' attention to the parts of the sentences that they have left out, as a way of focusing on general principles, e.g. omit introductory phrases, additional information, and examples; these can said during the presentation, but don't need to be written in the slides.

SUGGESTED ANSWERS:

1 One of the most challenging aspects of writing a presentation is the need to organize the information in a logical way.
Organize information in a logical way.
2 Choose attractive background and text colours that are comfortable for the audience to read.
Choose colours that are comfortable to read.
3 Presentation software can be fun to use. Be creative, but do not include too many effects which may distract your audience from your content.
Don't let creative effects distract from content.
4 Make sure the text is large enough that the audience can read it easily from the back of the room. Also, use a standard font that is not too complicated or distracting.
Use large, easy-to-read text and standard fonts.
5 Use positive statements like 'The figures show …' rather than vague language like 'The data could possibly suggest …'
Prefer positive statements to vague language.

5 Ask students to work with a partner to do this exercise. Encourage them to underline the key words first, as in Exercise 4, and then compose the points for the slide, using their own words or rewriting, where necessary. Circulate while they are working and assist.

Get students to write neatly or type their five points on a sheet of paper, and display them on a table or wall so that everyone can see them.

SUGGESTED ANSWER:

Three scenarios for our company's future.
Do nothing, continue to survive.
Invest in technology, develop new products.
Acquire Iticom, enter new markets immediately.
I recommend acquisition: risky, but enormous potential.

Output

6 2:48 Read the instructions with the whole class and get students to predict what the strengths, weakness, opportunities and threats might be for a software company in today's market. Play the recording through once so that students get an overview of the presentation. Ask students how many slides they would want to prepare– they may say four (strengths, weaknesses, opportunities, threats), but as suggested here, they should also prepare an introductory, or 'overview' slide.

Then, play the recording again. Pause at the end of each section to allow students to make notes on the main points. Get students to compare their answers with a partner. Play the recording again so that students can check their answers. Then take whole-class feedback, ensuring that everyone has the right information to prepare the slides.

Students work with a partner again to prepare their slides. Circulate and assist where necessary. When students have finished, play the recording again and get students to listen and imagine the speaker is working through the slides as he delivers the presentation. This will allow them to check if their slides work effectively alongside the spoken presentation.

SUGGESTED ANSWERS:

1 Overview:
- Strengths
- Weaknesses
- Opportunities
- Threats
- Proposal
- Questions and reactions

2 Strengths:
- a reputation for innovation and quality
- expert staff
- careful financial management (chart)

3 Weaknesses:
- not enough office space
- costs (chart of development costs)
- recruitment
- size: too small and vulnerable

4 Opportunities:
- recruit in eastern Europe
- do development offshore
- consolidation and diversification

5 Threats:
- possible takeover target

6 Proposal:
- take over Oranmore Video Games
  - growth and debt, less vulnerable
  - diversification, economies of scale
  - solve recruitment and space problems

RECORDING SCRIPT

2:48

Good morning everyone, and thank you for coming. Two months ago, you asked me to conduct a strategic analysis of the company's strengths, weaknesses, opportunities and threats. I'm here today to present my findings, and to make recommendations on the basis of those findings. I intend first to give a short summary of the company's position, and then to invite you to ask questions and give your reactions to my proposals. If anything is not clear, please feel free to interrupt me.
First of all, I'd like to remind you of the company's main strengths. Galway Software has a reputation for innovation and quality in developing highly-specialized customer applications. We are able to provide excellent service thanks to our small team of expert engineers and developers. What's more, our finances have been carefully and cautiously managed: as you can see from the figures on this slide, today the company is in good financial health with practically no debt.
However, there are also a number of weaknesses which must be considered. The first, small weakness is office space. We just don't have enough. The second, more significant weakness is costs. As this graph shows, our development costs have risen steadily, whereas market prices are falling. It is becoming increasingly difficult to maintain our profit margins. The principal explanation for these high costs is the high salaries we have to pay to attract experienced developers. A third, associated problem is recruitment: in spite of high salaries, we are finding it increasingly difficult to attract young engineers who prefer to join large international companies. This brings me to perhaps the most significant weakness, and a problem which I want to come back to in a few moments when I talk about threats, and that is our size. As a small company in a very specific niche market, we are vulnerable. If things went wrong with just a few of our big customers, we could have serious difficulties.
But before looking at the threats, let's move on to opportunities. In particular, new technologies and a changing world economy are opening up exciting ways of re-thinking our business activities. For example, the new member states of the European Union in Eastern Europe have excellent schools and universities: their young engineers are talented,

well-trained and keen to acquire experience in companies like ours. Another possibility is to do part of our development work offshore, in countries like India where labour costs are significantly lower than in Europe. Last, but certainly not least, we must look at opportunities in our own industry: competition is fierce, and a process of consolidation is under way. Many firms are forming alliances or launching takeover bids in order to exploit synergies, to make economies of scale and to diversify into new market segments. I believe these are opportunities we should not ignore and I will be making a specific recommendation in the last part of my presentation.
So, I've talked about our strengths, our weaknesses and our opportunities. I want now to explain why one of the opportunities I have just described is also a serious threat.
And finally, to look at threats in the context of the consolidation I referred to earlier, Galway Software, as a small, successful, well-managed company with no debt, is a perfect target for a takeover. It is only a matter of time before a big international firm comes knocking at the door with its cheque book open. ... Unless we move first.
In the last part of this presentation, I am going to recommend that Galway Software should itself launch a takeover bid. There are many good reasons for this. Firstly, external growth with a reasonable amount of debt will make us less vulnerable. Secondly, a takeover will allow us to diversify into new markets, to expand our customer base and spread our risks, and to make economies of scale. And thirdly, the ideal candidate, Oranmore Video Games, which is based just 20 miles away, currently has more developers than it needs, and has a lot of unused office space.
I'm going to give you a handout which gives more details of why I believe we should acquire Oranmore ...

Writing slides

7 This exercise allows students to personalize the work they have done on preparing PowerPoint slides to a subject which interests them. This could be related to their work, a hobby, or another topic of interest. They could, for example, choose to plan a presentation using the information they gathered in one of the Internet searches in this unit – on Alvin Toffler; vertical integration in the drinks industry; or bulls, bears and other animals on the stock market.

7.6 Case study
Calisto

Students consider the options open to a business in trouble and make recommendations in a presentation about how to resolve them.

Internet research

An Internet search for key words 'Avis: We Try Harder' will reveal how this car rental company took on the market dominance of its rival, Hertz, in the 1960s and through clever market repositioning and brand-building dramatically increased its profits.

Students could do this research before they begin the case study as a lead-in activity and to provide ideas for the discussion and presentation in Exercise 5. Or they could do it afterwards, to provide information on a real-world case study. They could write a short report on the story behind how Avis improved its market position.

Discussion

1 Do this as a whole-class activity. Explain *EBIT* (Earnings Before Interest and Tax: a commonly used way of measuring the profitability of a company).

Get students to compare the businesses in terms of their profits, costs, sales, etc. This analysis will feed into the exercises that follow.

SUGGESTED ANSWER:

Reysonido has lower operating costs than 1MM and Calisto. Reysonido has the lowest cost of sales while IMM's are very high.
IMM has the highest sales. (etc.)

Reading

2 Read the article aloud. Ask students to guess the meanings of *meteoric*, *newcomers*, *charismatic*, *slick*, and *trumpets* from the context, before they check the meanings in the *Glossary* on page 157 in their books. Then check answers to the questions with the whole class. Ask students to suggest what kind of advertising Dylan might have used that could be described as 'slick' and what kind of discounting might be called 'aggressive'.

ANSWERS:

1 By using direct sales, slick marketing and aggressive discounting.
2 The challengers have all lost market share and several smaller players have gone out of business.
3 IMM is the only company which has managed to reverse the trend of falling market share.

Listening for gist

3 2:49 Get students to look at the notes before they listen to the presentation. Do the activity with the whole class. Play the recording. Pause at appropriate points to allow students to tell you, in a few words, what the options are.

See answer for Exercises 3 and 4 on the next page.

RECORDING SCRIPT

2:49

President: As you know, this year Calisto has lost 1.5 million dollars. Obviously this situation cannot continue. Unless we take action now, we will go out of business next year. We have several options to consider. Our first option is to adopt the same strategy as IMM. IMM have reduced their operating expenses by 20% over the last two years. However, they have achieved this by ruthlessly cutting jobs: one fifth of IMM's staff have been made redundant. Here at Calisto we have a long tradition of looking after our staff, and I do not wish to choose this option unless there is no other alternative.

Our second option is to follow the example of our friends at Reysonido, and buy European technology which would reduce our cost of sales by 10–15%. However, we estimate that this investment would increase our operating expenses by half a million dollars a year. A third option is to cut our prices in order to increase sales. We estimate a price cut of 10% might increase next year's sales to $16.5 million assuming, of course, that our competitors do not reduce their prices. However, our cost of sales would increase to just under nine million dollars.

My friends, there are three more options which I have not yet discussed with you, but which I would like you to consider carefully. Option number four is a merger. IMM have offered us three million dollars, which, in view of our desperate situation, is a very reasonable offer. If we agreed to a merger with IMM, the new company would be the new market leader, and be in a far better position to compete with Dylan. However, there would no doubt be some redundancies in order to make economies of scale.

As I said at the beginning of my presentation, I will take questions at the end. Now, option five. This is a high-risk strategy, but we must consider all possible solutions. In order to compete with Dylan, we need to be bigger; one way to obtain that critical size is by acquisition. Our fifth option is to acquire Reysonido.

Reysonido are likely to accept a takeover bid of around four million dollars. As well as synergy and economies of scale, this acquisition would also give us another bonus: access to the technology which means Reysonido's cost of sales is 10% lower than our own. Of course, we would need to borrow the money, and the repayments would represent around half a million dollars per year over ten years: not so unrealistic with combined sales of 25 million, I believe.

The final option is one which I sincerely hope you will not choose. That is, to close the company, and sell off our assets to pay our debts. I have kept it until last in order to stress that it is a serious option.

All right, I'm sure you are anxious to ask questions. After that, I would like us to consider all the options in detail; everybody's contributions will be valuable. Thank you.

Listening for detail

4 Play **2:49** again while students complete the notes. Check answers by getting students to form complete sentences, using a combination of their own words and the words they heard in the presentation, e.g. *Our first option is to cut jobs. IMM has adopted the same strategy. This would reduce our operating costs by 20%.* This will be useful practice for the discussion activity in Exercise 5.

ANSWERS:

Exercises 3 and 4

	Options	Notes
1	cut jobs	– same strategy as IMM – would reduce operating expenses by 20%
2	buy technology	– same strategy as Reysonido – would reduce production costs by 10–15% – would increase operating expenses by $0.5M per year
3	cut prices 10%	– next year's sales: $16.5M – cost of sales would increase to just under $9M
4	merge with IMM	– price: $3M – advantages: the new company would be the new market leader – disadvantages: some redundancies
5	acquire Reysonido	– price: around four million dollars – bonus: access to technology, cost of sales 10% lower – repayments: $0.5M per year over ten years – combined sales: $25M
6	close the company	sell off our assets to pay debts

Discussion and presentation

5 Read the instructions with the whole class. Remind students of the work they have done in previous modules that will help them here, e.g. the vocabulary work in module 7.2, future forms and expressing likelihood in module 7.3, presentations in modules 7.4 and 7.5.

Set a time limit for the presentations, e.g. five minutes, so that each group has the same amount of time.

Circulate while students are working and assist where necessary.

When students are assessing which is the best presentation, they could use following criteria, which you could write up on the board as a checklist:
Did the speakers present their information in a clear, structured way?
Did the slides follow the guidelines given in section 5?
Did the speakers support their arguments in a convincing way?

Students could also add their own criteria, if they wish.

FURTHER PRACTICE

For homework, students can use the presentation in Exercise 3 for further practice in preparing presentation slides (see module 7.5, Exercises 4 and 5).

8 International trade

Digital resources for Unit 8

eWorkbook

Language practice: interactive & printable grammar, vocabulary, listening & pronunciation practice activities, extra printable reading & writing worksheets
Listen: Student's Book audio, language practice audio
Watch: video & video worksheets
Tests: interactive multiple-choice test
Resources: word list, grammar help & writing tips

Teacher's Resource Disc

Video: video & video worksheets
Audio: Student's Book audio
Tests: progress test Unit 8, review test 2 (Units 5–8)
Resources: PowerPoint Unit 8, business document Unit 8, photocopiable worksheets, Student's Book answer key, Student's Book glossary

Subject background

Why export? The two most important reasons are likely to be under-used capacity (exporting will allow you to increase production, reduce unit costs and increase profits) and diversity (relying on just your own domestic market is risky because the market may decline; there may be seasonal factors, etc. Selling in other countries allows you to spread the risk and develop opportunities abroad).

Before getting started, there is a lot of initial research to be done on the foreign market. The main concerns will include:

- background information (economic situation, political stability, currency risk).
- market size and likely product demand.
- competitors' products already in the market.
- tariffs or import restrictions (duties, quotas, taxes).
- distribution channels and methods (agents, distributors, wholesalers, retailers).
- technical, safety, environmental and other standards required by law.
- packing and packaging issues (climate and time in transit, handling methods, need for different packaging to suit local market).
- sales literature and support material (translations needed).
- servicing arrangements (if needed).
- customer satisfaction policy (money back / replacement schemes).

A major question is then going to be the nature of the distribution channel. Options to consider will include:

1 Direct selling from manufacturer to customer without an intermediary.
2 Domestic export firms operating in foreign markets (with their own agents, local offices, etc). These firms will take your goods on a wholesale basis and do all the sales and paperwork. However, you have no control over the market and your products may receive little attention compared to others.
3 Agents working exclusively for you in the foreign market. An agent receives a commission for sales made on your behalf. The advantages of using agents are that you gain the services of an experienced local person with contacts and market experience. The disadvantages are that the agent will take a high commission and may lose interest quickly if sales do not arrive quickly.
4 Distributors – a distributor is different from an agent. A distributor is a customer – they have rights (usually exclusive) to purchase your products and resell them in their market. They are like a foreign wholesaler. An agent is just an intermediary and never actually buys any products on their own account.

With agents and distributors there will be many issues to discuss and negotiate on an ongoing basis. These include:

- which products are to be sold.
- prices in the foreign market.
- performance targets.
- payment of local marketing costs.
- transportation (taking into account speed, cost, security and efficiency).
- getting paid (cash in advance, letters of credit, bill of exchange, open account, etc.).

There are other more specialized export options:

5 Licensing – this means selling or leasing some industrial or commercial expertise (for which you own the patent).
6 Franchising – this is a form of licensing for products which do not have patents.
7 Joint venture – this is a company owned jointly by two or more companies – for example a foreign company with a local partner.

Useful websites

On the net, good starting points to research international trade are these two government sites (one UK and one US):
http://www.businesslink.gov.uk
http://www.unzco.comlbasicguide
The World Trade Organization site is also useful (explore the link to Resources):
http://www.wto.org
For the activities of individual companies, look at:
http://www.corporateinformation.com

8.1 About business

Export sales and payment

This module explores the theme of international trade and payments. Students also practise negotiating skills and using diplomatic language.

Internet research

A search using 'Big Mac Index' will reveal it is an informal way of comparing the purchasing power of two currencies. It was introduced by *The Economist* magazine in 1986 in a light-hearted way, and has been published more or less every year since then. One way of predicting exchange rate movements is that the rate between two currencies should naturally adjust so that a sample basket of goods and services should cost the same in both currencies. In the Big Mac Index, a Big Mac hamburger from the McDonald's fast food restaurant chain is used as the single sample item.

Students could be asked to compare their own currency with one or more others using the Big Mac example. This research could be done at the end of this module.

LEAD-IN ACTIVITY

To get students thinking about overseas sales and payments, ask if they have any experience of shopping in a foreign country or if they have bought anything online from a company in another country. What happened? How did they pay? Did they have any problems with payment, shipment or delivery?

Alternatively, ask students about the use of credit cards in their country. Are they widely used? How many credit cards do people usually have? What do they use credit cards for? Are there any problems in their country with consumer debt?

Discussion

1 Circulate while students are discussing the question and assist where necessary. Make a note of any useful vocabulary to share with the whole class at the feedback stage. Ask one student in each pair to give you one aspect of the difficulty of selling in overseas markets. Make a list on the board.

SUGGESTED ANSWERS:

quotas, import taxes, exchange controls, local regulatory bodies like FDA, local customs for payment terms, difficulty of providing after-sales service, language barrier, corruption

Scan reading

2 Check that students know what a pinball machine is (a game in which small metal balls are shot across a board and points are scored when the ball hits a pin with lights). Ask some questions to establish the context, e.g.:
Are pinball machines popular in your country?
Where do you usually find them?
Do you play on them?

Get students to read the first paragraph of the article. Ask some simple questions to set the context, e.g.:
Why did Eisenhart Games expand into markets outside the US? (because of competition from video games and computers in the US)
What is Eisenhart's share of the Middle East market? (35%) If necessary, explain *take on board* (take notice of, learn).

With lower-level classes, students could read the article one paragraph at a time and identify the mistake.

ANSWERS:

1 wasting a lot of time chasing payments
2 trying to sell on price
3 not managing an agent
4 not taking an enquiry seriously

Reading for detail

3 Students work with a partner to find the answers. They should underline the relevant phrases in the article. Students could also pick out any examples that Daryl Vincenti gives to illustrate his points.

ANSWERS:

1 Use a credit agency to check out your customer's creditworthiness and to insure against non-payment.
2 Be flexible, learn to think outside the box.
3 Don't assume that what works well on your domestic market will automatically go down well in another.
4 Be prepared to modify product specifications to meet local conditions.
5 Focus on different aspects of the marketing mix.
6 Focus on one market, rather than trying to sell all over the world.
7 Put in a lot of time, get out there and meet your customers.
8 Remember that appearances can be deceptive.

Listening for detail

4 2:50 Read the questions with the whole class. Students work with a partner to note down the answers to the questions. Play the recording as many times as necessary. Note that the terms *open account* and *letters of credit* are explained in Exercise 5. Check answers with the whole class.

With lower-level classes, pause the recording after the answer to each question to give students more time to write.

ANSWERS:

1 Information and insurance.
2 There is information on over 50 million businesses worldwide, which allows N&H to provide information about financial performance, payment and possible problems.
3 They give a quick guide to how safely you can do business with a company or in a country.
4 70% of European firms, less than 5% of American firms.
5 Trading on open account with no need for letters of credit.
6 Between 0.25 and 1% of sales.

RECORDING SCRIPT

2:50

Interviewer: Mr Sullivan can you tell us first what exactly credit agencies do?
S: Well, basically, we offer a range of services in two main areas: information and insurance. Some of our clients are interested in information to help them manage credit risk, and others come to us for insurance. But many companies, like Eisenhart Games, need both information and insurance.
I: What sort of information can you provide?
S: We have details of over 50 million businesses in countries all over the world. So, for example, we can help Daryl by telling him how businesses and countries in the Middle-East are doing financially; we can tell him if his prospective customers pay, and how quickly they pay; and, in particular, we can warn him if one of his customers gets into financial difficulty.
I: And you give each company a rating which indicates how reliable they are?
S: Yes, companies – and also countries – are given a rating. This gives us a quick guide to how safely you can do business with a particular company or in a particular country. Actually,

there's much more than just the rating. Clients like Daryl receive detailed credit reports which help them decide if and how to work with different companies.

I: I see. Now, what about credit insurance? Is that something new?

S: Well, it's relatively new over here in the States, but not in Europe. European companies have been using it for a long time. Seventy per cent of European companies use credit insurance, whereas in the States the figure is below 5%.

I: Why is that?

S: Essentially because European firms have to export, because their internal markets are too small. Until now, the majority of American firms have done most of their business in America, so they didn't need credit insurance unless the customer was very risky. Nowadays, companies like Eisenhart need to export, so they're discovering the advantages of credit insurance. For example, it means that in Saudi Arabia, Daryl can trade on open account, with no need for letters of credit, which take a lot of time and are relatively expensive.

I: I see. Talking of expense, what does credit insurance cost?

S: Well, of course, it depends on the contract. The more risk the insurer takes on, the higher the premium will be. But, on average, I would say, for international credit insurance, between a quarter and 1% of sales.

Reading for detail

5 Give students a few minutes to put the methods of payment in order, then check answers with the whole class. Get students to give reasons for their answers, if they can.

ANSWERS:

4 Open account 1 Advance payment 3 Bills for collection
2 Letters of credit (L/Cs), also known as documentary credits (DCs)

Discussion

6 Students work with a partner. Check answers with the whole class. Students may have different answers, but should be able to give reasons for their choice.

SUGGESTED ANSWERS:

1 Open account	4 Bill for collection
2 Bill for collection	5 Open account
3 Advance payment	6 Letter of credit

7 Students work with a partner. Remind them of the discussion in Exercise 1 and the points raised in the article on page 101. Circulate and assist where necessary. Take whole-class feedback and make a list of problems and solutions on the board.

SUGGESTED ANSWERS:

Problems:
Different customer expectations, financing and producing to meet increased demand, transport, payment, currency exchange, pricing and margins, tax and VAT issues, managing agents / distributors, insurance.
Possible solutions:
Pricing – item might be too expensive for some markets and priced too low for others. Would need to check going rate of similar articles in individual markets and adjust pricing accordingly.
Transport – increased risk of damage to / loss of goods in transit – get insurance.
Problems with payment – could go for advance payment, etc.

8.2 Vocabulary
International deals and payments

This module practises verb–noun collocations, phrasal verbs and other vocabulary to do with payments.

Internet research

One definition of a 'thesaurus' is that it is a list of words showing similarities, differences, dependencies, and other relationships to each other. It will include synonyms (words with the same meaning), antonyms (words with opposite meanings) and collocations (combinations of words that are used together). With care, a thesaurus can be used to broaden one's vocabulary and provide variety in one's writing.

Students could do this research before they do this module or as a follow-up activity when they have finished.

Collocations

1 Students complete the first part of this exercise individually or with a partner. Allow them to use dictionaries, if they wish. Circulate while they are working and assist where necessary. Check answers with the whole class.

ANSWERS:

1 an invoice	2 goods	3 an application
4 conditions	5 a deal	6 a payment

Then, ask students to pick out any collocations that are new to them or that they are unsure of, and review their meaning and use.

Do the second part of the exercise with the whole class, making two lists on the board under the headings: <u>Buyer</u> and <u>Seller</u>.

SUGGESTED ANSWERS:

1 the seller issues / the buyer queries / settles an invoice
2 the seller provides / loads / ships the goods
3 the buyer submits / the seller vets / approves an application
4 the buyer states / the seller meets / complies with the conditions
5 the buyer and seller negotiate / make / sign a deal
6 the seller chases / the buyer makes / meets a payment

Phrasal verbs

2 and **3** Students work alone to do these exercises, then compare their answers with a partner. Check answers with the whole class by getting students to read the correct sentence aloud, followed by the definition.

ANSWERS:

Exercise 2
1 <u>Check up on</u> your new customer's creditworthiness.
2 <u>Take out</u> insurance if you have doubts about getting paid.
3 Do not let customers <u>get behind with</u> their payments.
4 <u>Chase up</u> invoices as soon as they become overdue.
5 Act quickly if your customer is <u>getting into</u> difficulties.
Exercise 3
a) 2 (take out)
b) 5 (getting into)
c) 1 (check up on)
d) 4 (chase up)
e) 3 (get behind with)

Listening

4 2:51–2:55 With higher-level classes, play the five conversations straight through and get students to make notes on their answers.

With lower-level classes, pause after each conversation to allow students to decide on their answers.

Check answers with the whole class. Accept any reasonable answers, as long as students include the correct target vocabulary.

SUGGESTED ANSWERS:

1. A Slovakian company has submitted an application for credit. Bruno asks his colleague to check up on them.
2. The company is going to check up on a shipment. They need to do this to comply with the conditions in the contract.
3. Francesca's boss asks her to chase up a payment from Kawasaki; she doesn't want them to get behind with their payments.
4. Mr Takahashi queries the invoice. He asks for more time to pay. The company seems to be getting into difficulties.
5. The companies talk about how the goods will be shipped. In the end, they reach a deal.

RECORDING SCRIPT

2:51–2:55

1

A: Bruno, have you seen this letter from those people in Slovakia?
B: No, what do they want?
A: Well, they say they're ready to place a large order now if they can pay next year.
B: Well, you'd better do some research on the company. Make sure they can pay! But be discrete. We don't want to upset them.

2

C: I'm still worried about sending these parts by sea. They're quite fragile, you know.
D: Well, don't worry. We're meeting the insurance people tomorrow. If anything goes wrong, we'll be covered.
C: But the insurance premium will be expensive, won't it?
D: Probably. But we have to do it anyway. It's one of the conditions in the contract. No insurance, no deal.

3

E: Francesca, have we received a payment from Kawasaki?
F: No. And I've already sent two reminders.
E: Two? Listen, could you give them a call? If we're not careful, they'll be late every month, and I don't want to have the same problems we had last year.

4

F: So, could you send the payment as soon as possible, Mr Takahashi?
G: Well, it's just that there seems to be a small problem with your invoice. It's more expensive than we expected.
F: I'm sorry, Mr Takahashi, but the invoice is for exactly the same amount as our quote, which you accepted.
G: Ah, yes. Well, exceptionally, as we are regular customers, could you perhaps wait two or three weeks? We just have a small cashflow problem at the moment. I'm sure you understand, Ms Trevi. It's nothing to worry about ...

5

H: Well, we'll accept your terms providing you deliver direct to our factory.
I: Hmm ... Our customers normally collect the goods from the port of entry.
H: But you said yourself these parts are fragile, so surely it would be better for the same forwarder to deliver all the way to the door? That way there's less risk of damage.
I: Well, you have a point there, I suppose.
H: And this will be a regular order, so it means a lot of business for the forwarder. I'm sure you can negotiate good terms with them.
I: Yes. Yes, you're right. OK, then. It's a deal.

Collocations

5 Do this as a whole-class activity, listing the collocations on the board. Make sure that you have listed the collocations needed for Exercise 6.

ANSWERS:

credit line, credit terms, credit period, credit sales, credit card, credit insurance, credit policy
insurance claim, insurance policy, insurance sales
customer credit, customer loyalty, customer portfolio

6 Students complete the sentences individually. Check answers by getting students to read the complete sentences aloud.

ANSWERS:

1. customer loyalty
2. credit policy
3. insurance policy
4. customer portfolio
5. credit insurance
6. insurance claim

Defining words

7 Student Student As' information is on the page so ask Student Bs to cover the crossword until they are ready to start.

To help students get started, do a few definitions with the whole class. Choose one of the terms in Exercise 1, e.g. *negotiate a deal*, and give students a simple definition, e.g. *this means that two people or companies discuss things until they reach an agreement*. Students have to guess the term. Continue with one or two more terms, e.g. *vet an application, ship goods*, and get students to suggest definitions.

Students could use a dictionary or thesaurus to help them with any new words or phrases. While students are completing the crossword, circulate and assist where necessary.

When they have finished, get students to practise using the expressions by forming sentences of their own which include them.

ANSWERS:

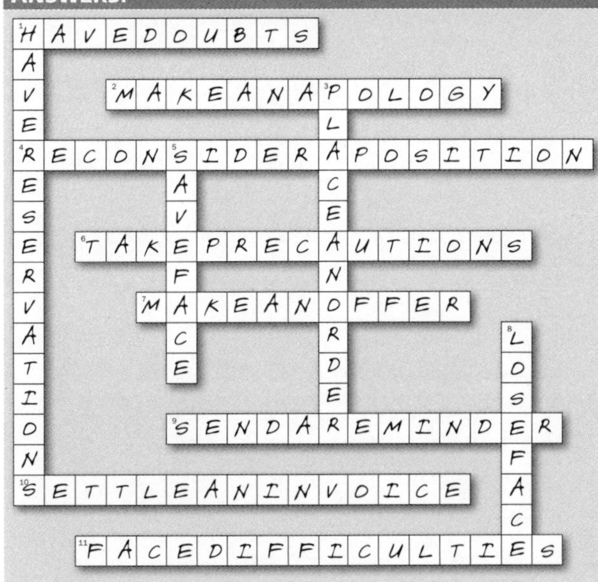

FURTHER PRACTICE

Get students to close their books. Using some of the key words in this module, write a list of scrambled words on the board and get students to unscramble them, e.g.:

oeiivnc	(invoice)
napmyet	(payment)
rditec	(credit)
rdirmnee	(reminder)
oontiaemcpsn	(compensation)
mlaci	(claim)
lyocip	(policy)
olptfroio	(portfolio)
poverpa	(approve)
uniacenrs	(insurance)

When they have unscrambled the letters, get students to suggest collocations for them.

8.3 Grammar

Prepositions

This module practises prepositions of time, verb + preposition and noun + preposition combinations in the context of international trade.

Internet research

A search for 'how to become a millionaire' will reveal several websites offering advice. The words that students choose will vary, but some possible answers might be: *take control of, decide on, make good use of, be certain of, willingness to, the best strategy for.*

Students could do this research before they do the speaking activity in Exercise 6 or after they have completed this module.

Prepositions of time

1 Start by reading the notes on prepositions in the *Refresh your memory* box with the class. Get students to make simple sentences using some of the phrases in the box.

Model the activity first by asking three or four questions across the class, and eliciting responses with prepositions. Once students have got the idea, divide them into pairs to ask and answer the questions. In feedback, elicit a few good examples of the use of prepositions from students and write them on the board.

If students seem unsure of the prepositions or would like further practice, work through some or all of Exercises 1–8 in the *Grammar and practice* section (page 136 of the *Student's Book*, answers on page 116 in this book).

POSSIBLE ANSWERS

1 at 9 / at 6
2 in the morning
3 in January
4 in the summer
5 at Christmas / at Easter / in January
6 in the summer
7 at 8 / at 1 / at 7 in the evening
8 in the evenings / at weekends / on Sunday
9 at the weekend / on Friday
10 on the 30th / on the last day of the month
11 some companies aren't that efficient
12 in the summer / in January

Dependent prepositions

2 Students work with a partner. They should refer back to the earlier exercises to remind them of some of the prepositions. Check answers with the whole class.

ANSWERS:

2 comply sympathize <u>resort</u> associate (with)
3 pay wait vote <u>object</u> (for)
4 depend rely insist <u>attend</u> (on)
5 result invest <u>borrow</u> succeed (in)
6 suffer emerge hear <u>account</u> (from)
7 <u>discuss</u> apply look apologize (for)
8 consist <u>react</u> approve think (of)
9 listen belong leave <u>relate</u> (to)
10 fight insure protect <u>ask</u> (against)

EXTENSION ACTIVITY

Divide the class into pairs and get each pair to draw two 3x3 grids, each one on a separate piece of paper like this:

In the squares of one grid they should write nine verbs, and in the other grid nine prepositions, selected from the exercises in this module.

Collect all the completed grids and put the verb grids in one pile and the preposition grids in another pile. Mix each pile up and distribute them around the class so that each pair receives one of each.

The pairs see how many combinations of verb + preposition are possible from the words on the grids and make a list on a separate piece of paper. They can use their dictionaries to check their answers, if necessary.

When students cannot think of any more combinations (or you could set a time limit), they should pass their grids to the pair on their left and repeat the procedure again with a new pair of grids. They continue in this way until they have found 20 correct combinations. (You can adjust this total according to the level of your students or the time available.) The game stops when the first pair reaches this total. Circulate while students are working and check their answers. Get the winning pair to read out their verb + preposition combinations.

Listening for gist

3 2:56–2:65 Play the ten short dialogues. Allow students to choose the correct words and add the prepositions individually, before checking answers with the whole class. Get students to pick out the words or phrases they heard which helped them arrive at the answer.

With lower-level classes, do this as a whole-class activity. Give students a few minutes to check the meanings of the words, using their dictionaries or referring back to earlier exercises. Play one conversation at a time and get students to choose the best word from the box, adding the correct preposition.

To consolidate understanding, students work with a partner to produce similar short conversations to show the meaning of these expressions.

ANSWERS:

1 investing in
2 apologizing for
3 damage to
4 aptitude for
5 dependence on
6 Complying with
7 insuring against
8 satisfaction with
9 hearing from
10 access to

RECORDING SCRIPT

2:56–2:65

1
A: It seems to me that with interest rates so low, property is still a better choice than the stock market.
B: Yes, you're right. I think a small flat in the town centre should give a good return.

2
C: I think you should talk to her. She's still upset.
D: OK, OK. I'll call her and tell her I'm sorry. I didn't mean what I said.

3
E: What state is it in after the accident?
F: Well, it could have been worse. Apart from a broken windscreen and headlights, there are only a few scratches on the paintwork. I was lucky.

4
G: It's amazing. She already speaks seven different languages, and she's picking up Chinese really fast!
H: Yeah, some people just have a gift, I guess.

5
I: You desperately need to get some more contracts. Relying on just one big firm is so dangerous.
J: Yes, I know. But we've always done most of our turnover with them.

6
K: The Americans are much more demanding. The Food and Drug Administration are terribly strict. But if you want to sell in the States, there's no other way.
L: Yes, there's no choice. We'll have to adapt the product to their norms.

7
M: What if we deliver the goods but they don't pay?
N: Well, we have a policy which covers that risk. For a small percentage of the value of the goods, we will guarantee to pay you if the customer defaults.

8
O: Well, sales are up 300%, we've reduced costs, our stock price has almost doubled and shareholders are delighted! Everything's worked out perfectly!
P: Yes. It doesn't get any better than this.

9
Q: Have you had any news from Taiwan?
R: No, not a word. It's strange. Usually they're in touch at least once a week.

10
S: Hey, Terry. Have you changed the passwords? I can't get into the database!
T: No, I'm having the same problem. I've tried everything but the system won't let me in.

Speaking

4 Divide the class into pairs or groups of four (to play 'doubles'). Student or Pair A say a verb and Student or Pair B returns as in the example. Get students to score their game as in tennis (15–0, 15–15, 15–30, etc). You could help students by giving them a list of verbs to use in their game. In a small class, you could make it an open class team game. Team A serves a word, Team B returns, etc.

Listening for detail

5 2:66 Get students to read the schedule and try to predict the prepositions. In most cases, there is more than one possibility. Play the recording. Pause at appropriate places to allow students time to note down their answers. Check answers by getting students to say the complete sentence aloud.

ANSWERS:

2 by 6.30
3 at 23.10
4 not until 9.15 / at 9.15
5 at 7.30 or later
6 by 7.45
7 until Saturday
8 between tomorrow morning and Friday
9 on Saturday evening
10 before flying back / on Saturday
11 within three weeks
12 during the flight

RECORDING SCRIPT

2:66

Paul: Oh, Jenny, did you pick up my tickets?

Jenny: No, I'm picking them up this evening. I have to be there before six, so I'll be able to drop them off here by 6.30.

P: That's great! What time's the flight?

J: It's at 23.10. But it's OK – check-in doesn't open until 21.15. You've got plenty of time.

P: Hmm ... I've got the finance committee tonight. That usually goes on until at least half seven. I'll only just have time to go home and pick up my suitcase. I probably won't see the kids for a week now. They'll be in bed by quarter to eight. When do I get back from the States again?

J: On Sunday morning. You've got six meetings between tomorrow morning and Friday. That leaves you a day to visit New York, and you fly back late on Saturday evening.

P: Well, I don't think I'll have much time to visit New York. I've got the Merosom pitch to prepare for next Monday. I'm going to be jet-lagged on Sunday, so I'll have to do it before flying back.

J: Oh, yes, that's right. When do you expect Merosom to announce their decision?

P: Well, they said within three weeks. By the way, have you got the files for the New York meetings?

J: Yes, they're all ready. Do want to look at them now?

P: No, I've got another meeting!

J: Well, you'll have to read them during the flight, then.

P: Hmm ... I suppose so.

J: OK. Well, I'll get on, then, unless you've got any other questions?

P: Er, yes, just one. When am I going to sleep?

Speaking

6 Read the instructions with the whole class, including the instructions at the back of the book to make sure that students understand what to do. Each group should then choose one of the topics to discuss, or you could allocate a topic to each group.

Circulate while students are speaking and assist where necessary. Make a note of any mistakes in the target language for remedial teaching later.

Higher-level classes or groups who finish early could repeat the activity using a different subject and/or by choosing different words to put on another six slips of paper.

8.4 Speaking
Negotiations – diplomacy

This module explores the intercultural aspects of negotiating style and practises ways of using language diplomatically in negotiations to achieve a successful outcome. On the Teacher's Resource Disc, you will find more related practice material, including a video (with worksheets) featuring an example situation for students to analyse and discuss.

Internet research

The anthropologist, Edward T. Hall, describes what are known as high- and low-context cultural factors. In a high-context culture, many contextual elements help people to understand the rules of society. In a high-context culture, meaning is not always put into words, and, for example, non-verbal clues will be as important. As a result, a lot of things are taken for granted. This can be confusing for people outside the culture who do not understand these 'unwritten rules'.

In a low-context culture, very little is taken for granted. Meaning is made explicit and put into words. This means that more explanation is needed, but there is also less chance of misunderstanding, particularly for people from outside the culture.

'Chronemics' is the term given to cultural attitudes towards time. In a monochronic culture, time is tightly controlled and measured. Punctuality is seen as a virtue and careful planning and scheduling are common. Monochronic cultures tend to be low context. In a polychronic culture, time is regarded more flexibly; meetings may not start on time and there is less concern for getting things done according to a schedule. Polychronic cultures tend to be high-context.

It would be best if students did this research before they start this module as it provides useful input for Exercises 1–4.

Discussion

1 Read the information in the box with the whole class. If students have limited experience of these countries or regions, do this exercise with the whole class, encouraging them to share experiences they have from business trips, holidays, reading, etc.

Get students to describe the kind of culture they live in, according to the descriptions in the box and the information they found in their Internet research.

SUGGESTED ANSWERS:

China H, USA L, Australia L, N Europe L, Middle East H, Latin America H, UK L, Japan H

The following scale is suggested in GLOBALWORK: Bridging Distance, Culture, And Time by Mary O'Hara-Devereaux and Robert Johansen

High-context cultures ↑

Japanese
Chinese
Arab
Greek
Mexican
Spanish
Italian
French
French Canadian
English
English Canadian
American
Scandinavian
German
German-Swiss

↓ Low-context cultures

Listening for gist

2 2:67–2:69 Play each extract one by one, getting students to note down what went wrong in each case. Check answers by getting students to give you at least one cultural factor and one example of a phrase which might have caused difficulties. Higher-level classes could also be asked to say how the individuals might have felt at the end of the conversation.

ANSWERS:

1 They fail to understand each other's different cultures regarding time and decision-making. The American is not sensitive to high-context communication style in Japan.
2 Frau Meier does not understand that Amal does not share her concern for deadlines and her all-or-nothing view of the project.
3 Misunderstandings lead to conflict.

RECORDING SCRIPT

2:67–2:69

1

A: I'm afraid I think we might need more time to explore all the implications and perhaps include some of our senior management in the discussions.
B: Mr Yamada, I've already been in Japan a week, and I have a plane to catch this evening! If you don't want to do this deal, just say so! I mean, when I get back, I have to tell my boss we have a contract, or explain why I failed to get one!

2

C: We feel that there are still quite a large number of difficulties to face in this project, and these will take a very considerable amount of time and money to resolve.
D: OK, Amal, let's sit down and work out a schedule.
C: I am not sure that at this stage a schedule is appropriate, in view of the considerable cultural differences between our companies.
D: Well, we need to start work soon if we want to meet the deadlines.
C: Frau Meier, perhaps we should talk again in a few days, by telephone?
D: Are you saying you're quitting the project?!
C: If you insist on putting it in those terms, then, yes, I think probably that is best.

3

E: And you pay the shipping costs.
F: No, as I told you, our prices are ex works. You pay for shipping.
E: So you don't want to sell us your machine tools?
F: No, why do you say that? I never said that!
E: Your terms with Auckland Industries last year included shipping, I believe.
F: Yes, but that was a much larger contract.
E: So our order isn't very important for you.

3 2:70–2:72 Play the recordings and get students to listen for the ways in which the negotiators changed their language and approach in order to avoid misunderstandings, e.g. they use less direct language and a less confrontational approach.

ANSWERS:

This time they check and correct misunderstandings and reformulate their positions; in this way they are able to defuse potential conflict.

RECORDING SCRIPT

2:70–2:72

1

A: I'm afraid I think we might need more time to explore all the implications, and perhaps to include some of our senior management in the discussions.
B: Uh-huh. Yamada-san, correct me if I'm wrong, but you seem to be saying that you're not completely convinced by this deal.
A: I'm afraid there seems to be a slight misunderstanding, Mr Bryson. Let me put it another way. We are as enthusiastic about this deal as ever, but here in Japan, it is very important to take the time to consult everybody, and to be sure there is a consensus.
B: Ah, yes, I understand. It's important for me to keep my Board informed too.

2

C: I'm afraid we feel there are still quite a large number of difficulties to face in this project, and these will take a very considerable amount of time and money to resolve.
D: OK, Amal, have I got this right? You're saying that you're not sure we have the time or the money to make this project a success?
C: That's right. Especially in view of the considerable, er, cultural differences between our companies.
D: So, would I be right in saying that you are considering withdrawing from the project?
C: No, I'm sorry, Sabine, that isn't quite what I meant. What I was trying to say was, we need to take our different approaches to these problems into account, but I'm sure we can find solutions.
D: Yes, I'm sure we can. Perhaps we should talk again in a few days, by telephone?
C: Yes, that would be fine.

3

E: And if I've understood correctly, you will pay the shipping costs.
F: I'm sorry, perhaps I haven't made myself clear. The price we quoted was ex works. But we can quote including shipping if you like.
E: But didn't you say you would give us the same terms as for Auckland Industries last year?
F: Ah, I see, yes. Well, allow me to rephrase that. What I meant was, we would be very happy to give you the same terms as Auckland, if you were in a position to order the same volume.

4 2:70–2:72 Play the recordings again, pausing if necessary to allow students time to complete the phrases. Check answers with the whole class. Get students to repeat the phrases, using the appropriate pronunciation, stress and intonation.

ANSWERS:

Checking understanding
Correct me if I'm wrong, but you seem to be saying that …
Have I got this right?
Would I be right in saying that …?
If I've understood correctly …
Correcting misunderstandings
I'm afraid there seems to be a slight misunderstanding.
I'm sorry, that isn't quite what I meant.
Perhaps I haven't made myself clear.
Reformulating
Let me put it another way.
What I was trying to say was …
Allow me to rephrase that.
What I meant was …

Diplomatic language

5 Do this as a whole-class activity. Get one student to say the direct statement and another to say the matching diplomatic statement. Make sure students use appropriate stress and intonation in the diplomatic statements.
Play 2:70–2:72 again so that students can hear the diplomatic statements in context.

ANSWERS:

1 b) 2 d) 3 a) 4 c)

6 Do this as a whole-class activity. Get students to review the phrases in Exercises 4 and 5 to help them complete the summary.

As preparation for Exercise 7, get students to identify the characteristics of the direct language, e.g. short sentences, absence of qualifiers or softeners, unambiguous messages.

ANSWERS:

Diplomatic language often uses:
modal verbs like *could, would, might, should.*
softening adverbs like *maybe* or *perhaps.*
qualifiers like *a bit, rather, a little* or *quite.*
introductory warnings like, *I'm sorry, actually, I'm afraid.*
(negative) questions rather than statements.

7 Students work with a partner. Remind students to use the features of direct and diplomatic language they have practised. Circulate and assist where necessary. Check answers by getting students to read out the statements they have written, using appropriate stress and intonation. Accept any reasonable answers.

SUGGESTED ANSWERS:

1 I don't want to risk going to Columbia for a meeting.
2 Perhaps you feel that it's a little too soon to formalize our relationship, if not everybody is convinced?
3 You must be able to make a better offer than that.
4 Do you perhaps have some reservations about doing business with my company?
5 If you people can get out of bed earlier we'll actually get some work done!
6 I'm afraid I don't remember actually using those words.
7 Look, I know lots of people think business trips are essential, but mostly they're a waste of time.
8 You wouldn't have doubts about our ability to pay our debts, would you?

Negotiating

8 With lower-level classes, read the instructions with the whole class and elicit from them the kinds of things they might want to negotiate about. You could also remind students of the work they did in Unit 5 on bargaining in negotiations and the value of trying to reach a win-win conclusion.

While students are speaking, circulate and assist where necessary. Check that they are using the target language appropriately.

Allow students time to prepare and practise their conversation. Then take whole-class feedback. Ask what students agreed to do. Get one or more confident pairs to present their conversation to the rest of the class.

Alternatively, with higher-level classes, get one or two pairs to do their negotiating in real time, i.e. without preparing it beforehand. The rest of the class listens and comments on the performance and the outcome, giving two things that worked successfully and two things that could be improved.

8.5 Writing

Requests and reminders

This module explores formal and informal language use in the context of correspondence to do with payments.

Internet research

A search for 'factoring receivables' will reveal that this is one way companies can improve their cash flow. For a fee, a factor provides a business with an advance payment based on their accounts receivable and invoices. The factor then waits to collect payment on the invoice and accepts any risks attached to it. This allows the company to get the cash flow and working capital it needs, without having to wait. Many businesses use factoring, among other things, to generate instant working capital; to help them predict and manage cash flow; and to increase sales by offering customers competitive extended credit terms.

Students could do this research as a follow-up to the work done in this module.

Discussion

1 Encourage students to give reasons for their answers, and to add any stories or anecdotes of their own to illustrate their answers. Take feedback from the whole class.

Model

2 Read the instructions with the whole class. If necessary, explain or elicit the meanings of the four terms.

Students do the exercise with a partner. Check answers by getting students to give you the number of the email and the phrases that helped them decide.

ANSWERS:

a request [4] a reminder [1] a refusal [2] a final demand [3]

Analysis

3 Students work with a partner. They can use their dictionaries to check any unknown words. Check answers with the whole class by getting students to read the sentences aloud and to tell you in what kind of correspondence it would be found.

To check that students have fully understood these formal sentences, get them to rephrase them in a less formal style, e.g. (1) *Could you extend credit terms of 60 days?*, etc.

ANSWERS:

1 I am writing to enquire whether you would be able to extend credit terms of 60 days.
2 I am afraid group policy does not allow us to give more than 30 days' credit.
3 We are pleased to agree to the terms you propose.
4 May I remind you that the sum of €21,552 is still outstanding?
5 We wrote to you on November 4 regarding the balance of €12,650 which is still outstanding.
6 Would you let us know your decision as soon as possible?
7 We would appreciate your early settlement of this outstanding balance.
8 We shall have no alternative but to pass the matter on to our legal department.

a request [1], [6] a reminder [4], [7] a refusal [2]
an agreement [3] a final demand [5], [8]

Language focus

4 Do this exercise with the whole class. Get students to read out the more formal phrase or sentence.

ANSWERS:

1 a) 2 b) 3 b) 4 a)
5 b) 6 a) 7 a) 8 a)

5 Students work with a partner to complete these emails. Remind students to check that they have the correct spelling of the words they use. Circulate while students are working and assist where necessary. Check answers by getting students to read the complete emails aloud.

ANSWERS:

1
In view of the increase in our volume of business, I am writing to enquire whether you would be prepared to extend credit terms of 60 days. Would you let us know your decision as soon as possible?
2
With regard to your request for improved credit terms, I am afraid that group policy does not allow us to extend more than 30 days credit.
3
Further to your email of 17 July, we are pleased to agree to the terms you propose, and we look forward to receiving your order.
4
May I remind you that the sum of €101,000 is still outstanding on your account. We would appreciate your early settlement of this outstanding balance.
5
We would like to apologize for the delay in sending the enclosed cheque. This was an unfortunate oversight due to circumstances beyond our control, and we can assure you that it will not recur.
6
We wrote to you on 11 April regarding the balance of €15,550 which is still outstanding. Unless we receive payment within seven days, we shall have no alternative but to pass the matter on to our legal department.

a request [1] a reminder [4] a refusal [2]
a final demand [6] an apology [5] an agreement [3]

FURTHER PRACTICE

Get students to rephrase the emails in Exercise 5 in a less formal, but still polite way.

Writing

6 Give students a few minutes to read the instructions so that they can see the context for the correspondence they will write. Then get each student to read part 1 of their instructions.

While students are writing the first email, circulate and assist where necessary. Remind students to check what they have written for the best choice of vocabulary and formality of language before they deliver their correspondence. They should refer back to the exercises in this module if they need help.

With higher-level classes you could set a time limit for each phase of the correspondence. When students have finished, get them to group each set of correspondence, i.e. three sets of four pieces of writing, and review them. Did they use and maintain an appropriate level of formality? Were there any grammatical errors? Are there any parts they could improve?

EXTENSION ACTIVITY

This activity practises some useful money idioms. Write the idioms and their explanations on the board in random order and get students to match them. The idioms and the explanations are given below:

Idiom	Explanation
loaded	*have a lot of money*
hard up	*don't have much money*
nest egg	*money that someone has saved*
on a shoestring	*with very little money to spend*
pay through the nose	*pay a high price for something*
tighten your belt	*live on less money than usual*
ready cash	*money that is available to spend*
spend money like water	*spend too much*

Once students have correctly matched the idioms and explanations, they can be used in various ways, e.g.:

- One student says the idiom, another says the matching explanation.
- One student gives the explanation, another says the matching idiom.
- Students work with a partner or small groups to make short dialogues which include the idiom.
- Students pick an idiom and describe a situation which illustrates it.

Ask students if similar money idioms exist in their own language; get them to translate them into English and explain them.

8.6 Case study
Jeddah Royal Beach Resort

This case study explores issues to do with credit and cash flow at an international resort hotel. Students practise writing letters to customers about credit facilities.

Internet research

An Internet search for 'collecting debt' will provide information on how to recover debts, including how to act within the law to contact a debtor; what to do if a debtor disputes the debt or refuses to pay; how to go about taking legal action. Students will also find websites for debt collection agencies who, for a fee, will undertake to recover debts on behalf of clients from debtors all over the world and who will provide legal advice if the client needs to pursue a debt through the courts.

Students could do this research before they start this module or after they have finished it, as a follow-up task.

Discussion

1 Do this as a whole-class activity. Make a list of the ideas on the board or get a student to do it.

SUGGESTED ANSWERS:

telephone and fax, restaurant and bar bills, leisure activities, limousines, airline tickets, cash advances, etc.

Reading for detail

2 Students read the article silently and answer the questions, then compare their answers with a partner. Check answers with the whole class. You could also ask students to consider the disadvantages of an in-house credit card for customers (e.g. it encourages them to spend more than they can afford; they lose track of how much they have spent; they don't pay attention to how much things cost).

ANSWERS:

1 Giving credit develops customer loyalty and makes it easier for customers to spend freely on the hotel's additional services.
2 to develop customer loyalty to their hotel or group and to avoid paying commission to credit card companies
3 It's easier to make bookings, it speeds up check-in and check-out, there are no exchange problems, no need to carry cash.
4 Credit Manager of the Jeddah Royal Beach Resort: his responsibilities include vetting applications, credit control and debt recovery.

Listening for detail

3 2:73 Read the instructions aloud. Get students to look at the database records and predict what the conversation is going to be about.

Play the recording through once so that students can complete the database entries. Check answers by getting students to form sentences, e.g. *Ms Koepple works for Cool Breeze, a record company. Her company credit rating is unknown. She doesn't have a current credit limit,* etc.

ANSWERS:

Customer: Ms Koepple
Company: Cool Breeze, record company
Company credit rating: good I average I poor I <u>unknown</u>
Current credit limit: 0
Credit limit requested: $20,000
Notes: very friendly, wants to organize a big conference for executives

Customer: Mr Kobayashi
Company: Kobayashi Auto Sales
Company credit rating: <u>good</u> / average / poor / unknown
Current credit limit: $50,000
Credit limit requested: $100,000
Notes: difficult, unpleasant, Frederick doesn't trust him

Customer: Mrs Saman
Company: Black Nile
Company credit rating: good / average / <u>poor</u> / unknown
Current credit limit: $30,000
Credit limit requested: $100,000
Notes: charming old lady, very influential

RECORDING SCRIPT

2:73

Frederick: Good evening, Riaz!
Riaz: Oh, hello Frederick. Everything OK?
F: Yes, fine, thanks. I just wanted to give you these applications, if you've got a moment?
R: Yes, of course. Have a seat.
F: Thanks.
R: OK, so what have we got here?
F: Well, first of all, there's Ms Koepple in room 406. She's with Cool Breeze. It's a record label based in Buenos Aires. Now, I know you don't like record companies, but ...
R: Yes, Frederick, and you know very well why I don't like record companies and those vulgar rock groups they send us, always causing damage and disturbing the other guests. Argentina, you say?
F: Yes. But Ms Koepple says they want to organize a big conference for their executives. There won't be any rock groups or that kind of thing, just corporate executives. So, they're applying for our credit card.
R: Well, it's true we need to develop in the conference market. It's good business, and it often brings in more business by word of mouth. But Argentina ... OK, leave it with me and I'll look into it. How big is Ms Koepple's bill?
F: Well, she's been here for four nights. Leaving on Saturday. She's spending a lot of money – maybe six thousand dollars so far. But she's very nice, very friendly. I'm sure she won't leave without paying.
R: Hmm ... She's applying for a credit limit of twenty thousand. Let's keep an eye on her, anyway. Let me know if her account goes over ten thousand dollars, OK?
F: Sure.
R: What else have you got there?
F: The next one is Mr Kobayashi from Tokyo. Remember him?
R: Oh, yes. The second-hand car salesman?
F: Yes. He's a really difficult customer. We've had to move him to a different room three times this week because he didn't like the view, or it was too far from the restaurant ...
R: Well, he may be difficult, but his credit's good. He seems to have built himself quite an empire over there. Kobayashi Auto Sales is doing very well. We've never had any problem with his people.
F: Well, I wouldn't buy a car from him. He never looks you in the eye, never smiles, never says thank you. He wants us to raise his credit limit, but I don't trust him.
R: Let me see. From fifty up to a hundred thousand, eh? All right, I'll think about it.
F: Right. And this last one is our old friend Mrs Saman and her team from Egypt.

R: Oh, no. Are they still coming here? I thought we stopped their credit last year.
F: No, the company paid up in the end, remember?
R: Yes, I do now. Charming lady, of course, but that company – what's it called? Black Nile, that's it. They invented the concept of the slow payer! I think it took 18 months to get them to pay their last invoice. What does she want now?
F: Well, she wants us to raise their credit limit to a hundred thousand, too.
R: Oh, no way!
F: But there are ten of them this time, and she's such a wonderful little old lady!
R: I should really suspend their credit and insist on cash in advance. They're on, let's see ... thirty thousand dollars. It's just too big a risk. Have you seen the latest cash-flow figures? Our customers are taking longer and longer to pay, and uncollectibles have gone over 3%! I'm getting a lot of pressure from management to take firm action.
F: Well, be careful: Mrs Saman told me yesterday that her brother is a very senior government official. And remember, we have a lot of guests from Egypt now. We don't want to upset them.
R: Yes, that's true. You never know who Mrs Saman might talk to. She's a very influential old lady. All right, leave it with me, Frederick. I'll let you know what I decide tomorrow.

4 Read the questions aloud. Students try to answer them, on the basis of what they remember from the first listening. Play **2:73** again. Pause if necessary to allow students to note down their answers. Check answers with the whole class.

SUGGESTED ANSWERS:

1 Because they are vulgar, cause damage and disturb other guests.
2 about $6,000
3 $10,000
4 Because he has changed rooms three times.
5 He never looks you in the eye, never smiles, never says thank you.
6 The hotel almost stopped their credit because they took 18 months to pay.
7 Mrs Saman's brother is a senior government official; they are both influential in a country which is an important market for the hotel.

Discussion

5 Do this as a whole-class activity. You could remind students of the work they did in Unit 7, and encourage them to use some of the vocabulary they practised there, e.g. *fall, drop, jump, rise,* etc.

With lower-level classes you may need to remind students of adverbs which can be used to describe the nature of the change, e.g. *rapidly, slightly, significantly, sharply*. These were practised in Unit 7.

ANSWERS:

1 decreasing rapidly
2 increasing slightly
3 increasing significantly
4 increasing sharply

6 Give students a few minutes to discuss the three questions. In question 3, review the situation for each of the three customers by looking at the database entries in Exercise 3. Students should also take into account the circumstances surrounding each customer and the likelihood of further business mentioned in the conversation.

Students could listen to the conversation again or read it in the recording script on page 151 in their books. Circulate and assist where necessary. Take whole-class feedback.

SUGGESTED ANSWERS:

1 Cash payments are decreasing; this is probably the price of the hotel's policy of offering credit cards to encourage customer loyalty.
Credits of less than 4 weeks are only increasing slightly; almost 40% of customers pay within 30 days of reception of their invoices.
Longer credits are increasing significantly, perhaps because a number of (larger?) customers are taking advantage of a competitive market to exploit the hotel's credit policy and pay more and more slowly. The increase in uncollectibles suggests some poor decisions have been made in allowing credit to unreliable customers.

2 The hotel could improve its cash flow by:
- reducing credit to existing customers.
- avoiding giving credit to new customers.
- vetting customers more carefully before giving credit.
- paying suppliers more slowly.
- invoicing more quickly.
- giving discounts for cash payments.
- using a debt collection agency.
- factoring (selling invoices to a factor or agent in return for cash – the factor collects payment for the invoices and accepts any credit risk attached to them).

Writing

7 Remind students of the language they practised in module 8.5, i.e. the level of formality required in this kind of correspondence; the useful phrases in Exercises 3 and 4 that they could reuse.

Students write a first draft, which they exchange with another student for feedback. When they are reading each other's drafts, students should check for grammar, spelling, appropriate use of language, and a clear message. Circulate while students are writing and assist where necessary.

Students then revise their texts using the feedback. Display the finished texts on a table or on the wall so that students can read them all. If you wish, get them to choose the best two or three letters and give reasons for their choice.

Review 7 and 8 Answer key

Review 7

(page 112 in the *Student's Book*)

Mergers and acquisitions

1

1 due diligence
2 liabilities
3 merger
4 acquisition
5 variable costs
6 fixed costs
7 assets
8 liquidity
9 economies of scale
10 turnover

2

1 variable costs
2 fixed costs
3 liquidity
4 liabilities
5 turnover

3

1 climb
2 dip
3 fluctuate
4 stabilize
5 deteriorate
6 slide
7 rise
8 soar
9 jump
10 peak

4

1 considerable
2 dramatic
3 moderate
4 sharp
5 significant
6 slight
7 sudden

5

1 because of
2 due to
3 thanks to
4 as a result of

6

1 we're going to enter
2 you'll have
3 I'm meeting
4 I'll turn

7

1 let's move on
2 next slide shows
3 notice from the chart
4 seem to suggest
5 as a result of
6 resulted in
7 However
8 whereas

Review 8

(page 113 in the *Student's Book*)

International trade

1

1 d) Don't sell on price rather than quality.
2 a) Be proactive with local distributors.
3 b) Make a firm commitment to export.
4 c) Think outside the box.
5 g) Trade on open account.
6 e) Sign an exclusive deal.
7 h) Be prepared to modify product specifications.
8 f) Invest time, effort and money.
9 j) Ask a credit agency about a customer's creditworthiness.
10 i) Chasing payments can be done by the credit agency.
11 l) Focus on one market, rather than trying to sell all over the world.
12 k) Don't assume that what works in your domestic market will also work abroad.

2

1 creditworthiness
2 chasing

3

1 reach
2 assume
3 chase
4 state
5 check in
6 move behind with

4

1 reach
2 ship
3 issue
4 comply with
5 chase
6 get behind with
7 check up on

5

1 During
2 In
3 from
4 until
5 within
6 at

6

1 Let me put it another way.
2 Correct me if I'm wrong, but you seem to be saying that you are not convinced.
3 I'm afraid there seems to be a slight misunderstanding.
4 Perhaps I haven't made myself clear.
5 Would I be right in saying that you want to withdraw from the project?

7

1 I think we might need more time.
2 I'm afraid there are still quite a large number of difficulties.
3 Perhaps we should renegotiate one or two parts of the contract.
4 Won't that be rather expensive?

8

1 According to
2 now overdue
3 early settlement
4 outstanding balance
5 Further to
6 regret to inform
7 have no alternative
8 pass this matter

9

1 overdue
2 outstanding

10

outstanding

Grammar and practice Answer key

1 Corporate culture

(pages 122 and 123 in the *Student's Book*)

1

past simple: said, happened, recognized, was, had, saw, didn't mention
past continuous: was doing, was working, was filling in, was entering
past perfect: had asked, had given, had applied for, hadn't found out

2

You use the past perfect to show that one event happened before another.
You use the past continuous to describe an activity in progress that gives the background to the main events.
You use the past simple to describe the main events of the story.

3

1 was revising, called
2 didn't hear, was reading
3 saw, was talking
4 was working, met

4

3 (we only know by the context)

5

1 got, had already worked
2 had just finished, called
3 was, hadn't seen
4 hadn't met, listened

6

1 finished / had finished
2 had already started
3 was / had been
4 had bought

7

1 b) 2 c) 3 a)

8

2 (return to a previous subject)

9

actually = in fact
after that = the next thing that happened was
apparently = it seems that
eventually = in the end
obviously = of course

10

1 was working
2 had just left
3 was serving
4 hadn't arrived
5 came
6 asked for
7 wanted
8 took
9 was sitting
10 placed
11 had never been
12 saw
13 was
14 had become

11

1 from *One day* to *naive*
2 from *Anyway* to *my life*
3 from *Of course* to *them all*
4 from *But, even today* to *that day*

13

1 You should ~~to~~ do it today.
2 You ought to do it today.
3 He should~~s~~ do it today.
4 ~~Do I should~~ Should I do it today?

14

1 You should speak to your supervisor.
2 You must speak to your supervisor.

15

1 apply
2 applying
3 to apply
4 apply

16

1 That sounds like a good idea.
2 That might be worth trying.
3 I'm not sure about that because …
4 No, that's not a good idea.

2 Customer support

(pages 124 and 125 in the *Student's Book*)

1

Present simple
Do you work there?
Does she work there?

Present continuous
Are you working there now?
Is he working there now?

Past simple
Did you work there before?
Did she work there before?

Past continuous
Were you working there then?
Was he working there then?

Present perfect
Have you ever worked there?
Has she ever worked there?

Past perfect
Had you already worked there?
Had she already worked there?

Modals
Would you work here next year?

Rule:
You form *yes/no* questions using:
auxiliary verb + subject + main verb

2

1 Did you buy
2 Do you have
3 Have you tried
4 Are you sitting
5 Will you reinstall

3

1 Yes, I do.
2 Yes, I am.
3 No, I didn't.
4 No, I haven't.

4

1 How much does
2 Why are
3 how far will
4 How do
5 what will

5

1 What
2 Which
3 Which
4 What

6

1 d)
2 c)
3 b)
4 a)

7

1 Who did you meet
2 Who met you
3 Who spoke
4 What did he speak

8

1 I wonder if I could possibly leave a few minutes early today?
2 a) grateful
b) appreciate

9

1 b)
2 a)
3 d)
4 c)

10

1 of course
2 certainly
3 sure

11

1 c)
2 a)
3 b)

12

Actually / To be honest

13

1 b) 2 e) 3 c) 4 d) 5 a)

14

1 You mustn't do it.
2 You have to do it.
3 You don't have to do it.

15

1 don't have to
2 mustn't
3 have to
4 mustn't
5 don't have to
6 have to

3 Products and packaging

(pages 126 and 127 in the *Student's Book*)

1

1 an, a, a
2 the, the, the
3 –, –, –

2

1 a
2 the
3 no article

3

1 a, the
2 the, a
3 the, an
4 a, the

4

1 –, the
2 The, –
3 –, the
4 –, the

5

1 FedEx® is an international company that / which operates in the transportation business.
2 Charlie Wang is a dynamic man who / that runs the New China Packaging Company.

6

Here is the package we designed last week.

7

You can leave out *who*, *which* or *that* in a defining relative clause if they are followed immediately by a pronoun or noun.
You must keep *who*, *which* or *that* if they are followed immediately by a verb.

8

1 These are the views of the consultants whose report was used by the government.
2 Look at this article about that German manufacturing company whose production was outsourced to Slovakia.

9

2 ✓
4 ✓

10

A non-defining relative clause simply adds extra information.
In a non-defining relative clause you use commas around the clause.
In a non-defining relative clause you cannot leave out who or which.
In a non-defining relative clause you cannot use *that*.

11

2 task force, focus group
3 sales forecast, hearing aid
4 market leader, stock control
5 price range, customer feedback

12

1 product design team
2 action film hero
3 staff development strategy
4 computer software engineer
5 customer feedback program
6 bridge construction project

13

2 a nice-looking action film hero
3 a long-term staff development strategy
4 a self-employed computer software engineer
5 a web-based customer feedback program
6 an over-budget bridge construction project

4 Careers

(pages 128 and 129 in the *Student's Book*)

1

1 d)
2 c)
3 b)
4 a)

2

1 A: Do you work on Saturdays?
B: No, luckily I don't work on Saturdays.
2 C: Are you going for an interview today?
D: No, I'm not going today – the interview is tomorrow.

3

1 comes, is coming
2 have, am having

4

1 am doing
2 have
3 check
4 is staying
5 am waiting
6 do

5

1 The soup tastes delicious!
2 The soup is boiling. ✓
3 Sorry, I'm not following you. ✓
4 Sorry, I don't understand you.
5 What are you saying? ✓
6 What do you mean?
7 This book belongs to me.
8 This book is selling for €15 on Amazon. ✓
9 Please don't interrupt me – I'm doing a grammar exercise. ✓
10 This grammar exercise is easy – I know all of the answers.

6

1 c)
2 b)
3 a)

7

- The present perfect has several uses, but it shows that the speaker is looking back from the present to the past.
- The present continuous has several uses, but it shows that a present action or situation is temporary.
- The present simple has several uses, but it shows that a present action or situation is permanent.

8

1 since
2 for
3 during
4 for
5 many years ago

9

- for: used with periods of time; used with the past simple and present perfect; answers the question 'how long?'.
- during: used with periods of time; used with the past simple; answers the question 'when?'.
- since: identifies the point an event began; used with the present perfect.
- ago: used to say how far back in the past something happened; used with the past simple.

10

1 just
2 already
3 yet
4 ever
5 never

11

1✗ 2✓ 3✓ 4✗ 5✓
6✗ 7✓ 8✗

- When you talk about people's experiences up to now, you use the present perfect or present perfect continuous.
- When you focus on the action itself, not the result, you use the present perfect continuous.
- When you focus on the result, not the action, you use the present perfect.
- When you say 'how many' you use the present perfect.

12

1 have been sending off • haven't had
2 have sent off • have been applying
3 has just received • has failed

13

1 went up
2 have gone up
3 go up
4 have worked
5 worked
6 work

14

1 want
2 applied
3 have been waiting
4 have decided
5 am sleeping

5 Making deals

(pages 130 and 131 in the *Student's Book*)

1

1 b)
2 c)
3 a)
4 a)

2

1 Sentence a) is called the zero conditional and the time reference is general.
2 Sentence b) is called the first conditional and the time reference is future.
3 Sentence c) is called the second conditional and the time reference is future.

3

1 If we continue talking, I'm sure we'll find a compromise.
2 If I agree to that price, can you sign today?

4

1 b)
2 c)
3 a)

5

The first conditional refers to a likely event in the future. In the *if* clause you use any present tense (simple, continuous or perfect) and in the main clause you use *will* or other modals or the imperative.

6

1 I'll
2 we might be able to
3 I should be able to

7

When the *if* clause comes at the end, you leave out the comma in writing.

8

1 S
2 D
a) uncertainty
b) certainty

9

1 Unless
2 If
3 If
4 Unless

10

1 Unless we leave now, …
2 Unless he agrees to our terms, …

11

1 a)
2 d)
3 c)
4 b)

12

1 If I was the boss of this company, I would improve communications by having regular meetings.
2 If we paid a 50% deposit now, would you reduce the price to €25,000?

13

The expressions *providing, provided, as long as* and so long as all mean if and only if. They emphasize the condition. They have a second conditional form, so they are followed by a verb in the past simple.

14

1 I suggest we ~~to~~ buy the cheaper model.
2 I recommend ~~it~~ that we have a short break.
3 I advise ~~that~~ you to look again at the figures.
4 What do you suggest ~~me~~?
5 I recommend ~~you~~ not parking here.

6 Company and community

(pages 132 and 133 in the *Student's Book*)

1

1 a)
2 b)
3 b)
4 A lot of illegal immigrants were employed last year.

2

1 b)
2 a)
3 d)
4 c)

3

Ending 1 makes a better link.

4

1 Car parts are made here.
2 The river is being polluted.
3 The law was obeyed.
4 I have been offered the job.
5 Fake goods were being sold.
6 This policy can be changed.
7 We might be fined.
8 This will be decided later.

5

1 The environment has been put at the centre of our future planning.
2 The idea of corporate social responsibility was introduced by Johnson & Johnson.
3 The elevator is serviced every week.
4 The elevator was serviced last week by that guy with the crazy look in his eyes.
5 A hundred new employees are being hired this month.
6 My flight was delayed.
7 My flight was delayed by a major security alert involving 80 Chechnian terrorists.
8 The environment must be protected.

6

A terrible gas leak occurred in Bhopal in 1984 – it seems that the disaster was caused by an act of sabotage.

7

1 e)
2 b)
3 c) and d)
4 a)
5 g)
6 f)
7 h)

8

1 ✓
2 ✓
3 ✓
4 ✓

9

She said that they'd give me their answer today.

10

1 She said that she would do that.
2 She told me that she would do that.
3 She said to me that she would do that.
4 She asked me what I would do.
5 She asked me if I would do that.
6 She asked me what I was doing.
7 She asked me when I would arrive.

11

2 She announced that they were stopping all production.
3 He reassured me that they had fitted new filters.
4 She replied that they could do absolutely nothing.

7 Mergers and acquisitions

(pages 134 and 135 in the *Student's Book*)

1

1 b) 2 a) 3 e) 4 c) 5 d)

2

'Good morning, ladies and gentlemen. I've called this press conference because of the rumours circulating in the media about our M&A strategy. Over the next few years our bank will become a major player in Central Europe, and naturally we will look at strong local banks as possible targets for acquisition. But we won't make any decisions until we have studied the market carefully. There has been much comment about possible job cuts, but I want to reassure you that the staff of a bank are amongst its most valuable assets. When we do make a move, there won't be significant job losses at the bank we acquire. In any case, we will deal with this issue at the time, and I have no further comment to add now.'

3

1 There will probably be significant job losses.
2 There probably won't be significant job losses.

4

1 b)
2 e)
3 a)
4 c)
5 d)

5

1 d)
2 b)
3 e)
4 a)
5 c)

6

1 prediction
2 plan
3 prediction
4 plan
5 prediction
6 plan

7

1 Citibank are going to make a bid for Tatra Banka.
2 We're not going to have enough time.

8

am flying, are coming, are giving

9

1 are going to make
2 will probably start
3 I'll come back
4 we're going to go

10

1 it will definitely
2 it's almost certain to
3 it's likely to
4 it might
5 it might just
6 there's not much chance it will
7 there's no way it will

11

1 There's a good chance the merger will go ahead.
2 The merger will definitely go ahead.
3 The merger definitely won't go ahead.
4 The merger might just go ahead.
5 The merger is almost certain to go ahead.
6 It's highly likely the merger will go ahead.
7 We fully expect the merger to go ahead.

12

1 T
2 F (*could not* means 'it is impossible')
3 T

8 International trade

(pages 136 and 137 in the *Student's Book*)

1

1 at, after
2 from, until
3 on
4 by
5 for, during
6 within

2

1 by
2 at
3 during
4 While
5 During
6 In the last year
7 Last year

3

1 lunch
2 the summer
3 the morning

4

1 Ø
2 Ø
3 Ø
4 Ø
5 Ø
6 Ø

5

1 by
2 until
3 until
4 By

Until means 'up to'.
By means 'on' or 'before'.

6

1 on time
2 in time
3 in time
4 on time

In time means 'with enough time'.
On time means 'at the right time'.

7

- In the end means 'eventually' or 'finally'.
- At the end refers to the last part of something.
- By the end means 'at' or 'before the end'.
- Towards the end means 'near the end'.
- At last shows pleasure because something happens that you have been waiting for.

8

1 S
2 S

9

1 e)
2 c)
3 d)
4 a)
5 b)
6 g)
7 j)
8 f)
9 h)
10 i)

10

1 complained to, apologized for
2 rely on, hear about
3 conform to, succeeded in
4 insist on, look forward

11

1 invest in
2 consists of
3 comply with
4 depends on
5 insure against
6 apply for
7 suffer from
8 agree with

12

1 in
2 for
3 for
4 to
5 with
6 on
7 for
8 on
9 to
10 for

13

1 involvement
2 substitute
3 ratings
4 dealings
5 damaging
6 levy
7 tax
8 credit-worthiness

Macmillan Education
4 Crinan Street
London N1 9XW
A division of Macmillan Publishers Limited
Companies and representatives throughout the world

ISBN 978-0-230-43791-3

Written by Antoinette Meehan, Frances Watkins, Paul Emmerson and Mike Sayer

This edition published 2013
First edition published 2007

Original design by Keith Shaw, Threefold Design Limited
Page make-up by MPS Limited
Cover design by Keith Shaw, Threefold Design Limited

The authors and publishers are grateful for permission to reprint the following copyright material:

Material used from *Unlocking Your People's Potential* by Eddie Davies (Fenman Training, 1995), copyright © Eddie Davies 1995, reprinted by permission of the publisher; Word definitions taken from *Macmillan English Dictionary For Advanced Learners* copyright © Macmillan Publishers 2002, reprinted by permission of the publisher; Material used from website -*www.openoffice.org Community*, reprinted by permission; Material from 'Ten Tips for Creating a Career That Lights Your Fire' taken from http://www.passioncatalyst.com/passioncatalyst/article1. htm, reprinted by permission of the publisher; Material used from 'Help Desk Call' taken from Funny.co.uk 08.02.03; Material used from 'Methods of Payment in International Trade' taken from www.sitpro.org.uk; Information from 'Groupon's call centre in the cloud' taken from website www.information-age.com; Material used from 'The Johnson & Johnson Credo' taken from www.jnj.com.; Material used from 'Good neighbours are good for business' copyright © OECD observer No. 248, March 2005 from http://www.oecdobserver.org/news/fullstory.phdaid/1583/Goodneighbours-are-good-for-business-html.

Printed and bound in Thailand

2019 2018 2017 2016 2015
11 10 9 8 7 6 5 4 3 2